122554

D1572611

Limited Classical Reprint Library

THE RESURRECTION

OF CHRIST

BY

H.C.G. MOULE & JAMES ORR

Foreword by
Dr. Cyril J. Barber

Klock & Klock Christian Publishers, Inc.
2527 GIRARD AVE. N.
MINNEAPOLIS, MINNESOTA 55411

JESUS AND THE RESURRECTION

EXPOSITORY STUDIES ON
ST JOHN XX. XXI.

BY

H. C. G. MOULE,
Principal of Ridley Hall, Cambridge

Foreword by
Dr. Cyril J. Barber

Third Edition

Klock & Klock Christian Publishers, Inc.
2527 GIRARD AVE. N.
MINNEAPOLIS, MINNESOTA 55411

Originally published by
Seeley & Co. Limited
London, 1898

Copy from the personal library of
Dr. Cyril J. Barber

ISBN: 0-86524-062-0

Printed by Klock & Klock in the U.S.A.
1980 Reprint

232.5
M86Ir

L.I.F.E. College Library
1100 Glendale Blvd.
Los Angeles, Calif. 90026

FOREWORD

A few years ago Dr. Alan Cole made a very astute remark to a group of clergymen. His words, however, extend far beyond the ministerial profession and find their application in the life of every believer. He said,

> I constantly dread for all of us what I have seen in some, an intellectual development that outstrips the spiritual development, and a spiritual insight that is not matched by the moral strength that alone leads to spiritual progress.

Most of us know more about the Bible and the dynamic of "Christ in us" than we presently practice. Our major problem is not one of ignorance of God's will, but of failure to apply the teaching of Scripture to areas of our lives which have not yet been brought under the Holy Spirit's control. How then may we close the gap between our knowledge about the lordship of Christ and our experience of living under His sovereignty? Where may we find someone who, having bridged the gap between interpretation of Scripture and its application in his own experience, can properly explain the practical teaching of God's Word to those who desire a more fulfilling Christian life?

One of the ablest mentors we could ever hope to find is Handley Moule, at one time Professor of Divinity, Cambridge University, and later Bishop of Durham, England.

Handley Carr Glyn Moule (1841-1920) was the eighth son of the Rev. Henry Moule and his devoted wife, Mary. His early life admirably fitted him for service to others. In reflecting on his home and its influence, Moule wrote, "Happy, thrice happy, was my lot to be that mother's last cradled little one," nurtured in an atmosphere of belongingness and in an environment where God was loved and His Word obeyed. And so in the providence of God, the young child who was destined to become one of the world's finest expositors by balancing accurate exegesis with penetrating exhortation, was reared in surroundings of piety and discipline, warmth and affection, and where leisure was given over to the cultivation of the mind.

All of the sons of Henry Moule who survived infancy were educated at home. They all became lovers of good books and all were versed in the classics (Greek, Latin and English). An interesting account is given us by one of Handley Moule's biographers of him as a young lad, walking down a country lane with one of his elder brothers, and translating Hesiod's works.

In 1859 Handley Moule went to Cambridge where he successfully passed the entrance exams and completed his B.A. and M.A. degrees with distinction. He excelled in classical literature and, having taken a keen interest in theology, went on to earn the University's B.D. and D.D. degrees. While engaged in this latter pursuit, Moule also mastered Hebrew and, for the rest of his life, loved to study the Scriptures in the original languages.

While at Cambridge, Moule came under the influence of the renowned exegete, Dr. J.B. Lightfoot, and the vision of becoming an accurate expositor of God's inspired Word never left him.

031658

L.I.F.E. College Library
1100 Glendale Blvd.
Los Angeles, Calif. 90026

In time, Dr. Moule was invited to join the faculty of his *alma mater*. In addition to his lectures which were well-received, he ministered every Sunday evening at the Round Church, where crowds of people flocked to hear him. Following each service, men from the university were invited to visit with him in his apartment for a "reading from the Greek Testament." After singing a hymn they would kneel in prayer and then be taught by this most gracious and gifted of teachers. The Gospel of John was one of Dr. Moule's favorite portions for these evening gatherings, and the present volume is a product of them.

As an expositor, Professor Moule's great objective was to make the subtle, and sometimes complex, thought of the writer stand out by means of a clear, lucid explanation of the text. His greatest achievement was on Romans in *The Expositor's Bible,* but no less significant were his *Ephesian Studies: Lessons in Faith and Walk, Philippian Studies: Lessons in Faith and Love,* and *Colossian and Philemon Studies: Lessons in Faith and Holiness.*

Dr. Walter Lock, writing Handley Moule's biography in the *Dictionary of National Biography,* expressed his view that Dr. Moule's works were the most scholarly expression in that generation of true Evangelical Christianity. A contemporary, J.B. Harford, said, "He was a theologian both by instinct and training," and the respected Australian clergyman of our own day, Dr. Marcus Loane, adds, "His theology had been firmly planted on the rock of Scripture with the sure hand of the expositor and the historian."

I am personally delighted that the writings of this devout man of God are being reissued, and I trust that they will bring blessing to others as they have to me.

Cyril J. Barber
Author, *The Minister's Library*

CONTENTS.

JESUS

AND

THE RESURRECTION

I

THE DISCIPLES.

MANY years ago—it was in 1869—I received a kind letter from the late Lord Chancellor Hatherley, formerly Sir W. Page Wood. I had been much helped in thought and faith by his small but valuable book, as well worthy of attentive study now as ever, *The Continuity of Scripture*,[1] and I ventured to thank him. His reply contained the following sentences :

" I thought that many young and ardent minds become embroiled in controversy before they have had the thought or inclination to make *proof* of Scripture by its effects on their own hearts when read with a simple, prayerful wish to believe. In my youth (I cannot express the benefit thus derived from Holy Writ) I used, when under trial, to read say two or three

[1] Murray, 1868.

B

chapters of the New Testament, specially the
closing chapters of the Gospel of St John, and
never found my doubts so cleared as by that
expedient. I have now for more than thirty
years perused the whole Volume yearly. I fear
I may not have time now allowed me to expose
the very shallow reasoning powers of some very
eminent continental scholars. Their learning I
admire; but at the bar we often find a man's
logic swamped by his learning; and so it is in
divinity."

I quote these words of that good man and
great judge, one of the greatest of all our
masters of legal evidence, to introduce a few
short studies on these same last pages of St
John. Their object is not criticism specially,
nor speculation, but reverent verbal enquiry,
carried on " with the simple, prayerful wish to "
realize, and so the more gladly to " believe."
Whatever such studies do, or fail to do, may
they lead us a little nearer to Him who is the
Life and the Light—Jesus Christ, our Sacrifice,
our Hiding-place, our Resting-place; our
Strength for watching and for work; our
Panacea for all temptation ; our Resurrection ;
our Heaven in prospect.

We begin with a translation :

Now on the first day of the week Mary of Magdala comes early, while it was still dusk, to the tomb, and sees the stone taken out of the tomb. So she runs and comes to Simon Peter, and to the other disciple, whom Jesus loved, and says to them, They have taken the Lord out of the tomb, and we do not know where they have put Him. So they went out, Peter and the other disciple, and set out for (ἤρχοντο εἰς) the tomb. So they were running (ἔτρεχον), the two together; and now the other disciple ran forward (προέδραμε), quicker than Peter, and came first to the tomb; and, stooping from the side, he sees lying the linen cloths. He did not go in, however. So Simon Peter comes, following him, and went into the tomb, and views (θεωρεῖ) the linen cloths lying, and the napkin that was over His head, not lying with the linen cloths, but apart, rolled up and put in a separate place. So the other disciple, who came first to the tomb, then went in, and he saw, and believed. For not as yet did they know the Scripture, that of necessity He would rise from the dead.

Verse I. Τῇ δὲ μιᾷ (*Now on the first day*). We observe the connecting "*now*," δὲ. It points to previous details, and reminds us that the Resurrection is indissolubly linked, in significance as in fact, to what precedes—the Cross. It is these two which make the one glory of the work of Christ. It is "the Living One *who became dead*" (Rev. i. 18) who is our Peace, and can lay His hand on us and say, "Fear not."

So this brief particle leads us back, over some forty hours, to that mid-afternoon of the Friday when the Lord expired; to the short interval before sunset, when Joseph and Nicodemus had buried Him in the adjoining garden, watched, perhaps from under the city wall,[1] by some of the Galilean women; then to the hushed interval of that sunset, and evening, and night, and following day. That interval the disciples spent in grief and tears, and apparently in different places, isolated into groups. For Peter and John, having with them no doubt the Lord's Mother, seem to have been found apart from the rest when Mary Magdalene sought them; and Thomas was definitely withdrawn; and the women, again, appear to have set out, on the Sunday morning, from different points. Then

[1] I venture to assume the rightness of "General Gordon's site" of the Crucifixion, outside the Damascus Gate. An interesting controversy has lately (1892) been carried on in *The Times* and other papers, over the question whether an old tomb near that site is or is not the very tomb of Joseph. The weighty judgment of Canon Tristram is given for a probable affirmative.

we are led to the evening of our Saturday—the close of their Sabbath—when, as the sun set, the women, or some of them, at once set out to buy and to prepare the odours with which to complete the work of Nicodemus. So we reach the middle of that night, and the breaking of the First Day morning, when from their various lodging-places the women came—Mary of Magdala, Mary "of Joseph," Salome, and perhaps others too.

As we review that interval, I would touch on one point only in the picture of the disciples drawn for us in the Gospel narrative; I mean the collocation and the contrast, so startling yet so deeply truth-like, of the total failure of their faith and the survival of their love.

When the Lord rose, perhaps no living person, excepting (surely) His Mother,[1] consciously and intelligently "believed on His Name." No living person, except her, trusted His promise to rise again, and understood His death in the light of it, resting the soul upon His sacrifice. So this very passage tells us, in regard of no less personages than John and Peter. But such a statement would have been the very last

[1] And possibly the Family of Bethany. None of them appear at the tomb. I owe this remark to the suggestion of the Rev. G. F. W. Munby.

thing which a fabricator would have excogitated, and the very last which would have arisen unconsciously in minds (such as many historical critics assume all the minds of the primeval Church to have been) pregnant with legend, or facile vehicles for the growth of myths. Who in that simple age, with its literary "helplessness," would have thought of *constructing* an utter collapse of faith in the central circle of the disciples just when Jesus was accomplishing His alleged victory—a collapse just *because of* the Cross, which so soon became somehow the hope and glory of His followers?

But knowledge and reflection now show us how true to history, to time, and conditions, and the human soul, all this picture is. All the prepossessions of those men and women, and their cherished wishes, lay in the direction of a triumph not through death at all. The attention they ought to have given to their Master's words about His death had been all the while distracted and neutralized by these intense expectations and preferences. When the stern fact of the Crucifixion came, their confidence was not only surprised, but crushed; and so it would have remained, if Jesus had not risen again.

And yet—they loved Him. They must have been tortured with worse than doubts about His

Messianic character, if, indeed, in those dis-
tressing hours they had mental leisure to *doubt*
amidst their absorbing *grief.* But *some* formidable questionings, not only about Him, but about
all they had known or hoped about God, must
have mingled with their tears. And yet—they
loved Him. Women, Apostles, all, in one
degree or another, they loved Him still. And
in this too there is a deep and verifiable truth
of the human heart. Mere grief and alarm may
easily be imagined over the unlooked-for death
of any strong leader. But the leader these
persons had lost was JESUS—the Man JESUS,
such as the Gospels draw Him. Such a Chief,
even had He misled them in the end, must still
(it is true in the logic of the heart, which alone
is in question here) be loved, for the time, with
an intensity only the greater for His fall. Take
the case of Magdalene. Jesus, contrary to her
dearest longings and most confident expectations, had died :—what could she believe? But
Jesus, whatever else had happened, had liberated
her from awful physical and mental suffering
(Mark xvi. 9) :—how could she not love?

May I draw a somewhat evident lesson? Let
us give continual thanks for the broad, strong
foundations of fact and reason, of cogent and
manifold proof, which lie beneath the assertion

of the Creed, that He who died for our sins rose again the third day. History has nothing else in it so firm and solid, in the historical sense, as that position. But the human mind is a strange and subtle thing, and it is possible that we may, in certain states of it, find ourselves doubting, as it were, against our reason ; seeing the steps and links, but so as to fail to combine them at the moment into a result of conscious and invigorating certainty. Then let us be thankful indeed if we bear about in us another part of the vast evidence of Christianity, that is, of Jesus Christ ; the thing which kept the adherence of those disciples tenacious when for a dark season their full faith was gone. This Jesus Christ has, somehow, touched, and changed, and set free my soul, my being. He, and only He—His Name, His Person—has had a power over me which is like nothing else. The more I have seen, trusted, loved Him, the more always I have stood clear of sin, of self. I cannot but love Him still. And as for these haunting doubts, I will at least drag them into the light of His love, and look at them there. If I feel for a sad moment, "They have taken away my Lord," I will at that very moment remember why, among other reasons, I can call Him "my Lord" at all ; He, or if not He, then nothing, has freed me from many more than seven sins. Is not doubt about such a Power a self-detected fallacy already ?

But on the other side, we must not press too far the resemblance between Mary's case and our own. What was, after all, this passionate love of the disciples when their faith was gone ? In a great measure, it was only passionate. It was affection for a Being whom they had (on their then hypothesis, Luke xxiv. 21) much mistaken ; affection for some one who, if the faith had been " vain," was less than the Son of God ; affection indeed for Jesus of Nazareth, but for a Jesus infinitely short of His reality—a dead, a vanished, a disappointed Friend.

So, warm as it was, that love could not well have persisted. As time went on it must have been infected with the bitterness of an ever-growing pain at the loss, the blank, *the mistake.* Many of the company would be tempted to forget Him, if they could. Some would have come to dread, perhaps even to hate, the spectre of His memory. Those who still loved would love on, not in joy and strength, but in gloom. It was the love more of nature than of grace— let us not fear to say it—which brought Mary to the tomb. The heavenly love—the joyful, holy, undecaying love—was yet to come : love stirred from its depths by light and power divine. But in order to this she had yet to know Jesus as the Risen One, who was dead, but is alive for evermore.

As such we know Him, and have felt His power.

Let us stand by the side of Mary of Magdala, with that knowledge and consciousness in our grateful hearts. Let us look into that tomb, and see it full of light—the seat of Angels, the gate of heaven. Let us turn round with her, and see the reason of it all—the Lord Jesus risen indeed; Jesus calling us by our name, while we answer, *Rabboni*, My Master, O my Master!

11

MARY MAGDALENE.

IN the previous chapter mention was made of
the "three days" which came between the
Lord's death and His resurrection, the silent
interval referred to in the δὲ of our ver. 1. Let
us so far return to that point as to remind ourselves of the extreme importance to us of that
interval from one particular point of view.
"The third day I will rise again"; that promise
of delay was pregnant with many mercies.
Putting aside all thought and question (never
by us on earth to be answered with certainty)
what the Lord Jesus Himself might have to do
in that mysterious time, we see at once that the
interval was momentous, not only for our greater
assurance of His literal death, but—this is the
point here in my mind—for our better apprecia-
tion of the real state of mind of His followers.
Their blank surprise, their despair, their mistakes, their broken faith but not broken love—

all are before us now, for all had time to come out. And thus we are able to estimate better the massive solidity of the evidence of the Resurrection, looking at the absolute contrast between the former and after states of the disciples. The disciples between the Friday and the Sunday—the disciples after the Sunday, thenceforward for ever—what a difference! Before, all is misunderstanding, bewilderment, helplessness ; after, all is one strong consistency (if we except a passing check, soon much more than repaired, in the case of one person, Thomas) of holy certainty, peace, energy, and joy.

But now we draw near the scene of Resurrection.

Perhaps it was soon after midnight, the vernal midnight, that the Lord arose. Indeed, as soon as the sun of Saturday had set, and the first moments of the First Day had come, the letter of His promise permitted Him to return ; for the νυχθήμερον (the twenty-four hours) could be represented by ever so small a fraction of its course. But as a fact the Revival took place not long before the discovery of its occurrence. In one place (Mark xvi. 9) we read distinctly that "Jesus rose early" (πρωΐ), in the early morning, on the first day of the week. It was probably a very silent Resurrection. It was not till the great Angel, afterwards, came down that the stone was rolled fairly away, and the earth shaken around the place of burial. It may be that in a way unknown to us, and unknowable, the Body of the Resurrection was made able to pass through the stone while the stone yet lay unmoved in the doorway.[1] But, however, It passed out from the cell. HE stood up, in His veritable, immortal Body, dropping aside, so that they lay on the floor, just as and where they had been worn, the long linen cloths which had so recently pressed "an hundred pound weight" of spices round His lacerated limbs[2]; and so He re-appeared, "in the power of an indissoluble life," "according to the working whereby He is able even to subdue all things unto Himself" (Heb. vii. 16; Phil. iii. 21).

[1] I own the greatness of the difficulties which beset this theory, which *seems* to put an essential difference between the Lord's Risen Body and our body. Yet it must be observed that the theory does not suppose the contradiction of any apparent necessary law of thought. It does not suppose any ubiquity, or practical ubiquity, of the Body, nor that the same space would be occupied by the atoms of the stone and of the Body; but that the sacred material of the Body was so subtilized by the action of the Lord's Spirit that the dense stone became, relatively to It, a network of large interstices. See further below, p. 87.

[2] Where had the spices gone? Had they been, as it were, consumed by that contact?

In that resurrection life "He dieth no more." The human Form, flesh and bones, which stepped forth in the light of dawn into Joseph's garden that wonderful morning, was alive eternally. Identical in continuity with the Body of His birth and His death, it was in a state infinitely new, "a spiritual Body." For it, time was as it were no more. Eighteen centuries have not worn it into age, nor shall the coming æons do so. In it, He is "this same Jesus," yesterday, to-day, and when He comes again. And every moment of its holy permanence is proof both that we are accepted in His death and are being saved for ever "in His life" (Rom. v. 10).

So did the Risen Saviour triumph in the deep silence of that early morning. Meanwhile the disciples were weeping and groaning because of His death, and were coming to bid His remains the last farewell.

Verse 1. *On the first day of the week,* τῇ μιᾷ τῶν σαββάτων. The Greek plural σαββαθὰ is a transliteration of the Aramaic *shabbâthâ*, and has no plural meaning. Μιᾷ for πρώτῃ is Hebraistic.

Cometh Mary the Magdalene, Mary of Magdala, or Migdol, a place (probably) near Tiberias, and still perhaps to be identified. This much-favoured disciple is mentioned fourteen times in

the Gospels, and always (except only Luke viii.
2, where she is seen, along with "many other
women," accompanying the Lord through Galilee, and assisting Him with her personal means)
in connexion with the story of the Passion.
There is no real evidence to identify her with
the "woman that was a sinner." From the
Magdalene (Mark xvi. 9) Jesus had "cast out
seven devils." But this tells us nothing for
certain of any special impurity in her life. All
it does is to account most instructively and
nobly for her deep, devoted, energetic love.
That love began with this simple but mighty
motive—gratitude for immense blessings, pro-
foundly certain to her consciousness. She had
been a tortured, perhaps a terrible, demoniac;
now she was at rest, and Jesus was the cause.
So she came to the sepulchre early, in the dusk,
earlier than the Apostles; brought by no super-
human courage, but by grateful love.

She did not come alone. "The other Mary,"
wife of Clopas, mother of James the Less and
very possibly sister of the Virgin,[1] was with her;
and other women came to the same spot about
the same hour, Johanna and Salome among
them. But, with one minute exception, which

[1] See Smith's *Dictionary of the Bible,* s. v. "Mary of
Clopas."

we shall notice as it comes, their presence does not appear in this narrative. In it we have the whole scene from *Mary's* point of view; and deeply truth-like it is, when we remember Mary's condition of feeling, that that point of view should have regarded herself and her own experiences alone. As she told the sacred incidents over, when she went to the disciples with the message that "she had seen the Lord," she would speak as one whose whole being had been concentrated on what He had said to *her*.

She came *early, while it was still dusk, to the sepulchre;* finding her way to the walled garden whither she had seen Joseph and Nicodemus convey the Body, and there deposit it, rolled in that mass of linen-folded spicery, inside the chamber cut in the rock, at the back or the side of the enclosure. The sun was near his rising; but it was dusk still in the nooks and corners of the place.

And now, *she sees the stone taken out of the sepulchre.* This view, very probably, was not from the garden itself. A glance as she approached it would be enough to show her the black void recess. And perhaps, accordingly, she did not now go up to the tomb at all, but hastened on alone, leaving whoever might have come with her, or have met her, to follow or not as it might happen.

However, the stone was moved. " *The* stone," says St John, though he had said nothing about a stone before.   To be sure, the definite article may be accounted for by the fact that every rock tomb would have *its* stone.   But knowing as we do from the other Gospel narratives how large a part "the stone" did play on that momentous morning, I cannot help seeing here one of the many details in which St John, in his Gospel, *takes for granted* the main Evangelic narrative, and passingly and without anxiety uses his reader's knowledge of it.

Verse 2. *So Mary runs.*   How much eager speed there was that hour!   The holy woman, the two Apostles, all *run*, from the sepulchre, or to it, in the self-oblivion of great grief or of great hope.

And she comes to Simon Peter, and to the other disciple whom Jesus loved; so John describes himself, with a *naiveté* inimitable, and altogether unlike a fabricator (when we have regard to the literary conditions of the early generations of Christianity[1]), about fourteen times.

[1] It cannot be too often remembered, when we study the inner marks of the authenticity of the Scripture narra-

C

So she found Peter and John in company; perhaps in the same house, though the repetition of the πρὸς before τὸν ἄλλον μαθητήν *slightly* suggests that she may have called at two doors. Very beautiful is the sight of this special intimacy of the two Apostles. We seem to see it first when they go (Luke xxii. 8) to prepare the room for the Last Passover; then, when they stand together at the door of the Palace of the Priest; again in this incident; again in the following chapter, and again and again in the early passages of the Acts. How different was each from each—how helpful each to each manifestly became ! And we may specially note how deeply "the disciple whom Jesus loved" had learnt in that wonderful friendship to "love his brother also." John had never actually denied his Lord; Peter, probably in John's hearing, had repeatedly denied Him. Many a "saint" of later days would, I fear, have thrust Peter away from all fellowship with himself. But not so John. At once, before the Resurrection, before the hope of it, while there was yet no joy in his own heart, John has joined himself to Peter; has

---

tives, of both Testaments, that anything like finished and really deceptive personation of the past (if I may use the phrase) is a very modern literary phenomenon. Is it much older than Sir Walter Scott?

taken him to be his brother as well as the Virgin to be his mother.

If for us, in our day, the sense of our Redeemer's love, our rest upon the bosom of His forgiving friendship, does anything, it will make us condemn and renounce the spiritual self-righteousness which shuts up sympathy. It will make us feel how wonderfully welcome to the Lord is "whosoever cometh," even if he comes fresh from some grievous fall, some denial of the blessed Name. It will make us so far like Him who loved us, that while we shall see and feel sin, as sin, more and more keenly and painfully (and not least, the sin of not loving the Lord Christ, and submitting the whole being to Him), we shall more and yet more truly love, and seek to help, others for whom our aid may avail, however strange the case, however great the fall.

So, to Peter and to John, Mary of Magdala comes running.

And she says to them, They have taken the Lord out of the sepulchre, and we do not know where they have put Him.

I turn the aorists by perfects; not of course forgetting an important grammatical difference; but remembering that the genius of the Greek tongue places an act or event in the complete past more promptly than the genius of English. Accordingly we have often, for the sake of English, to represent the Greek completed past by the English past connected with the present.

They have taken. The expression is quite indefinite. It appears to be fairly equivalent to the *on* of French ; *on a enlevé le Seigneur;* Joseph, Joseph's servants, any one, had done it. Mary may have thought of the soldiers, who had already left the place pell-mell. But probably she did not even know of their having been there, nor of the seal upon the stone. The guard had not been sent to the place till the Sabbath ; and the women had kept the Sabbath most strictly (Luke xxiii. 5, 6[1]), moving about very little.

They have taken away THE LORD ; wonderful word ! It was only the Corpse ; yes, but to Mary this was JESUS. And she was right. The body, as much as the soul, is an integral part of perfect man : it is so with the Christian, it was so with Christ. We are amply justified in mourning, loving, honouring the precious bodies of our departed dear ones ; they *are* a part of *them.* And truly we are justified in longing, in praying, for the Resurrection hour

[1] Their Master, it appears, had taught them no neglect of the Commandments.

when they shall actually, and eternally, be part of them again.

And WE *do not know where they have put Him.* Here, surely, we have a distinct, though minute, indication of the presence of other seekers along with Mary. Some even devout scholars (I think Dr Sanday is among them) say that we cannot argue thus; that the memory of the aged Apostle could not charge itself with the presence or absence of a mere syllable (a mere μεν, if Mary spoke Greek). But it seems obvious to remark that to recall a syllable may mean much more than merely to recall the sound. The word is bound up with the thing. Not so much the sounds spelt οἴδαμεν cling to the mind as the represented idea of the more-than-one who "did not know."

Anywise, St John has carefully written οἴδαμεν, "we know," and (to speak of no deeper considerations) it is in harmony with his whole style to imply details which he leaves un-recorded, because recorded otherwise already. I take it that he makes Mary here conscious of having approached the sepulchre with her friend, and now to refer to their united thought.

We know not where they have put Him. What strange words, at such a moment! What a sublime "irony," in the Greek sense of that word, about them! Let us try to enter into the anguish and bewilderment of this blessed forerunner of our faith and lover of our Lord. Intensely devoted to the Person of Jesus; bound to Him by ties of the tenderest gratitude, by her knowledge that reason, and rest, and friends, were all the special gift of Him who had disencumbered her soul of the seven foul spirits; bound to Him also by long-ing hopes, cherished visions (in the light of true prophecy) of His passionless triumph and world-wide glory and fame; longing, no doubt, for all this wholly for His sake, and not at all for her own; she now saw Him murdered, buried, and— stolen from her. And her only resource was to run to two poor men, as hopeless and helpless as herself, and even more paralysed. And yet, she loves. She is energized by love; she will still do anything for "the Lord."

How shall it be with us? We know im-measurably more (it is strictly true) about Christ Jesus than Mary at that moment did. We know him as the Eternal SON given for our sins, according to the Scriptures. We know Him as the Risen One, according to the Scriptures, living at this hour—and for ever— for us, with us, in us. He is revealed to us as the Ascended One, our Mediator and Head at the right hand of Eternal Love. Ah, what should be our thanksgiving as we contrast it all with the anguish and despair of Mary at that moment? What should be our gladness, as we come daily and hourly to Him, and receive, instead of deserved condemnation, HIMSELF, and all the fulness of our salvation in Him? It is for us to be strong with a strength greater than that of the Magdalene that hour; for hers was a love full of darkness and distress, ours is a love which is full of joy.

III

PETER AND JOHN.

WE arrive at ver. 3, and address ourselves to consider some verbal details of the text in that verse and some verses which follow, and then to pause for reflection on their contents.

It may be noticed in passing that the Greek text before us in this neighbourhood is remarkably free from various readings—at least, from such various readings as in the least degree call for comment in such a study as this. The margin of Scrivener's Testament (for example) shrinks to a narrow compass here, giving only seven variants, none of them of the least practical moment for our purpose, through the first twelve verses of the chapter. This is a relief to the reader who is, above all things, looking for spiritual edification. Not that even the minutest details of a critical "apparatus" are to be despised or regarded with impatience from another view point; they are witnesses to the mass of material which exists for the determination of the text of the New Testament, a mass (need I say?) incomparably greater than that which survives in the case of any classical author. Still, it is not unwelcome to find that our examination of some passage of peculiar sanctity and glory need not be interrupted by the note which registers some *itacism*, or the presence or absence of a *subscript iota*, or the like.

Verse 3. *So Peter went out* (ἐξῆλθε). That is, he left the house where he was lodging; or he left the city gate; or the word very naturally includes both. The gates of Jerusalem were not shut, apparently, at the time. The Master and His followers had found no difficulty in leaving the city on the night of Thursday, though undoubtedly it was late when they walked to Gethsemane. The vast concourse of the Passover necessitated such laxity.

If ἐξῆλθεν includes a reference to *the house*, that house very probably was the Passover abode of St John. Not that it would be a house of his own; that would be a possession most unlikely in the case of a Galilean countryman. But St John's connexion with Jerusalem had something special in it; he was "known" (γνωστός) to the High Priest (xviii. 15), and it is at least very possible that near kindred of his were domiciled at Jerusalem, and that, if so, he lodged with them on his visits there.

So Peter and his friend *went out,* and now *they were coming to the tomb* (ἤρχοντο εἰς τὸ μνημεῖον). The Greek tense and preposition indicate that they were on the way, and now nearly there—not merely in a direction to reach the place, but almost arrived. They had left the northern gate, and were perhaps not a hundred yards on the road from that "green hill" which to us is "far away," but close to which was the Arimathean Councillor's garden wall.

Verse 4. *So they were running, the two together* (Ἔτρεχον). Either they had been going at full speed all the way, or the nearness of what they craved to see now quickened their pace ; but the former alternative is more likely. And now, near the goal, the other disciple προέδραμε, ran in advance, took a start forward (we observe the aorist, of course) *quicker than Peter.* He does not give the reason why, though he of all men knew. "Because he was the younger man" is an account sometimes given ; but we know nothing at all of the ages of the Apostles relatively to one another. Tradition and pictures commonly make St Peter an elderly man beside

the Lord Jesus and beside St John ; but it is at
least as likely that the company were much of
an age with one another and with their blessed
Leader.   In xxi. 18, if I read aright the bearing
of the words there, "when thou *wast young*,"[1]
Peter is regarded by his Master as a young man
still.   But did not the feet of Peter flag because
his heart was heavy and his conscience heavy-
laden?   It was less easy for him than for John
to hasten to that tomb to which he had, so it
might have seemed to his troubled soul, almost
betrayed his Lord.   However this might be, John
did outrun his friend, *and came first to the tomb*
—to the scene which still, no doubt, bore traces
of the presence and then of the flight of the
sentinels, who not very long before, perhaps
not an hour before, had been so sorely scared
by the rocking of the ground and by the Angel's
glory, and had rushed in confusion into the
sleeping town.   All was silence now.   And now
stooping from the side (παρακύψας), *he sees lying
the linen cloths.*

Such a *sideway* stooping is implied by the
structure of the sepulchre.   It would be the only
way of looking into a horizontal cavity, through
a low orifice, without so placing the body as to
get in the observer's own light.   As it was, he

[1] See below, p. 190.

got a view of the interior, and this was what he saw, in the twilight of the cell, doubly dusky in the early morning shadows : τὰ ὀθόνια κείμενα, the long folds, or strips, of fine white linen (ὀθόνη) lying in the grave-niche. This was not what should have been had the sacred Body been still there. *Then* he would have seen a solid white mass, an ample roll ; *now* he found a length of laid-off linens, thin and empty. And here of course was part of the mystery and surprise : the Body was gone, but the winding-sheet was left ! Of this Mary had said nothing ; her eyes and mind had observed only the removal of the stone, and her account would prepare them to find merely a vacant grave. So it was an unlooked-for riddle to explain what was there, as well as what was gone ; and with that sight and its perplexity there stole perhaps the first subtle ray of Resurrection hope into the mind of John. It was indeed a disappearance, but not a mere disappearance—certainly no hurried " snatching " of the elaborately enfolded Corpse. The long, long linens had been disengaged completely, and left in the place where what they held had been.

He did not go in, however. Why not ? There is not much need to ask any one who has ever looked into, or even upon, the coffin which con-

ceals a beloved form, or has visited the recent
grave which has received that coffin. No commentary is wanted by such readers to explain
St John's look, yet refusal to step, into the tomb
of his lost dear Lord and Friend. But with
that simple reason of the bereaved heart others
no doubt mingled. John was in a conflict now
of grief *and wonder*, and thought as well as
sorrow may have preoccupied him and left
him motionless for the moment. But however,
he *says* nothing about his reasons, and how can
we analyse them all? Very subtle is the influence of character on circumstance; we should
need to know John's character and Peter's far
better than even we do to be able quite to tell
what checked the one and what impelled the
other at that narrow door. But none the less
important is it to take note of these unexplained
details, just because they are unexplained.
Coming one after another as they do, set down
thus so simply and without anxiety, yet minutely,
they carry the very tone and accent of the eye-
witness. We seem to stand there watching;
the whole motion of the scene is before us; all
is near, real, natural, visible. And then we remember that this Fourth Gospel (whoever wrote
it) is no piece of modern literature, written in
our age, when imagination has trained itself,

more or less consciously, into an almost morbid activity, not least in the way of reconstructive narrative. It is the work of a far simpler and less self-conscious age, written (as we remarked in a previous chapter) centuries before the art of successful imitation of fact in fiction had developed itself, even in the centres of human culture. This quiet, while emphatic, minuteness of detail in a scene which yet the writer regards as vastly important would be, if I judge in the least aright, a literary impossibility in the first or second century, even for a trained *littérateur* —if the writing were not a record of observed fact. As it is, it is just the diction of him who knows that "that which our eyes have seen, and our hands have handled, concerning the Word of the Life, *that* we declare unto you" (1 John i. 1, 3) ; declaring it for a reason which lifts a narrator to a very different moral level from that of calculated fiction—"that your joy may be full ; that ye may believe that this Jesus is the Christ, and that, believing, ye may have life in His Name."

Verse 6. *So Simon Peter comes, following him, and went into the tomb.* Perhaps only a few minutes or even moments intervened. The backward Apostle cannot have been far behind his friend, who probably, as we saw, had run in front only when both were near the garden.

And now, at once, Peter stoops and enters. Again we conjecture the motive. Why did he pass in, and leave John at the door outside? There was something characteristic in the motive, for we remember the parallel action, xxi. 7, where Peter is the disciple to hurry to the shore. In this case was not the heart whose intensity of emotion checked the feet on the way, just the heart to find itself unable to linger a moment when the feet had reached the goal? However this may be, here again is the touch of historical, not poetic or constructive, detail.

And he views the linen cloths lying. He takes his view, he gazes : θεωρεῖ, far more than βλέπει (ver. 5), means a deliberate look—the look of one who is taking in the scene and something of its significance. And what does he say about it ? For indeed we seem to hear him speaking from within the cavern, and telling his friend outside, point by point, what he finds : "Yes, here are the winding-sheets as you saw them ; and here, too, what you did not see, is the napkin, the *sudarium*, which was fastened round His head. It is put here, or left here, apart, by itself ; not thrown on the rest, but rolled up (ἐντετυλιγμένον), in a separate place (εἰς ἕνα τόπον [1])." *He views the linen cloths lying, and the napkin that was over His head, not lying with the linen cloths, but apart, rolled up and put in a separate place.*

Here were fresh signs of something very different from what they and Mary had feared. Here was no hostile invasion of the grave, no rough and careless removal; rather all the marks of order and attention, we might almost say of neatness. If, in that moment of profound feeling, there was time to think (and thought often goes quickest at such times), John might have thought how entirely unlike this was to the work of enemies, and that to remove the Body at all was extremely unlike the work of friends. Who would have done it? Joseph of Arimathea—the very man who had laid the shrouded Body there with such reverent pains? Any other members of the circle of disciples or supporters? Such a thought as this last most certainly would not have occurred to John, in the entire absence of probable motive. All alike were unexpectant of a Resurrection; all alike were in the depth of distress and disappointment, and probably also in much alarm for their own safety. All, if they had leisure or

[1] Literally, of course, "*into* one place"; brought to it and laid *in* it.

courage for much such reflection, must have been thankful that their beloved Master had found (by no means of theirs, for they had none) an honourable burial. Certainly, in any case, *they* would not have stripped the cloths away.

Enemies had not so gently unwound the corpse. Friends would not have unwound it at all.

Verse 8. So, with the dawn of a blissful hope in his soul, and probably with a sudden throng of memories in his mind—memories of words spoken by Jesus, and of prophecies He had half explained—*the other disciple, who came first to the tomb, went in.*

And he saw (εἶδε). Here is a third verb, with βλέπειν and θεωρεῖν. And it is used in its proper place : ἰδεῖν tends to indicate a sight which is also intelligence. He saw the facts and their meaning.

And believed. Here was infinitely more than an empty grave, an absent corpse, an unused winding-sheet, a folded napkin. Here was— Resurrection. He believed, he accepted without direct sight the certainty, that there was life here, after death. He believed the *fact* that Jesus lived again, and he believed the *truth;* he recognized a *divine* fact, a fact of prophecy. For how does he proceed?

D

Verse 9. *For not as yet did they know the Scripture, that of necessity He would rise from the dead;* that by a supreme necessity, in the predestination of the eternal plan of Messiah's work, He would die and rise again.

The Scripture (τὴν γραφήν) : a singular which seems almost always in the New Testament to refer to some one *passage* of the Old. We are not told what "Scripture" to St John just then shone out as *the* Resurrection promise ; but as we read the Pentecostal Sermon of his friend (Acts ii.), we may well suppose that Psalm xvi. may have been the place.[1] But whatever "the Scripture" was, "they" had not understood it.   But now John—at least John —did.   The ray of fulfilment lighted up the prophecy.   The fact, once seen, began at once to kindle into the glorious truth.   The grave was vacant, and so vacant that it was plain that Jesus had not been lifted away from it by other hands ; He had *left* it.   And so at once the strangely-hidden secret was solved ; the impossible, the incredible, the unwelcome had become

[1] The "Scripture" for a *third-day* resurrection is undoubtedly, on our Lord's own testimony, the narrative of Jonah.   But the third day is not immediately in view here.—The testimony of this brief passage to the apostolic belief in definitely predictive prophecy is very impressive, by its very passingness.

the glorious truth of life. Jesus, the Dead, was risen.

He believed—with a faith decisive and new, as an experience in his mind. What a wonderful candour there is in the admission, "as yet they did not know"! This aged saint and prophet does not shrink from telling the world that for three long years, spent in his Saviour's company, he had laboured under an immense mistake about that Saviour's work. He had laid his head upon the breast of Jesus Christ, and yet had never understood that He had come on purpose to die and to rise again. This is no ordinary frankness; it is, in fact, nothing less than the simplicity of transparent truth, the truthfulness of a man to whom the reality, the glory, the blessedness of his Master are so precious that he cannot pause a moment to think of his own reputation in telling his Master's story. Rather, he is glad to recall the contrast, because it was even more happy than humbling —the contrast between his own strange blindness in the old days and the sunrise of joy and life upon which he now entered, and which he owed entirely to his Lord. We are welcome to know anything, everything, about John's slowness, dulness, oblivion, ignorance, about his poor insight into Scripture, his earthly view of the

Kingdom, his temporal ambition, his unbelieving despair, if the contrast may only lead us, for
whom he writes, and whom he loves by anticipation as fellow-believers, to a full view of the
sacrifice, the victory, the life, the love of the
Lord Jesus Christ. " He knoweth that he saith
true, that ye might believe."

So, with all the quiet simplicity of truth, he
closes this part of the story. Ver. 10 : *So the
disciples went away again to their own abode*
(πρὸς ἑαυτούς). That was all—all, at least, that
we are to know for the present. We have seen
them in the moment of their first faith long
enough to confirm our faith ; but how they felt,
what they said, on the way home, and at home,
what Peter said to John about the denial in this
new light, and what John said to Peter, what
Mary felt and said when they met her beneath
the roof of John's abode—all this we do not
know. It is all written, not for effect, but for
fact ; for truth, for faith, that we too might
believe.

For my own part, after tracing out again the
details of this section of St John's story, one
thought comes uppermost in the mind—the
thought how invaluable to the enquirer after
Jesus Christ, and also, at least as much, to the

believer in Him, are the strong, definite lines of
the narrative of His triumph. Here we have
been standing almost entirely aside from explicit
Christian doctrine, and looking simply at events.
Some of them have been very small events in
themselves: the grief and hurry of one affectionate woman ; the actions of curiosity and search
on the part of two perplexed and anxious men ;
and then the fact that they had mistaken certain
venerable writings ; and then their quiet retire-
ment to their abode again. No instruction ; all
narrative.

For that very reason, how invaluable it is in
its proper place ! How good it is for me, for
many reasons, for reasons the very deepest, to
be able to touch this paragraph, and handle it,
and feel in it the texture of mere fact ; to find
myself in contact, not with a poetic cloud, however coloured, but with the angles of the Rock
of Ages ! The material is hard, for it is solid ;
hard with a hardness which sustains, not
wounds. It is the rock ; it is indissoluble fact.
I take no pains to make it stronger ; I neither
can nor need ; it is *fait accompli ;* Jesus is
risen.

Why is this fact-character of the Gospel so
very valuable to me? this objectivity, this view
of spiritual truth as bound up for ever with

events which really happened in time and place,
quite external to me and independent of me?

It is so because, on the other hand, my need
of the Gospel is a thing so deeply *internal.* I
know, with the most direct of all sorts of knowledge, I know as an inner fact, my essential
need of a SAVIOUR. I know my sin, and I
know my want. There is that in me which asks,
and must ask till satisfied, for pardon and for
holiness. And this asking is prompted by more
motives than one. First, as regards the question of pardon, there is the conviction (very
definite, stern, and unpoetical) that without
pardon there is danger, danger of an indefinitely
awful sequel to the fact of unforgiven sin. And
then, in a similar way, the desire for victory
over sin, and for the liberty of holiness, arises
in part from a very stern, simple source—from
the fact that sin met with compromise puts
a hopeless bar between me and the possession
of the peace of God. And then, in harmony
with these inner facts, springing up with them,
yet from an even greater depth, there are other
reasons. Somehow I know that I am made to
know God and to love Him, and that the heart
will not rest until it rests in Him.[1] It stands to
reason, in the deepest sense of reason. What

---

[1] Augustine: *Confessiones, ad init.*

but the Maker Himself, to the thinking thing
which He has made, can be the point of rest,
the ultimate centre, the never-disappointing
satisfaction, the spring never dry, the tree which
bears fruit every month? Positively or nega-
tively, the human soul is always athirst for God,
for the living God. Probably we, writer and
reader, have known more or less of both phases
of that thirst; the negative consciousness, as we
become aware of the insufficiency of anything
less than Him for rest and joy; and then the
positive consciousness, when grace shows us
that the Lord God, known, trusted, embraced,
is "all our desire," our joy which cannot waste,
our pure and purifying happiness.

So the soul asks, implores, the pardon which
it knows it will never merit. It asks, it thirsts,
for the knowledge of the Eternal Holy and
Happy One, and, in that knowledge, for a joy
which is absolutely unattainable elsewhere.

Now, the very fact that these realities of the
inmost heart of man are what they are, *internal*
facts, is what gives its peculiar preciousness to
the objectivity of the Gospel, to its character as
a compact mass of *external* events, achieve-
ments, done apart from us, done for us, by
Another.

When the soul cries out for God, it implores

not an echo, but an answer. A mere series of impressions roused by another series will not satisfy. No webs woven out of "inner consciousness" will bear the strain of the consciousness of conviction. No Saviour constructed out of the elements of self can be the Saviour from self, from the sentence hanging over it, from the bondage of sin within it.

Here the revelation of our Lord Jesus Christ comes in as it is. From the exactly opposite quarter it comes to meet me at the precise point of my need. It is not aspiration, or emotion. It is fact—outside, objective, the work of Another; done in history; done without thought, or choice, or leave of mine; while I was nonexistent; while I was yet to be, and was foreseen as yet to be, in all my sinfulness and extreme unworthiness of such benefits. And this work of Another, what is it? It is the death and triumph of the Eternal and Incarnate Son of God.

This is history, recorded and attested event. It no more depends on me for its truth than does the history of Cæsar, or of Cromwell. External to me stands this wonderful fact, Jesus Christ, slain and risen. I do not make it, but I take it.

He is, indeed, "the thing that I long for";

the propitiation for my sin, proved to be such
by His resurrection after His altar-death; the
adequate Cause, wholly by Himself, why even
I, touching Him, united to Him, should be not
only forgiven but accepted with divine joy by
the Father who infinitely loves Him.

He in His Person and Character is indeed
competent to fulfil my heart's longing for a satisfying Object of pure and worshipping love—
"chief among ten thousand, altogether lovely."

And this wonderful and all-blessed Lord thus
satisfies the human soul because He is not the
echo but the answer. He is not a splendid
figment of speculation. He is revealed through
events of history; in lines of fact which do not
depend on our moods, and cannot change. He
is revealed in a historical though supernatural
birth, a historical though sinless life, a historical while propitiatory death, a historical while
supremely miraculous resurrection. As He is
history, He stands clear of this sinful, anxious,
inner world of mine; and He is therefore able,
as He is the Truth, to be its refuge and its
peace. Jesus Christ, immovable in Himself, is
my point of rest, my spring of life.

Such are some of the thankful thoughts with
which we may stand by the empty sepulchre
while the Apostles walk away to their own

home. The garden, the rock, the cave, the winding-sheet, are no scene of romance ; they are historical : " Handle them and see." Jesus Christ has actually suffered and risen again in anticipation of my needs, and of my complete incapacity to meet those needs out of the resources of self.

Let us often walk to Joseph's garden accordingly. When the heart is heavy and weary, casting about for peace, or when it is preoccupied and earthly, and refuses to attach itself in conscious, affectionate faith to its one and perfect hope, Jesus Christ, then let us not go deeper into the heart, for it will only disappoint us, but let us return to the facts—to the Person who is our Life. Let us stand again beside the open and vacant sepulchre, and see again and trust again the risen Son of God. There let us leave behind alike self's sinfulness and its imagined righteousness, and calmly give thanks for His great glory and accomplished work, joining Bonar as he sings :

> Thy works, not mine, O Christ,
>   Speak gladness to my heart ;
> They tell me all is done,
>   They bid my fear depart.

IV

MARY AND THE LORD.

OUR last study closed with verse 10. We watched the departure of Peter and John from the garden to the city, as they retired with the new-born belief in their hearts that Jesus was risen, while the light of prophecy broke in on that astonishing fact and turned it into a glorious truth of redemption.

How brief, how unadorned, is the notice in the narrative : *So the disciples went back to their own abode* (πρὸς ἑαυτούς). Its simplicity is one of the many notes of truth in the passage. No creator of an unreal scene (writing within the first two centuries) would have thought of sending them away so quietly, with so little apparent *effect* in the story. Such simplicity, meanwhile, is quite in the manner of the Fourth Gospel. It is of a piece with the extremely simple sequel of the raising of Lazarus, and again with the noble brevity of verse 21 below : *So the disciples were glad, seeing the Lord.*

Here the narrator is already occupied, so to speak, with the next great fact in the chain of events, the appearance to Mary. Peter and John have done their part, they have borne their witness to the Resurrection by telling us what they found in the tomb ; now it is time for Mary's witness.

Once more we pause to observe the holy carelessness of the Evangelist about his own apostolic prominence, or Peter's, apart from the relation which he and Peter bear to Christ. The two leading Apostles, and their new resurrection-faith, are in his view merely a fragment of the witness to Jesus. And if the solitary woman left weeping by the empty cave can serve as well, or better, for the next fragment of that witness, let Peter and John move away unnoticed, and let Mary fill the scene.

"We preach not," and we depict not, "ourselves, but Christ Jesus as Lord, and ourselves your bondservants, because of Jesus" (2 Cor. iv. 5) ; such is the uniform spirit of the Apostles and Evangelists. For our little sphere, let it be always our spirit too. If we would have it so, we must be always learning their secret ; we must have for ourselves the Lord Jesus as the one grand certainty, satisfaction, joy, and hope.

The quiet self-forgetfulness of St John's treatment of narrative (a spirit which appears, indeed, though in different forms, far and wide in Scripture narrations generally) is a phenomenon full of importance. Certainly it is a literary paradox, this balance, this calmness, when we remember at the same time the prodigious character of the events related. The morning of the Resurrection is described with the same simplicity and absence of effort as the conversation by Jacob's Well. How does this simple and unanxious manner tell as an inner evidence of truthfulness? Somewhat thus, if I read aright. Had the story of the Resurrection, and the whole circle of Gospel miracles, been a creation of imagination, a result merely of mental and spiritual emotion, then the emotions and impressions (to produce the results which followed) must have been very vehement experiences of highly excitable minds. And if so, if this were all, then these same minds would have been left, on the hypothesis, to work out their emotions as they might, uncontrolled, uncorrected, by the word and power of a risen Redeemer. The issue of such conditions would surely be not only hopeless divergences but wild exaggerations. But what we have as a fact before us is at least substantial consistency of statement and great calmness of manner. To any one who watches carefully the ways of man this is good moral evidence, not that nothing extraordinary had occurred, but that the wonderful something which had occurred had come with amplest warrant of its reality, and had become a permanent and most powerful, while elevating and calming, factor in the minds of the narrators.

The Evangelist writes of the Resurrection with dispassionate calmness because the Resurrection was an objective fact, absolutely certain ; and because the Risen One had come back not merely to be seen and vanish, but to teach, to control, and to abide with His disciples' souls for ever.

This same quietness of manner, with the same explanation, may be traced back into the narratives of the Crucifixion-time, where the Evangelists display an altogether wonderful calmness and (if I may use the word) fairness of tone in describing the conduct of the enemies and murderers of their Lord.

But it is more than time to proceed in our study of the text, from verse 11 and onwards.

But Mary was standing at the tomb, weeping, outside. So while she wept, she stooped from the side (to look) into the tomb, and beholds (θεωρεῖ) two angels, in white, seated, one at the

head and one at the feet, where lay the body of
Jesus. And they say to her, Woman, why do
you weep? She says to them, Because they have
taken away my Lord, and I do not know where
they have put Him. And with these words she
turned backwards, and beholds Jesus, standing,
and did not know that it was Jesus. Jesus says
to her, Woman, why do you weep? whom do
you seek? She, thinking that it is the gardener,
says to Him, Sir, if you carried Him off, tell me
where you put Him, and I will take Him away.
Jesus says to her, Mary! Turning, she says to
Him, Rabbouni, which means, Master (Διδάσκαλε).
Jesus says to her, Do not touch (feel) Me, for I
have not yet gone up to My Father. Go to My
brethren, and say to them, I go up to My Father
and your Father, and My God and your God.
Mary of Magdala comes, reporting to the disciples
that she has seen the Lord, and that He said
these things to her.

Verse 11. *But Mary was standing at the tomb.*
Εἱστήκει, she had taken her place, and was now
there. Probably she had followed the Apostles
out from the city, but more slowly. She would
be left behind naturally by the pace of the two
eager men, young as probably they both were;
and besides, she would hurry less, as she knew
the fact, which they had yet to assure themselves

of, that the tomb was empty. She entered the garden after them, perhaps unnoticed by them, and not much heeding their looks and words as they entered successively and saw what the cavern had to reveal. We need not wonder at the absorbed unconsciousness of one another which those disciples, men and women, showed that morning. After all these Christian centuries, and after our personal Christian education, it is hard for us, even when we have found the Saviour with joy for our own, to realize what was the first grief for His death and the first joy for His resurrection. Those were moments which to an unknown degree threw minds and hearts back on themselves.

So, for the time, Mary was to the Apostles, and they were to her, as if they were not. Was Jesus stolen away? was Jesus risen again?— that was all.

The loving and desolate Galilean woman remains, then, as she thinks, all alone. If she just noticed the silent departure of ‚Peter and John, it only said to her the worst—the Lord was not in the tomb, the Lord's body was gone. So she "stood," seemingly as if paralysed : not kneeling, making no gesture of misery ; standing, just as she had come, κλαίουσα, weeping, alone. And yet, like other sorrowful disciples since.

she was not alone. Angels were just in front of her, and the Lord was just behind her. And the very thing which caused her tears, His absence from the place where she sought Him, was soon to be her blessed surprise, her sudden and endless joy.

So *Mary was standing, at the tomb, weeping, outside.* Thus the words follow each other in the Greek.

Verse 12. *So while she wept, she stooped from the side to look into the tomb, and beholds two angels, in white, seated, one at the head and one at the feet, where the body of Jesus lay.*

Again detail follows detail with a peculiar and thrilling simplicity. While weeping, she bent her head and looked in; the look not of curiosity, but of bereaved love, which in a sad unreasoning way cares for the bare spot where the beloved has been. And now her wet eyes, gazing fixedly ($\theta\epsilon\omega\rho\epsilon\tilde{\iota}$), see two human figures in the dark place; for simply human in form, surely, all Angels are in Scripture when they appear in intercourse with men; the winged aspect is seen only in symbolic or mystic surroundings. There they are, two youthful watchers, as we may suppose them to look (Mark xvi. 5, $\nu\epsilon\alpha\nu\acute{\iota}\sigma\kappa\omicron\iota$), seated, in quiet dignity, one at each end of the niche in the cavern-wall,

E

where the holy Body had lain in its linen folds. They were ἐν λευκοῖς, in white clothing, white and more than white, positively bright[1] ; so we gather from Luke xxiv. 4, ἐν ἐσθήσεσιν ἀστραπτούσαις. We may compare the word στίλβειν used for the white raiment of the transfigured Lord Himself, Mark ix. 3. Such a radiance, or something like it, shone in that garden sepulchre, touching with light its rocky roof, and walls, and floor, and "the linen cloths" as they lay there. There, before this weeping disciple, this once possessed and miserable woman, sat revealed those two inhabitants of the heavenly home. And listen ; to reassure her, to tell her that it is no delusion generated by her glancing tears, they speak to her, perhaps one by one, in human words, and with gentle, I might almost say respectful, sympathy : *Woman, why do you weep ?* Γύναι, as all know, is a word of perfect courtesy, a word of as much possible respectfulness as Κύριε would be in an address to a man. *Woman, lady, why do you weep ?*

It is a moving thing to observe the sympathy of Angels with men and women, as Scripture so very often brings it out. "These things" (the

---

[1] See Trench on the word λευκός in his commentary on Rev. ii. 17.

salvation of sinners by the Son of God) "Angels desire to look into " (1 Pet. i. 12) ; and indeed we find it to be so with them whenever the veil is lifted. They are no mere official dignitaries of the court of heaven, just stooping to hand a message of reprieve to pardoned rebels of an alien race. They come as brethren to brethren, as servants to fellow-servants, as lovers and worshippers of the Son of God to those who, in the midst of sin and death, yet love and worship Him also. Aye, they come as to those whose nature He has taken, and who do not grudge sinful man that inexplicable and inexpressible privilege, but love him for it. So Mary, this weeping child of a sinful race, all weakness, all mistake, is to these heavenly ones an object of holy sympathy. To them she is one whom Jesus Christ loves, and who loves Him, and it is enough. *Why do you weep? Whom do you seek?*

Verse 13. But for Mary all this is, for the present, nothing. In her then state of thought and feeling, the appearances and the voices were to her as things of every day, commonplace, indifferent. She just answers, *Because they have taken away my Lord, and I do not know where they have put Him.*

Nothing could be more curiously truth-like

and truthful than this indifference of Mary of Magdala. It was quite another thing than the startled *fear* of the women when (Matt. xxviii. 5, 8) the Angel appeared on the stone. That was a shock, a sudden sight, on their first arrival. Here grief had had time to deepen, and to fix itself on the absorbing fact of the absence of Jesus. And such was the bitterness of that absence of the Body which (to her mind at that time) was so soon to be dust—such was the grief of its absence, because He was her Lord, that the sight of two Angels, and their audible voices, were to her, wonderfully yet naturally, as nothing.

What would it be to us if our Lord, as we have learnt to know Him, were removed? What if Jesus were found absent from our heart, our life, our earth, our heaven? If He—not the slain, but the slain and living, Lamb of God, our Lord, were found to be non-existent, or existent no more for us? Would not our souls so fail as to find no rest, no remedy anywhere else? Should we not really feel that heaven itself and its inhabitants, without Him (*per impossibile*), would be blank, unsatisfying, even formidable? Yes, for heaven is not the cause of our pardon, nor the source of our life, nor is the angelic race our Saviour and King.

And if indeed He is, as He is, such that
nothing can ever possibly take His place for
us, what a place should His be in the heart!
Henceforth we will more than ever watch and
pray against even the transient pain, so heavy
and so paralysing, of even seeming to find Him
absent, sin having taken away our Lord, and
we know not where He is gone.

Verse 14. *And with these words she turned
backwards, and beholds* (θεωρεῖ) *Jesus, standing,
and did not know that it is Jesus.*

She turned backwards, bent her stooping head
towards the garden, not the cavern. It is vain
perhaps to ask what made her turn. Chrysostom
gives a singularly beautiful explanation—that, as
the Lord appeared, the Angels did obeisance,
and Mary turned to see *to whom.* Or, as some
have guessed, she felt that subtle consciousness
of some one near her which we have all probably
felt at times. But was it not simply the aimless
movement of a new disappointment? The long
look into the cave has told her that Jesus is not
there, and now she will look away, and go
away.

St John, we may be sure, is here recording
exactly what Mary told him. " So I turned my
head, and there behind me stood, as I thought,
the gardener."

And she sees Jesus, standing. The word θεωρεῖ is again used. Even here, though certainly at first sight it is less easy to read than usual, we do read its distinctive meaning, the "seeing" of a deliberate gaze.[1] The look she gave was but sidelong, for see below, ver. 16, where she "turns herself" again more completely. But it was steady. She deliberately and distinctly saw some one there.

Whence the Lord had come we do not know. How long He had been there, whether up to that moment He had been visible to any one, whether He now appeared in His familiar form, we are not told. But He was there, none the less because Mary did not know Him and so little realized all that He was.

There stood the Lord of death and life, fresh from bearing that disciple's sins and ours, from those unfathomable and unknown sorrows of His Soul (ἄγνωστα παθήματα) which went to make the ransom of our souls ; just come from the unseen world "in the power of an indissoluble life" (Heb. vii. 16). There He stood before her. And He was "the same Jesus" still ; the same in corporeal and spiritual iden-

---

[1] See this meaning at once unmistakable, and spiritually most important, in John vi. 40.

tity, the very Body which had been torn by the
Roman scourges and nails, the very Soul which
had been exceeding sorrowful unto death ; the
same Humanity under the same Personality,
glorified but identical. And He was the same
too in moral identity, the unalterable Lord
Jesus in faithfulness, patience, and love. He
dies for His doubting and mistaking followers ;
He rises for them, and finds them mistaking
and despairing. They, if I may say so, are still
themselves, and more than themselves, in their
imperfections ; He is still Himself, and more
than Himself, in His perfections. He is about to
deal with Mary, and with the two, and the ten,
and Thomas, as indeed "this same Jesus"; so
we shall see in due time. There is strong
consolation in this picture of the moral identity
of the risen Lord.

But she did not know that it is Jesus. Though
essentially the same, He was to her now different. Partly, no doubt, it was simply a case
of imperfect sight. She did not see Him full ;
perhaps she did not look *in His face* at all ;
and she was in tears. But also we have here,
surely, one of the many cases (Matt. xxviii. 17 ;
Mark xvi. 13 ; Luke xxiv. 16, 37 ; John xxi. 4)
where we trace a change in the aspect of the
Risen Saviour, and also that it was His pleasure

sometimes not to be recognized, checking the
message of the eyes to the mind.

In passing I see here again an evidence of
truth. A fabricated narrative would hardly
have gone out of its way to say that the Risen
One, after forty hours' absence, was at first not
recognized. It might even seem suspicious,
were it not true. *All* the Gospels record this
inability of the disciples to recognize their Lord
at once, and then go on to show how fully the
doubt was removed. And how *permanently* it
was removed ! After Thomas' recovery to faith
we detect in the first age of Christianity no
trace of the least hesitancy, no whisper of a
word of retractation of certainty, on the part
of any one of the professed witnesses of the
Resurrection. No heretic, no pagan, has
preserved the faintest tradition of any after
misgiving in the Church of the witnesses.

Verse 15. *Jesus says to her, Woman, why
do you weep? whom do you seek?*[1] Blessed
enquiries, from that Enquirer. When Jesus
Christ asks us about our sorrows their truest
comfort is already begun ; when He asks about

---

[1] "This first word of the Risen Lord to a mortal is an
inexhaustible text for the Resurrection, which it is the
business of the preacher to unfold. He has risen again
to comfort those who mourn" (Stier).

our loss, our blank, He has already begun to fill
it.   Happy those who, like Mary, are found by
Him, even if they are found grieving for Him
and missing Him.   We must not fear to tell
Him all our fears.   There is sure to be some
element of sin, however recondite, in them.
There was such an element in Mary's fears ;
she *ought* to have remembered His many
promises better, and trusted them more firmly.
She *ought* to have known that, come what
might, He must conquer and reign.   Yes, even
a Mary at the tomb had sin somewhere in her
unhopefulness.   Yet the Risen Lord came in
person to dispel it.   And to us He is ready to
come as personally to help us, not because we
deserve, but because we need ; because in our
guilty weakness we are so disappointing, if the
word may be allowed, to Him.   So we will
come, and speak out, keeping nothing back,
telling Him our worst misgiving, as simply as if
we could hear Him say, "Why do you weep?
What do you want?"

But Mary is slow to see the light of joy.
Perhaps already she has turned her eyes away
again.   She is so little conscious of supernatural
glories and joys close to her that she thinks
she sees there—Joseph's gardener !   A very

homely, unsentimental conjecture it was; certainly not the thought of a *femme hallucinée* such as Renan, himself hallucinated, supposes her to have been. She was quite sane, though very sad, when she said to herself, "It is the gardener." In great sorrow there is sometimes a cool, prosaic consciousness of trifling or common things around, as curious as it is real; the high wrought state of the mind leaves it open more than usual to the touch of even small impressions. So Mary would seem rapidly to have *calculated*, "It is the rich man's gardener; the Sabbath is past, and they may work. Joseph did not intend my Master's Body to stay permanently in his fine grave, only to rest there for a while, because it was so near; and now his servant has been told to take the Body away and bury it somewhere else." And then, with the resolve of a love which felt as if it could move mountains, she thinks she will take it into her own care, lift it, carry it, bestow it in some untroubled sepulchre, if she may but have it again. *Sir*, so the helpless mourner speaks, with the deference of helplessness, *if* you *carried Him off, tell me where you put Him, and I will take Him away.*

"*Him:*"—she uses no name; no need to do so occurs to her. Jesus, even slain and gone, fills her whole thought, and she assumes that it must be so with others too.

How truth-like again in every detail! the submissive sadness of the appeal, and, on the other hand, the blind energy of love, which undertakes, in the exhaustion of grief, to do the work of a strong man, removing and burying the Body.

So she plans a second interment for Jesus, while the living Jesus is there, and just about to lift her in the embrace of His manifested power and love.

Verse 16. *Jesus says to her, Mary!* The reading Μαριάμ, *Miriam*, is, on the whole, most probable here ; the specially Jewish form of the name, not *Maria*, its Greek equivalent. It is interesting to remember that the same Voice, at a later day, spoke to another heart by its own home-name, Σαούλ, not Σαῦλε (so in all the narratives of the great Conversion). It is observable, whatever inferences we may draw, that where the Evangelists record the Lord's utterance of an Aramaic word or sentence the occasion is almost always one where a specially close and personal appeal was needed. The Aramaic of the cry from the Cross is scarcely an exception.[1]

[1] See this handled very ably in Dr Alex. Roberts' *Discussions on the Gospels.*

But this is a minor point here; the all-important fact here is that He used the woman's *name*. The personal appeal, the voice to the individual, to that mysterious personality with which, as a fact, man so intimately connects his *name*—it is this we are to notice. It is no longer *Woman*, it is *Mary*. Any voice might have said the first; the speaker of this last, then and there, must be no other than the Friend who had set her free.

Turning, she says to Him, Rabboni, or more precisely, probably, (some think that we have here a *Galilean* form,) *Rabbouni.* This St John at once explains; *which means Master*, Διδάσκαλε, *Teacher;* but, of course, with the conveyed idea (in the Hebrew) of the greatness, the venerability, of the Teacher. The termination, it would seem (Rabboun*i*), may either be the possessive suffix (*My* Master), or an appellative (*O* Master); either alternative gives much the same impression of intensity and reverent endearment. With the word, she clasps Him as He stands. In that tumult of fear, love, and joy, to assure herself of the objective reality of His presence, she lays her touch, the touch which *feels* (ἄπτομαι), on His sacred Person, probably on the feet, towards which she bent. Compare Matt. xxviii. 9.

Verse 17. *Jesus says to her, Do not touch (feel)*
Me, for I have not yet gone up to My Father.
Go to My brethren, and say to them, I go up to
My Father and your Father, and My God and
your God. Mary of Magdala comes reporting
to the disciples that she has seen the Lord, and
that He said these things to her.

The two verses, 17, 18, I thus merely translate. It would be impossible in this chapter to
dwell on ver. 17, with its problems of reference,
and its depth of truth about the Father, the
Son, and the soul.

Let us for the present close with the delight-
ful effort to place ourselves in thought beside
those two persons, in the calm, silent morning of
that wonderful spring-time, in Joseph's garden.
Looking on them we forget, as the Gospel
forgets, the blessed Angels close at hand; JESUS
and Mary Magdalene have much more to do
than they with our salvation and peace. It is
indeed a place good to visit, and to visit at the
moment we have studied. We stand upon the
common earth; the ground of a garden, near
the walls of a still existing town, a garden whose
last traces are, some think, still visible. We
see the cavern tomb, and its round door-stone
rolled out. We look up to the common morning sky, through the garden trees. But in that

quiet place and hour JESUS Himself is making known, for the very first time, the success, the completeness, the glory of His salvation. It is HE who stands literally there, speaking to Mary, but now much more speaking to us, to you, to me, as we too "turn" to Him to hear His words about Himself. He points *us* to His own open grave; that is, to His accomplished victory for us, His finished atonement for our sins. He points us to His living Self, living immortally, eternally, living at this moment, and present with us, even when "we perceive Him not." He points us to the heavens above, and tells us that He is going thither, and that we, for whom He has died, and who have come to Him, and whose sins—including doubts and fears—He has wonderfully cancelled in His own blood, may be sure that for us that heaven is home. It is home for Peter, who denied Him; for the Eleven, who forsook Him; for Magdalene, who thought that His death was the end. It is home for us, unworthy; for He is there. Henceforth, the earth and the heavens are filled for us with light—the light of the redemption, the love, and the presence, of the sacrificed and risen Son of God.

V

FROM THE GARDEN TO THE CHAMBER.

OUR last study brought us to the close of the account of the interview of Mary Magdalene with the Risen Lord. In a passage so conspicuously rich in treasures of grace and truth, I make no apology for leaving some points quite untouched. But on two main points, which have been touched in some sort, so little has been said that some additional words must be said upon them now, and at more length.

I refer to two topics given us by the utterance of the Lord Jesus in ver. 17 : *Do not touch Me, for I have not yet gone up to My Father. Go to My brethren, and say to them, I go up to My Father and your Father, and My God and your God.*

(i.) The prohibition and command to Mary. I need not explain to my readers what difficulty this has presented to expositors. What was the touching? Why was it forbidden? What was the connexion (observe the "*for*") between the "Touch Me not" and the "I have not yet gone up to My Father"? These questions have been very variously answered.

Yet we may be sure that the first meaning, however, must have been intended to be quite simple. Addressed to that loving disciple, in that moment of supreme emotion, the logic cannot have been recondite or involved, in the blessed Speaker's purpose. In view of this, I incline to that explanation of the passage which connects as closely as possible the prohibition "Touch Me not" with the commission "Go to My brethren." We observe that the Greek verb is in the present, or continuing, imperative, not in the aorist subjunctive ; μή μου ἅπτου, not μή μου ἅψῃ. Accordingly, by familiar laws of Greek usage, it conveys an order not to forbear touching Him at all, but to forbear a longer, a prolonged, touching. She is not to linger over it : it is enough ; let her remove the hand which *feels* the sacred limb.

The verb ἅπτομαι occurs only here in St John. But its general usage assures us that it indicates here nothing like clasping or clinging, as when the women (Matt. xxviii. 9) "held Him by the feet." It means no more than simple touching. It occurs, for example, where the Lord (Mark

viii. 22) is asked to "touch" a blind man's eyes ;
and where the suffering woman (Matt. ix. 21)
plans to "touch" just the fringe of His garment.
Here Mary Magdalene may have just laid her
hand, in felt contact and no more, on His foot,
or on His hand ; not clinging, not embracing,
only *feeling*, as if to make certain that no vision,
but the living LORD, was there.   And it is this
then which He thus gently checked. We cannot
see in the prohibition accordingly anything
like a reproof, as if she had taken a liberty, as
if she had not been reverent enough.   The
thoughts familiarly associated with *Noli me
tangere*, as a quoted phrase, are quite out of
place here.

May we not paraphrase the purport of the
words of Jesus somewhat thus ? " Do not linger
here, touching Me, to ascertain My bodily
reality, in the incredulity of your exceeding joy.
I *am* in very fact before you, standing quite
literally and locally on this plot of ground,
not yet ascended to the heavens ; you need not
doubt, and ask, and test. And, moreover, there
is another reason why not to linger thus ; I
have an errand for you, Mary. I desire you to
go hence, and at once, for Me ; to go to My
brethren, and to tell them that I *am* about to go
up thither ; that in glorious fact I am risen, and

therefore on My way to the throne; going to My Father and their Father, and My God and their God."

She might be sure that He was literally, and still, on earth; so she need not any longer touch Him. She was to carry the tidings to the disciples; so she must not any longer linger at His side.

Here then we may further trace, with thanksgiving, a lesson for all believers, for all and sundry who (Rom. x. 9; Heb. xiii. 20) "believe in the heart that the God of peace hath brought again from the dead our Lord Jesus, that great Shepherd of the sheep." The lesson is, not to be too constantly and too anxiously tracing and retracing the evidence of the glorious fact of the Resurrection, vitally precious as that evidence is, and not to stay pondering and enjoying that fact for one's self only, and so, inevitably, with an imperfect realization; but to carry on to others the light and blessedness of the fact, of the truth, that He is "risen indeed," and ascended too; saying to them (as He shall give occasion to the glad and ready messenger) both with lips and yet more with a life full of His resurrection-life: "I have seen the Lord; He is risen, He is ascended, and our life is hid with Him in God."

Beautiful it is to observe, in the Gospel narratives of Easter, this instant commission to *all* the newly-enlightened disciples to tell to the rest, "as they mourned and wept," their glorious cause of joy, in simplicity, confidence, and love.

(ii.) And now *what was* the message which Mary was to carry, and for which she was thus to leave the tangible presence of her risen Lord? Strange to say, it is the message of His approaching departure. Not "I am come back," but "I am going away, I am going up."

Here is indeed a deeply spiritual aspect of the resurrection message. The return of the Lord Jesus bodily for a season to His people on earth, was much, unspeakably much, but it was not all; the Resurrection was the avenue to the Ascension. Or, to put it otherwise and perhaps in a safer way, as the blessed Death is seen in its comfort and glory only in the light of the Resurrection, so the Resurrection is fully seen in all its precious import only in the light of the Ascension. The Risen One is hastening on to His true place, the place of Rev. v. (where we are permitted to see the Ascension, as it were, from its heavenly side); He is going to be the Lamb *upon the throne.* The finished work of His Death and Rising, what was it but the beginning of His continuing work of Intercession? Let us not forget this in all our daily contemplation of, and intercourse with, our Lord; in our life in and on Him, who is at once our pardon, our power, and our holiness. After all, we are not so much to look back, as to look up, on Him who was crucified for us and rose again. His atonement is in one supreme aspect absolute, complete, never to be repeated. We rest on it as on "fact accomplished." We know that He did once, and now no more for ever, bear for us the unknown burthen of our guilt. But the application of His atonement, in some of its most precious aspects, is a thing incessant. Momentarily needed (for sin's prevention as well as cure), it is momentarily applied to the believer's soul; it is free and efficacious each day, and hour, and moment, for our reception, and possession, and enjoyment :

> His love intense, His merit fresh,
> As if but newly slain.

Our safety under that Shelter, once given in covenant, is ever being given in actual mercy and truth; and so too is our fruition of the once-pledged gift of His Holy Spirit, that gift so vitally connected (see Gal. iii. 13, 14) with our justification through the merits of the Crucified Jesus. And how do we joyfully know that this giving *is* thus continuous? We know it because Jesus Christ is not only risen, but ascended also. " It is Christ that died, yea, rather, that is risen again, who is even at the right hand of God, who also maketh intercession for us." " He, by the right hand of God exalted, hath shed forth this " (Rom. viii. 34 ; Acts ii. 33).

The Epistle to the Hebrews, in its great picture of the Lord Jesus as the true High Priest, emphasizes this in a very remarkable way. The Death, the precious blood, is everywhere in the Epistle ; but we read of the Resurrection only once (xiii. 20). The Resurrection, in the main argument, is merged in the Ascension ; and this because the intercession of our Aaron-Melchisedec is essentially bound up with His Ascension. He intercedes "for ever" as "a Priest upon *His throne.*" "When He had by Himself purged our sins, He *sat down* on the right hand of the Majesty on high " (i. 3 ; see iv. 14 ; vi. 20 ; vii. 25, 26 ; viii. 1 ; ix. 11, 12, 24 ; x. 12, 13 ; xii. 2, 24).

Thus the Ascension is, in deepest spiritual truth, the sum and crown of the work of Jesus Christ. Looking at it through the lens of Scripture, we see, gathered into one, the rays of the Cross and of the Resurrection, the atoning Work once and for ever done, and the ceaseless

Result, in the power of the Lord's endless life, ever flowing out, flowing down, from Him who, as our Mediator and as our Head, ever liveth to make intercession for us; to receive for us, to give to us.

Thus, although that very evening He is going to visit His brethren, and to fill them with the mingled natural and spiritual joys of His Resurrection, He sends on to them in advance the message of the coming joy, greater and wholly spiritual, of His Ascension. And note well the terms of the message: it is an Ascension not merely to heaven, but to a God and Father. And to what a God, what a Father! No mere Absolute or Supreme, no mere First Cause, unknown perhaps, and unknowable, except as an antecedent Somewhat demanded by the logic of phenomena. Jesus Christ is going into the depths of the unseen universe; yet whither He goes we know, for we know to Whom He goes. We have a double, nay, a quadruple description of HIM, to fix and to fill our thought. HE is Father, and He is God, each in two respects; first, in each case, in relation to Jesus Christ, then, in relation to His brethren. Here is a fourfold chain of truth, light, and love by which the believing sinner, coming to the sinner's Friend, lays hold of nothing less than the throne and of Him who sits thereon.

We observe, of course, and we have all done so a hundred times, the fact that the chain *is* not double but quadruple : not "our Father and our God" (the Lord Jesus never speaks so ; His nearest approach to it, and that is not really the same thing, occurs John iv. 22 : "*we* know what *we worship*") but "Mine and yours" in each case. It is the same relation, but predicated in different respects, when the Saviour and the disciple are respectively in view. Can we fail, in the whole light of Scripture, to see what the difference is? "*My* Father, as by eternal Generation, ἄχρονος γέννησις; *your* Father, by adopting and regenerating grace in Me : *My* God, as by Paternal Deity, by relations within the Godhead, and also in the bright mystery of Incarnation ; *your* God, as in covenant through Me ; Mine, and so therefore yours, yours because Mine."

We are led to touch, with reverence, on a truth implied in this passage, though not directly taught in it, the Filial aspect of the Godhead of Christ. I humbly conceive that the words, "My Father and My God," have as much to do with the Divine as with the Human nature of

the Son. Christ is God ; yes, in all the fulness of
the word. He is Eternal, Necessary, Uncreated,
Absolute in every sacred attribute ; Co-equal
with the Father in "majesty, power and
eternity," Blessed for ever. Yet He is THE SON.
He is, while God, Filial. Unbeginning, He is
yet eternally *of* the Father, and His blessed
Being is in just such a sense subordinate that
He is—with the "is" of eternity—the Son.
Thought is lost, or rather silenced, when we
come really in face of the revealed glory of
the Godhead. But when we have just spelt
out the revelation of It as it stands, we see in
that revelation two truths most bright of all for
us—the Godhead and the Sonship of the
Lord our Saviour. And in the light of that
view it is surely safe and Scriptural to see, in
a passage like this, words which befit the
voice of Jesus Christ speaking, not as Son of
Man only, but as God the Son.

But if the doctrinal value of these words is
thus large and precious, how great is their
practical power and sweetness in personal application to the Christian's soul ! Do we really
take in, to some degree, what it is to know God
the Father as the God and Father of our Lord
Jesus Christ, and *in this respect* our God and
Father too ? To know the Father in beholding

(θεωροῦντες) the Son? To love the Father in loving the Son? To rest on the Father in resting on the Son, on God the Son, on "the only begotten Son who is in the bosom of the Father"?

A very different view of God is this from that of *the mere* Theist. "The Absolute God," says Martin Luther,[1] "all men, who do not wish to perish, should fly from, because human nature and God Absolute are irreconcilable enemies (*infestissimi inimici*). From the Name of God we dare not shut out Christ. Not naked Deity but God robed and revealed in His word and promises we must lay hold upon, or inevitable despair must crush us. This God we can embrace, and behold, with joy and confidence; but Absolute Deity is as a wall of brass, on which we cannot strike without ruin."

How precious is that ancient, that old-fashioned faith, too often slighted under the unpopular designation "*orthodox*"—how precious, to the heart which craves, and discovers, a Saviour! In it the Lord is seen as not only God and Man, but *God the Son* and Man. He

---

[1] On Ps. li. 1; quoted by Professor Stanley Leathes, *Witness of the Old Testament to Christ*, p. 244. Dr Leathes remarks that Luther's "invaluable works were never more worthy of study than at the present crisis of the Church."

is revealed, He is believed in, as God the Son ;
not that we may worship Him less truly than
we worship the Father, or trust Him less, or
love Him less, but that we may all the more
truly worship, trust, and love Him and His
Father, who are One.   He is the Eternal Son :
who shall measure the love of Paternal Godhead
for Filial?   And—the Father "spared not His
own (ἴδιον) Son, but delivered Him up for us all "
(Rom. viii. 32) ; "so loving the world that He
gave His only begotten Son."   In the rapturous
Te Deum we address our Redeemer as the
Everlasting Son of the Father ; and in that
title we adore at once the love of the Giver and
the love of the Given ; and we feel that a
Subordination, not of essence, but of relation, a
Relationship just so far subordinate that it is
filial, only intensifies our adoration of the Godhead of our Saviour.   It shows us, through the
fact of His Filial Godhead, something of the
ocean of love within the Eternal Nature of the
Triune ; love in the divine Relationships within
It ; love in the outgoings towards us of such a
salvation from It.

Is this too much of a digression?   I know
not how to avoid it, for the very attraction of
the blessed theme.   The meditation of Him,
the Lord Christ the Son, is sweet ; joy in the

Lord is kindled at it.[1] In gazing on Him as the Son we understand *a little*, as in a glimpse, of what the Father meant when, from the heavens He called Him "My Beloved." And if by divine mercy we have been drawn to love the Beloved of the Father, shall we not be glad? Shall we not take home for ourselves the joy of this message which He sent on the Easter morning to the bewildered beings whom yet He was not ashamed to call His brethren—" I ascend unto My Father and your Father, and unto My God and your God"? It is the voice of the Beloved.

With such an errand, then, does Mary leave the garden.

> She first, all-happy Magdalena, bore
> From Joseph's grot the bliss unheard before,
> And still her tidings was the broken tomb ;
> And still, though ages roll,
> That message from the soul,
> And that alone, must chase the enfolding gloom.
> Jesus, our Lord, the First and Last,
> Thy rising work is past ;
> Then present is our strength and rest,
> And all our future blest.

She comes, reporting to the disciples that she has seen the Lord, and that He said these things to her.

She obeyed at once. Quietly, with the joy of

---

[1] See Psalm civ. 34.

love (we seem to see her), she gives up her literal contact with His presence, and goes from the company of the risen Jesus Christ to the very different company of His mistaken and troubled disciples, all of whom, save Peter and John (and they, perhaps, were still apart), still lay in the cloud of their awful disappointment, and were not greatly disposed to see light through it. St Luke (xxiv. 11) tells us of the report of the women (and probably Mary's special message-bearing is included in that brief summary) as seeming to the disciples λῆρος, "nonsense"; and of course they said so to the messengers. Perhaps the first theory of James, and Philip, and Andrew was what long after was the theory of Renan, that the report was the product of illusion, and the illusion the product of feminine emotion. However, Mary went, in that spirit of meek but mighty confidence which is given to the soul now, as well as then, by the certainty in itself of the life and the love of Jesus. " He that believeth shall not make haste" (Isa. xxviii. 16) ; "we which have believed do enter into rest " (Heb. iv. 3), a rest full of power. All through that forenoon, probably, she saw her Lord no more ; nor through that afternoon, which He spent upon the Emmaus road. And perhaps from time to time that day she heard much to distress her in the refusal of

" His brethren," many of them at least, to believe
Him risen. Yet we are quite sure that it was a
day of unimaginable joy for Mary Magdalene.
Her own load of hopeless grief was gone. If He
had dismissed her from His side, if He remained
hour by hour out of sight, what did it matter,
beside the gladness of knowing that He was
risen, and alive for evermore? An hour, a few
hours, ago she had loved Him with a love full
of despair ; now, with a love full of immortality.
Then it was comparatively a blind affection, now
she had a sunrise view of what He really was,
and of what He had done, and would for ever
do, for her. Then the past seemed all failure,
the present solitude and ruin, the future a cruel
gloom. Now past, present, and future were all
filled with the work, the love, the triumph of
her dear risen Lord. Then she could go to the
others only to mingle her fears and tears with
theirs, now she went as her Saviour's own commanded messenger to them, to constrain them
to believe and be glad because of Him, and she
bore witness to Him by her own joy. Her own
burthen was now gone ; how much better now
she could bear theirs ! Her own perplexities
were passed away now for ever ; how gently and
tenderly, while with confidence, she could now
wait for the time when He should be pleased

(as, of course, He would be pleased) either to open their hearts to her message, or in some other way to reveal Himself to them !

I do not apologize for thus dwelling on some of the possibilities of that day, as spent by the first messenger of the Resurrection.[1] Our own hearts, surely, see in them more than possibilities, and they carry lessons of living power to ourselves as believers, not in ourselves, but in a risen Redeemer.

Throughout that day of joy and trial there must have been, for Mary, a wonderful conquest of joy over trial. She would be " at leisure from herself," and very full of Jesus Christ. She would be specially softened and sanctified, cut off delightfully from sinning in word or spirit, by the unselfish, adoring sense of His triumph, simply *as His.* It was not only that *she* was personally relieved, rescued, I might almost say immortalized already, by what she knew for herself; she knew now also something of the glory, the victory, the joy into which He had entered who had once expelled seven devils from her. And this would more than fill the blank which *nature* might feel when His visible presence was left behind her in the garden. He, she knew, was safe in His own blood-bought

[1] See below, Appendix i.

victory, and was on His way to His own Father's
throne. He had suffered ; it had pleased the
Lord, the Father, to bruise Him (Isa. liii. 10) ;
He had died, going through all that death is,
and more than death can ever be now to His
followers ; He had had to bear it all ; His
Agony and Death were now irrevocable facts.
But so now also was His triumph. "The joy
set before Him" had come. He was in the
infinite repose of conquest over sin and death ;
He would need to die no more. And soon He
would be receiving the eternal tribute of the
praises of heaven, for He was going to the Father.

If all men disbelieved, yet was it all true *for
Him.* And, though they disbelieved, they too
would soon be worshipping with joy like hers ;
for He who had sent that message would not
linger long behind it.

Nor did He do so. The Evangelist who has
dismissed Peter and John now in turn dis-
misses Mary, never to name her again, for she
has done her work for us. He brings us face to
face once more with the Lord.

The day has drawn to its evening. Many
have been its alarms and surprises, and half
hopes, and troubled rumours, and obstinate
reasonings of unbelief. And, now, as the

shadows fall, the group of the Apostles, ten of the Twelve, and others (Luke xxiv. 33) with them, are together. There they are, gathered after scattering, and with some glad awakenings of faith and hope in their souls, for by that time the rumours of the Resurrection had begun to tell, and Peter and John were now with them (see Luke xxiv. 34).

They were assembled, perhaps in John's lodgings, perhaps in the chamber of the Last Supper. The Evangelist takes no pains to tell us, nor does he give us a single extraneous detail ; for instance, the manner of entrance of St Luke's two travellers from Emmaus, who came in a little while before Jesus appeared. St John gives the scene just so as best to show us the Risen Lord Himself. And we will close this chapter with the mere translation of the wonderful record.

Verse 19. *So when it was evening, on that day, the first day of the week, and when the doors of the place where they were gathered had been shut because of their dread of the Jews, Jesus came and took His stand in* (ἔστη εἰς) *their midst, and says to them, Peace be to you. And as He said so He showed them His hands and His side. So the disciples rejoiced* (ἐχάρησαν), *seeing the Lord. So Jesus said to them again, Peace be to you. Even as the Father has*

*sent Me out, I too send you. And as He
said so He breathed a breath towards them,
and says to them, Take (the) Holy Spirit. If
you remit the sins of any, they are remitted
to them; if you retain the sins of any, they are
retained.*

Of course all study of details must be deferred.
But let us at once carry away the fact of that
scene and its blessing. In the hush of the deep
evening, in that broad dimly-lighted chamber,
where the anxious group are listening for the
tread of the enemy, heavy or stealthy, upon the
stairs, and preparing perhaps for such defence
as Galilean courage even then might try, on a
sudden the Holy One Himself is there. And
we are there to see Him, and to be glad with
them in Him. It is our privilege, our right, our
possession. For us He has died and risen; He
is about to ascend for us; He brings for us the
gift of the Spirit.

To us He shows His hands and His side, and
we read there our salvation, as truly as Peter,
and John, and James, and all the once fugitive
disciples, read theirs there that evening. Like
them, we receive it wholly from Him. Like
them, we behold the Lamb of God, sacrificed,
risen, ascending to the heavens, and in that
view we, like them, looking on Him whom *we*

G

have pierced (Zech. xii. 10), step off from the unrest, the languor, the cowardice, of Christless self into the rest and joy of Jesus Christ.

One of the witnesses of that evening, many years later, wrote as follows (1 Pet. i. 3) to all the sharers of his faith : " Blessed be the God and Father of our Lord Jesus Christ, who, according to His abundant mercy, hath begotten us again to a living hope by the resurrection of Jesus Christ from the dead."

Why walk in darkness ?   Has the dear light vanish'd
    That gave us joy to-day?
Has the great Sun departed ?   Has sin banish'd
    His life-begetting ray ?

Lord, Thou art risen ; but Thou descendest never ;
    To-day shines as the past ;
All that Thou wast Thou art, and shalt be ever,
    Brightness from first to last.
Bonar.

VI

THE LORD IN THE CHAMBER.

IN our last study we only touched the narrative of the Saviour's appearance to the gathered company on the Resurrection evening. We now return to that narrative to consider it more in detail. And may He of whom we think approach us and speak to us through our meditation. In the evening shadows may He bring us His light. Even so come, Lord Jesus Christ. In the nightfall of change, of grief, of the sense of sin, and in spite of the doors which our ignorance or unbelief would shut, unwittingly, against Thee, come and speak to us that peace which the world, even at its best and purest, cannot give. Show us Thyself, and breathe into us Thy Spirit.

Verse 19. οὔσης οὖν ὀψίας : *So when it was evening.* The exact hour must be left uncertain, but probably it was an hour, or perhaps two hours, after sunset. The word ὀψία does

not necessarily denote late evening.   Indeed, in
Mark i. 32 (ὀψίας, ὅτε ἔδυ ὁ ἥλιος), it is explicitly
connected with the sunset.   So again in Matt.
xvi. 2, ὀψίας γενομένης λέγετε, Εὐδία, πυρράζει γὰρ
ὁ οὐρανός : there the ruddy splendour of the
sunset sky, with its afterglow, the sign of " a
glorious morrow," is connected with the ὀψία.
But on the other hand, to fix within *some*
limits the time reference here, we must remember that St Luke supplies us with a note in his
narrative of Emmaus.   There the two disciples
plead with their Stranger Friend to " abide with
them," because it was " towards evening (πρὸς
ἑσπέραν), and the day had declined " (xxiv. 29) ;
and then followed the meal, and the revelation
of Jesus, and their hurried return to Jerusalem,
which could scarcely have taken less than an
hour and a half in any case.   Then came the
Lord's appearance in the midst of the company
at Jerusalem, an appearance certainly identical
with that now before us.   If Emmaus had been
reached at sunset, or say an hour before it, the
arrival in the chamber first of Cleopas and his
friend and then of the Risen One may be
placed at a time ranging from one to two hours
after the sun had gone.
      This, in Palestine, with its short twilight,
would mean of course that it was now quite

dark—very dark indeed, no doubt, in the byways
of Jerusalem, and in the courtyards, and on
the stairs of the houses. Through those deep
shadows of the vernal night, if not already in
the late afternoon, the Galilean disciples had
found their way from their Passover lodgings
here and there to the central meeting-place.
Not the Apostles only had entered; there were
"those that were with them" (Luke xxiv. 34).
Perhaps it was a company of twenty or thirty.
The holy women, probably, were of the number,
just as we find them in Acts i. 14; the two
from Emmaus made part of the group at the
last moment; and there had entered also, very
likely, several more of the inner circle of
adherents. Not that a really large number,
however, would be there on that first day of
mingled hopes and fears. Thomas, we know,
was absent, and many another less conspicuous
disciple would naturally have felt and acted like
him, in helpless grief, not to speak of positive
fear for limbs and life.

We are not to think of the company as silent,
in solemn expectation of the coming joy. The
room, we gather from St Luke again (xxiv.
33—35), was a scene of conversation, of exclamation, of excitement. During the day now over
Jesus had been appearing at intervals to one

and another of His followers ; Mary, the other women, Peter (Luke xxiv. 34), Cleopas, all had seen Him. Each might fail at first to convince all the rest, but the concurrence of witness would of course, above all when Peter joined it, begin to tell. So it had done, even by the time that Cleopas and his friend reached the city.

What a conversation it must have been, as all thronged together to hear more from each ! And all the while they would be also listening, lest the gate of the court and the door of the room should be thrust open, and Roman guards or temple officials—" the captain of the Temple " and his men—should break in upon them.

So they mingled their joys and their fears in the large dimly-lighted room. (Lighted it was, in some measure, or they could not afterwards have *looked* so intently on their Master's scars ; but no more light than was needful would be used in that anxious hour.)

But now there came a sudden hush. For while they were in full conversation (St Luke tells us this) then, says St John, JESUS came and ἔστη εἰς τὸ μέσον—stepped into the midst, and there took His stand. Such is the brief account ; we shall gain little by striving to realize every detail. What would we not give to see, as if in living presence, through the

glass of a pictorial narrative, the RISEN ONE
as He was? To gaze on the very body of
His Resurrection, the "flesh and bones" which
He literally had, and in which the scars were
visible and palpable? To see the sameness
and yet difference in the frame and form of the
Great Shepherd brought again from the dead?
But we cannot, we must not. The wonderful
narrative strikes us alternately by its details
and by its silence. Notes of time, place, and
individual character are given in abundance,
but gratifications of mere curiosity, especially
about the aspect of our Redeemer, are with
equal care withheld. It is as it ever is with
Scripture ; the nature, the glory of Jesus Christ
we have given us, for this we need. We do not
really need a photograph of His form, and it
is not given. Enough to know that the sacred
Body was real, was human, was identical—that it
had been slain, but now was alive for evermore.

So we are constrained to look, not upon a
picture, but upon the fact—JESUS there, in the
midst of them.

How had He entered? St John does not tell
us. Possibly the simple reason of his silence
is that he did not know. He knew that the
doors (of courtyard and of room) had been
fastened, and yet that Jesus now stood in the

room. But whether with mysterious speed and silence He had opened those doors, or whether without opening them He had willed that the material of His risen Body should pass through their material, probably the Evangelist could not tell. Only it is plain that he intends us to think that there was *some* mystery in the matter.

We may incline to either of the two alternatives. The secret opening of the doors may seem the more in harmony of the two with the perfect simplicity otherwise of the narrative of the Resurrection visits. It would be mysterious and indeed miraculous ; for the doors were well fastened, manifestly, from within. But it would be, so to speak, the more conceivable, the more simple, act of power.

On the other hand, the possibility of the second alternative must not for a moment be denied as if it were (what no Scripture miracle will ever be found to be) a contradiction to the laws of thought. One plea for it is that it seems as certain as anything can be, without a distinct assertion, that the Risen Lord left the sepulchre *before the stone was moved.* Was *this* a contradiction to the laws of thought? It would be so were we called on to believe that the stone and the Body quite precisely filled the

same space at the same moment; the particles
of the one coinciding with those of the other.
But is there not open to us a different theory,
to be held with reverent modesty? Grant to
the risen Body a mysterious subtlety of material
(and remember that even the least subtle body
is not really solid, not really without interstices
between particle and particle), and we can
surely see the line of abstract possibility in
which the supposed miracle would run.

I make these somewhat obvious remarks just
because it seems to me that *no other* miracle,
recorded or predicted, even tempts us to doubt
it on *this* ground, the ground of apparent
abstract or mental impossibility. The raising
of the dead presents no such difficulty when the
Lord of life is the Agent, directly or indirectly.
But the conception of two bodies occupying
really, atom for atom, the same space, *is* a contradiction to the laws under which the Creator
has bid us think and know. And so it is worth
while to notice that at least one known fact, the
fact that no material body is in the strictest
sense solid, shows us that such a conception is
not demanded by the view that the doors that
night were not opened.

We may linger a moment or two longer over
this question, because the passage (on the latter

hypothesis) has been made use of very naturally in the search of arguments for the subtle tenet of transubstantiation. It has been almost assumed that if we can believe that the Lord's Resurrection body passed through a "solid" door, we can believe *anything* about it ; we can believe it to have nothing to do with laws of space ; we can believe it to be everywhere, or practically everywhere, and to be present in, with, under anything.

But, in the first place, such reasoning begins, surely, with a neglect of "*the proportion* of the faith." For one proof which Scripture gives us of mysterious qualities in the Lord's blessed Body of the Resurrection, it gives many proofs of, so to speak, simple qualities in it. And not one incident—not *this* incident, most certainly —can be adduced to show that it was ever in two places at the same time. Bodily, He was in Emmaus and Jerusalem, not at once, but successively, so far as anything goes that we know. "He *came*," and that one expression, used so often and so familiarly, denies the ubiquity of His Body. Subtlety of particles and organization, mysterious speed, mysterious invisibility, these are wonderful things, but not at all (in a strict sense of the word) inconceivable. The presence of a human body in

more than two places at once is strictly inconceivable. And is it not the case, as I said
above, that *never*, unless in this case alone,
does Scripture miracle imply what is strictly
inconceivable? If so, is not the ubiquitarian
theory, or anything like it, out of proportion
with the faith?

Is not that "faith," taken as a whole, in this
matter of Christ's Presence, as simple as it is
divine? The Lord our Saviour is indeed
ubiquitous as God, as God the Son. And His
Divine Nature is united to His Human Nature.
So He is everywhere present as God, being also
Man. But the Lord our Saviour is *corporeally
absent*, in the main aspects of Scripture doctrine; as to His blessed Body (His "natural"
Body, as the last rubric of the Communion
Office calls it; that is, His non-mystical Body,
His mystical Body being the Church), He is
markedly withdrawn from us for a season; with
the promise of a glorious return of that Body to
the range and ken of our senses, when He shall
" *come.*"

With deep and tender reverence toward God,
and sympathy towards man, let every discussion
about the nature and work of the Sacrament of
the Holy Table be carried on. There is nothing more perfectly irreligious than bitterness in

religion ; assuredly there is nothing which more
effectually shuts out from the heart the joyful
presence of Him who vouchsafes (Eph. iii. 17)
to dwell in it by faith. But to avoid a bitter
eagerness does not mean either to be indifferent
to objective truth, or to go on the principle that
a vague uncertainty is ever *in itself* a spiritual
gain. If, for instance, it is the fact, as I think
it is, that the New Testament indicates that
"the Body" of the blessed Communion is not
the Body as now glorified, but the Body as
once crucified,[1] it cannot be a gain to us to
think quite indistinctly about it, or not to be of
one mind with Scripture about it. And surely
it is happily possible to combine distinctness of
Scriptural conviction with that gentleness and
sympathy which the Scriptures, and which the
ordinance of the Holy Supper, so pressingly and
delightfully enjoin on the Christian, and which
the Christian who "abides in Christ" *shall* find
supplied out of the fulness of His Lord.

But now let us come back from this excursion.
Let us fix our glad and worshipping eyes on the
Risen One standing there in that room in the
midst of His followers. However He had come,
HE WAS THERE ; that was the point. Let us

---

[1] See at large the late Dr Vogan's learned book, *The
True Doctrine of the Eucharist.*

thank God if we can humbly say the same of
our hearts : However my Lord came in, He is
here now, dwelling in my heart by faith, manifesting to me His death for me, saying to me,
It is I ; thy sins be forgiven thee ; receive the
Spirit. However He came, whether He passed
through the door, or softly opened it, or broke
it down ; whether my conversion to Him was a
lightning-like burst of day in night, or a calm
sunrise hour, or a slow clearing of a misty sky
into the blue ; one thing I know, the Sun
shines now ; JESUS is here. He has come into
the midst, and I am glad, for I see the Lord.

He took His stand in their midst. What a
place was this for the Risen Lord to take !
He, so holy, so triumphant, comes " into the
midst" of that throng of unworthy sinners ! It
is indeed a wonderful sight, Jesus Christ come
back "into the midst of them." Yet it is His
chosen stand, willingly taken, with the willing
joy of love. They have grieved Him, but, with
a conquering Saviour's love, He loves them,
and so their company is sweet to Him. And
what He was, He is.

Sweet indeed is the sound of His first utter-
ance to them : *He says to them, Peace be to you.*
It is no mere salutation, but a divine reality.
The Speaker is also the Reason. " He is their

Peace" (Eph. iii. 14). "The God of Peace has brought Him from the dead, through the blood of the everlasting covenant" (Heb. xiii. 20), shed three days before.

St Luke, our welcome supplement to St John in this whole scene, tells us how much they needed that word. Their *first* sight of Him was full of alarm ; they thought that they were gazing on a disembodied spirit (xxiv. 37) ; so mysterious had been His coming, so sudden was His visible manifestation. And to have seen "a spirit," however it might have resembled the living Jesus—yes, even to have seen *His* bodiless human "Spirit,"[1] would not have been, properly, to see THE LORD. It would not have meant any victory over death. It would not have been, in the least, a Resurrection.

So also (let us remember, as we pass on) with the soul now. He who can and does speak Peace must be a living not a visionary Saviour. He must be the Christ, not of fancy, not of aspiration even, but of both history and revelation ; literally risen, living, coming. Not "a spirit," but the Lord.

And now, "this same Jesus," Reality not

[1] Observe this as a perfectly incidental witness to the *intelligence* of the disciples in their faith in the bodily Resurrection of their Lord.

Vision, speaks peace to these frightened and troubled hearts. What a peace it was ! " Peace, peace," as the prophet says (Isa. xxvi. 3), a double peace ; the peace of the finished Work and of the living Presence.

Absolute indeed was the *gift* of such peace. They had learnt effectually that He must and could give it, and only He. Nothing of their own could do so. The moment they lost (as they thought) HIM, what comfort had they from themselves ? They had worked miracles, they had preached a sublime message, they had been centres of spiritual influence. But all these things, divorced from Him " in the midst of them," could only by the contrast intensify their gloom. The fire and energy of Peter, the intense affection of Magdalene — were these sources of peace, on the supposition that Jesus was gone? No ; each fine characteristic of the disciple would become only the side which felt the loss most bitterly ; which felt most deeply that there is " no peace " apart from Him.

But now He came to give peace ; to speak it as His gift, and to prove its validity as such.

For (verse 20) τοῦτο εἰπών, *as He said so*, with the words, *He showed them His hands and His side*. The holy Body was robed, and so as to hide the hands and side. Now He drew back,

He lifted up, the raiment, and they saw the certificates of His agony. He showed the "glorious scars," partly no doubt *for identification.* As they gazed in the lamplight at those deep clefts (the narrative of Thomas's doubt and conversion shows they were still deep *hollow* wounds), bloodless, we must suppose, and with none of the fever of wounds about them,[1] yet still wounds indeed ; as they examined with their eyes (and fingers? Luke xxiv. 39) the rent side, and saw, as it were, the light through the sacred hands, they knew Him in truth for "this same Jesus." And that by itself was sweet indeed, even as it is now when the disciple's soul realizes that, after all these ages, it is dealing still with the same Person identically who died for us and rose again.

But also, surely, He showed them His wounds for a further purpose ; to bear in upon them the thought of *the way in which* He had brought them that peace which now was theirs. There He stood before them, their living Lord, immortally living. But He was also now what before He had not been, their living Lord who had for them been slain. Such was to be "His name for ever, His memorial to all generations"

---

1 The Risen Body is nowhere described as "flesh *and blood.*"

now. What a paradox! Never through the eternal ages will the Lord of Life be parted from the remembrance of His Death, and from the praises of His people because He died. And never let Him and His Death be parted in our thought and love now. While we realize with joy that He lives, that He is beside us and within us, let Him be ever to us still "the Lamb that was slain," "the Shepherd brought from the dead," the Lord who, "that He might indeed be Lord," be Master, "*died* and revived" (Rom. xiv. 9). When we use Him, in His indwelling power, as our life, and as our one way of victory over sin, still let Him be to us the Lord who "loved me, and *gave Himself* for me" (Gal. ii. 20).

He shewed them His hands and His side. So the disciples rejoiced (ἐχάρησαν, aorist, a definite *act* of joy), *seeing the Lord.* THE LORD; that name by which more than ever now they loved to call Him.

The two great blessings flowed together, in His presence; Εἰρήνη, Χαρά, Peace, Joy. Showing His wounds, He spoke the peace. Seeing Him, they knew the joy.

Verse 21. Jesus now speaks again. The outbreak of untold joy was, as to its expression, over; what a scene of tears, and wonder, and

H

shame, and recognition, and worshipping praise it must have been! But now He speaks again, and the word again, calm and articulate, is *Peace be to you.* Their very joy, in its deep agitation, needed this—a clear, definite assurance of the strong *basis* of such gladness, a certainty that it was caused from without, *His* gift, the issue of *His* work.

Speaking peace, He gives them at once, bound up with it in love, Duty. *Even as the Father has sent Me out, I too send you.* Even so. As I was to be His Representative in My work on earth, so you are now to be Mine. As I was His Ambassador in "the days of My flesh," you are to take My place. Ὑπὲρ Χριστοῦ πρεσβεύετε, "be ambassadors in Christ's stead" (2 Cor. v. 20). And be so in Christ's spirit. Your duty, your obedience, is to be your sphere of joy, as His was.

That duty, let us observe, was not given them till they had seen in Him their joy. "They rejoiced, seeing the Lord"; "Now send I you."

Such was our Lord Jesus Christ's commission to His true flock, His true Church. Assuredly it was not to the Apostles only, however specially; it was to all that "blessed company of believing people." "Even so send I you." Every believer is to be a messenger under that

commission, and to take the Risen Lord as his
message.

Then, with an act of divinely simple symbolism, He "conveys" to them (makes over to
them, as by an act and deed of gift, a physical
visible action at once to instruct and strengthen
their faith) the Holy Spirit. Their embassy,
their message-bearing, their representation of
Him, was to be done only and truly "in the
Spirit," if it was to be rightly done at all.

*He breathed a breath towards them, and says to
them, Take the Holy Spirit.*

Are we to understand that this action of the
Lord's, with His spoken word, did literally
then and there infuse the Spirit's power into
them? I dare not say not. But do not the
circumstances rather favour the view that the
incident was divinely symbolical, and was
rather a prophecy of Pentecost than a part-
gift before Pentecost? His *mission* of His
people into the world was, in a sense, not
to take actual effect till Pentecost. Was not
the same the case with this quasi-sacramental
"gift" of the Spirit to His people? Was it not
a guarantee rather than a then-and-there in-
fusion? If so, the case is instructive in the
study of sacramental truth.

But now, how does He proceed? Verse 23

If you remit the sins of any, they are remitted to them ; if you retain the sins of any, they are retained.

On these deep words I only lightly touch in a few brief paragraphs, calling attention to some leading considerations about them.

(i.) They are a commission to the Church, to the Church as the Representative and Witness on earth of the Risen Lord Jesus ; not to Apostles only, but to all true believers. We have already seen this, as we have recalled St Luke's evidence to the fact that other disciples were present with the Apostles.

(ii.) There must therefore be a sense, and that a very important and conspicuous sense, in which every true disciple is called upon to act on the Easter commission. Whatever remitting and retaining means, it has something to do, as God shall show the way, with every Christian's life and work.

(iii.) This consideration interferes not at all with the conception of an ordered, ordering, specially-commissioned Christian pastorate. The pastoral office is as old as Christianity. The same Risen Lord who, when He ascended on high, "gave some as apostles," also "gave some as pastor-teachers, to equip the saints for (their) work of service, for the upbuilding of

Christ's Body" (Eph. iv. 11, 12). And the Christian pastorate, despite all the defects and sins of Christian pastors, has assuredly proved itself, in fact, to be a mighty and salutary factor in the Church. To put only one most simple side of the matter forward ; the fact that a host of Christian men year after year are solemnly, by chosen representatives of the Church, separated and dedicated for their whole lives to special thought, special labour, special guiding function, special speech for Christ, has certainly had an effect beyond calculation in the coherence and force of the work of the Christian Church.

But to say that it is the special office of a class or order to proclaim the message of our Master is not to say that that message is not to be proclaimed by all who belong to Him.

(iv.) This declaration, this commissioned declaration, of His message, with its alternative of condemnation or pardon, death or life, is, I am convinced, the work here entrusted by Him to His Church.

That it does not mean, certainly at its heart and centre, a private judicial sacerdotal absolution or its reverse, I am sure. First, because the Scriptures, fairly interrogated, give no clear evidence that such a function was claimed or exercised by the Apostles, or enjoined by them on even the earliest presiding pastors. Secondly, because such a delegation to man of the judicial power of God, if it is not to be a mere name, a something worse than useless, would necessarily involve the need that the absolver and retainer should be, as such, inspired—gifted with a special discernment both of the nature of the sin of the soul and of the sincerity of the soul, and not of its sincerity only, but of its self-knowledge, its truth or its error in estimating and describing its sin.

I do not think that either Scripture or experience at all assures us that Christian pastors, as such, are by any means thus inspired ; that they have, as such, any supernatural intuition into the self-knowledge of the human soul.

But if it be the duty of every Christian, in his or her path of intercourse and influence, to " retain sins " and " remit sins " in the sense of pointing out, as a living witness, the Scripture terms of pardon and peace to a sorely needing world—here is indeed an intelligible as well as a most blessed commission ; and it is a work as to which the Acts and Epistles are full of suggestions, while they are silent about a sacerdotal function of confession and absolution.

Of the special and adapted bearing of the

words as used in the ordination of the Anglican
presbyter, and again in the formula which he
is directed to utter, under very peculiar and
guarded conditions, in the Visitation of the
Sick, I scarcely speak at all here. But it
may not be out of place to point out how
clear the witness of Church History is to the
fact that in such a connexion the drift of
the word is towards "remission" and "retention" *from the point of view of the Christian
Society;* towards guarding the central hearth,
so to speak, even the Table of the Lord, from
unworthy intrusion. And even thus, it may be
remembered, the formula was not introduced
into the Ordinal for the Presbyter till the
thirteenth century.[1]

But this is a digression indeed. I recur to that
view of the Lord's commission, which, alike for
the pastor and the layman, is at once the simplest
and the most sacred—the carrying to the world,
as by a messenger who is also a living witness,
of the message of the grace of God. Specially
for my ministerial brethren I venture thus to
point to it once more. May our idea of our
ministry never be lowered from this ; never

[1] See a learned sermon by the Bishop (Reichel) of
Meath, *The History and Claims of the Confessional,*
1884.

allowed to sink into the idea of a merely ad-
ministrative and ceremonial function, or into
that of only philanthropic enterprise. May we
live and labour as those who deal indeed with
sin and with salvation, and in our Master's
Name ; as those who know in our own instance
how the human heart needs remission, and how
it must and does find it in Christ alone. May
we minister as those who know their own souls
and their own Saviour, so as to enable them to
deal with the souls of others ; above all, who
can say, as those first disciples of the Chamber
could, " We have seen the Lord, who was dead
but is alive for evermore, and our heart is
glad in the sight of Him ; now then (2 Cor. v.
20, 21) we are ambassadors in His stead ; in
His stead we pray you, be reconciled to God.
For God hath made Him to be sin on our behalf
who knew no sin, that we might be made the
righteousness of God in Him."

VII

THE EASTER MESSAGE—THOMAS.

I DO not propose to retrace the lines of comment on verses 22, 23, offered in the last chapter. Let me only add to them the remark that if the conclusions then suggested are substantially true, we are led to the thought that the commission given to the Church is given to it, practically, as it is (Article XX.) *testis et conservatrix divinorum librorum,* "a" (the Article in its English does not say "the") "witness and keeper of Holy Writ." Such a witness and safe-keeper the Church is, undoubtedly ; a character too often either forgotten or greatly mistaken. Some Christians think of Scripture as bound up with the Church visible more than it is, some as bound up with it less than it is. Some extend the meaning of Article XX. so far as to make the witness and safe-keeper to be, *therefore and as such*, the only qualified *interpreter;* a gratuitous inference, as if a librarian as such were an adequate expositor. Some, on the other hand (it may be from a deep and joyful experience of the living power of the written Word), forget too much its intimate connexion and, so to speak, cohesion with the living, breathing Congregation of Christian disciples. No doubt it can happen, and in detached cases it does happen, that the Book acts altogether apart from the immediate action of the Church. I know, from first-hand report, of instances in which a Bible has been the solitary means through which Christianity, orthodox and living, has been learnt by one who was an untaught heathen when the Book almost literally fell into his hands. But even in such an instance we trace an indirect co-operation of the Christian Church; for without its existence it is most unlikely that Scripture, as we have it, would have been largely copied, preserved amidst the storms of history, and widely dispersed. On the human side, every copy of the Bible is connected with the existence of the Church, as a condition to its existence. And then, in the immense preponderance of actual experiences, the written Word is brought home to the individual by the spoken witness of the Church, coming (as of course it must ordinarily come) through the voice of some other individual, who in his turn has already been similarly approached. Practically, it is the Christian parent, or friend, or teacher, or expositor, who, in the vastly larger number of cases, is to the individual the "witness" as well as "keeper" of Holy Writ, saying, "This is the Word of God; I have received it; I pass it on to you." It is an individual who speaks, or writes, but an individual who, knowingly or not, has been helped to his or her own realization of the written treasure by the conditions and aids of Christian membership, and who is thus in some sense, in turn, an organ of that membership in its work of witnessing and keeping.

Doubtless, if every living witness and every Christian uninspired book were to vanish from the earth to-morrow, the Book would still prove its own undying and independent power. But would it, in the actual workings of human life, speak to man nearly as often, or as widely, as before?

It is one thing to dream (it *is* a dream) of a Church-interpretation of Scripture such that the reverent and prayerful soul *cannot* get at the true sense of Scripture without it.

It is another thing when what we assert is a connexion of Scripture with the visible Congregation of Christ, such that the world's acquaintance with the Word, reverence for it, and benefit by it, is indefinitely increased and assured by that connexion.[1]

It is then this character of the disciples of Christ, and of their Community, as the actual witnesses and guardians of the revelation of Christ, which is referred to specially, if I am right, in the passage before us. The revelation of Christ is above all things a revelation with a view to the remission or retention of sin. It reveals, with infallible certainty, the way of remission, the means to it, and, by consequence, how to miss it. The terms of the revelation are sure ; its absolution or condemnation is divine. When St Paul, for example, or St John so instructs me as to assure me, penitent and believing, that my sins are forgiven, I am to be as sure of it as if Christ stood by me and spoke the words. And when a Christian pastor, in his ministry, and when also a Christian friend, in

---

[1] It may not be out of place to refer to Augustine's well-known words, *Ego Evangelio non crederem nisi me Catholicæ Ecclesiæ commoveret auctoritas.* (*Contra Epistolam Manichæi quæ Fundamenti dicitur*, cap. v.) The ample teaching of Augustine on Scripture assures us that he by no means intended by this that the Church is above Scripture, or that Scripture owes its divine authority to the Church. But he felt it an all-important credential to Scripture that it came to him as a fact through the historic Christian Society as that Society's rule of faith.

conversation or by example, *brings home* to my
thought and heart such an apostolic—*i. e.* such
a divine—absolution, or, again, some corresponding apostolic condemnation of my state
or of an act in my state, he is doing me not an
accidental service, but one divinely instituted,
and implied in the fact that our Lord willed
that His followers should be a Community, and
should live and work with His Word in their
possession.

Two reflections may be offered before the
subject is quitted.

First, this *diffusion* of the witnessing and
keeping office over the whole Christian congregation is no contradiction to the divine institution of an ordained and thus far separated
Ministry—a Ministry which has a function full
of life and blessing, concentrating the witness
of the Congregation, and securing in a degree
otherwise impossible, or at best most precarious,
the order and the continuity of Christian worship.
Hence, as we have already remembered, the
commission to the Church is, in our Ordinal,
not unlawfully given with special emphasis to
the Christian presbyter ; though this was not
done in any known ordination ritual for pres-
byters before the thirteenth century.

Secondly, on the other hand, whatever is true

of the remitting and retaining efficacy of the Church's true witness to Scripture, and true articulation of the message of Scripture, this must be at least as deeply true of the direct witness of Scripture to the soul as the man reads it and ponders it for himself. Of the Oracle itself we may truly say, "Whosoever sins it doth remit, they are remitted unto them." I quote some wise words of Doddridge's, written on this passage one hundred and fifty years ago, in that often useful commentary, his *Expositor :* "Let us try our state by the character laid down in the inspired writings ; in which sense we may assure ourselves that if our sins are declared to be remitted, they are remitted. And if indeed they are so, we need not be much concerned by whom they are retained. . . . Men may claim a power which God never gave, and which these words are far from implying. But whatever the sentence they may pass, they whom God blesseth are blessed indeed."

This whole subject is one of continual, and in our time of acute and special, importance. A properly sacerdotal theory of the Christian Ministry, in all parts of such a theory, and not least in that of a judicial absolution supposed to convey divine forgiveness, puts a human intermediation between man and God where God would have man see the one Mediator only. It is a contradiction to the sacred first principles of the Gospel.

Meanwhile may our Lord in mercy shorten the days of controversy, and utterly abolish in us that which likes controversy for its own sake ; and may He lengthen, till they fill our lives, the sweet hours in which we for ourselves enjoy in glad consciousness, and so are able gladly to assert to others, the holy certainties of the re-mission of sins for the Name's sake of the Only Begotten of the Father, who died for us and rose again.

But now let us pass at once to some view of a scene which will indeed carry us into the pure light of a direct view of the Lord Jesus Christ, seen in His living glory. We arrive at the record of the doubt and the belief of Thomas, verses 24—29.

Verse 24. *But Thomas, one of the Twelve, whose name means Twin, was not with them when Jesus came. So the other disciples began to say* (ἔλεγον) *to him, We have seen the Lord. But he said to them, Unless I see in His hands the print of the nails, and insert* [1]

---

[1] Βάλλειν appears never quite to lose a certain *force* of meaning. Here ἐὰν μὴ βάλω is not merely "unless I *put*," but almost " unless I *push*."

my finger into the print of the nails, and insert my hand into His side, I will never believe (οὐ μὴ πιστεύσω). *And after eight days again the disciples were indoors, and Thomas with them. Jesus comes, while the doors were fastened, and took His stand in the midst, and said, Peace be unto you. Then He says to Thomas, Bring your finger hither, and see My hands; and bring your hand and insert it into My side; and do not become unbelieving, but believing. Thomas answered and said to Him, My Lord and My God. Jesus says to him, Because you have seen Me, Thomas, you have believed; happy such as saw not, and believed.* Ver. 30. *Now Jesus did many other signs besides in His disciples' presence, which have not been written in this book. But these have been written that you may believe that Jesus is the Christ, the Son of God, and that, believing, you may have life in His name.*

Of this passage I do not attempt any detailed exposition in this chapter; it will be more possible to do so in the next. At present I merely take up for notice some of its outstanding facts and lessons, asking the Risen Lord to grant writer and reader to realize His presence "in the midst," and to adore Him from the soul as our, nay as my, Lord and God.

We note, then, as often before, the concurrent brevity and minuteness of the record. Its brevity : no remarks or explanations are offered with reference to the absence of Thomas ; just the fact is given, as necessary to explain the sequel. We are left to conjecture for ourselves why he was away. And conjecture surely says that his absence at such a time cannot have been mere accident. It was probably an expression of individual character, an act of that peculiar independence passing into self-will which we trace throughout his sketched portrait in this Gospel. I should not think that the mind of Thomas was one in which there was a strong tendency to doubt the miraculous, a Sadducean mind ; but rather that he was a man decidedly apt to fall back upon himself, suspicious of over-influence from others, perhaps with something of that morbid honesty (if the phrase is permissible) which doubts because another believes, doubts because it fears, or seems to itself to fear, that it may accept reasons for belief which are good only for another. Such a character, I venture to take it, was expressed in that marked absence. Reports were about that Jesus had risen. Jesus he dearly, ardently loved (chap. xi. 16), whatever mistakes he made about Him. Perhaps the first notion of His Resurrection may

I

have struck bright and glad upon Thomas, as a notion. But with equal likelihood he may have decided against the reports for that very reason : " Too good to be true—so good that the wish must have fathered the assertion." So he would fortify himself with the reflection that his associates had done just this, had believed because they wished. Then he would unconsciously and easily pass from the spirit of grief to the spirit of pride, pride in his firmness and caution of thought, in his courageous willingness to be in the dark if dark it must be. Neither accident, nor intellectual scepticism, but grief passing into a sort of melancholy pride—such seems to me a probable account of the absence of Thomas.

All this, however, if true, is unrecorded by the pen of St John, in his tranquil brevity. Yet on the other hand, what minute traits of individuality we have in these few touches ! How truly Thomas stands out as a real character, altogether different from Peter, for example, and from John ; not for a moment to be taken for a mere reflection or echo of another personage. This is not only proof of veracity, of the firm reality which lies as a rock beneath the beautiful narrative. It is not only evidence that we have a record of facts before us, indicated in these brief touches not of art, but nature—for such nature-copying art *was not*, most surely, in Christian circles (if anywhere) when this Book was written. It is a phenomenon not only of fact, but of instruction and consolation. The individualities of the Apostles Peter, John, Thomas, Nathanael, Paul, are representative. And the fact that they were, each and all, subdued to the same adoring love of Jesus Christ is a representative fact. Were the Apostles for us so many mere names, so many lay-figures attired in Galilean costume and grouped around the Lord, their recorded faith would *teach* us very little. But they are "men of like feelings" with us, ὁμοιοπαθεῖς ἡμῖν (James v. 17), like present-day people in their marked differences from one another. And the Lord Jesus found them all out, and they all found out Him ; the one Lord, absolute and unalterable, and yet precisely the right Friend and Saviour for each of these persons.

Such a record as this may be used in the divine hand to remedy two very possible mistakes.

(i.) We are apt sometimes, in thinking, praying, speaking for the benefit of the souls of others, to forget too much the differences of character ; to expect and to demand that characters the most diverse from our own shall not only reach the same results, but shall reach them by the same steps, in the same order. A man who has suffered much from intellectual clouds and conflicts, sometimes perhaps to be traced to indolence and half-heartedness, is often tempted to insist, as it were, that some friend now seeking after Christ shall feel just the same difficulties before he attains the light. Strange to say, such an attitude is possible, instead of that of the prayer and longing that into the light we now enjoy, holy and happy, this soul may step by any path our Master shall choose, and the sooner the better, if it be His will.

A mind, again, which has had little or no experience of such trials (and this exemption is sometimes a sign of mental health and strength, not of blindness or immaturity) is apt not seldom to grow impatient and unsympathetic in contact with one of the opposite cast. Let it not be so. True, you are not obliged to experience the conflict with the legions of doubt. But you should thoughtfully watch that conflict, and pray, like Moses on the hill, while Joshua was battling in the valley. You should recognize with respect a different character, training, position ; not to doubt whether such a heart needs the same

Christ and the same salvation, but to bear with its different pace, its circuitous route, as it comes towards Him and to Him.

(ii.) On the other hand, are not Christian believers often tempted sorely in the other direction, tempted to too keen a suspicion, too serious an estimate of differences of character, in the presence of Christianity and Christ? Are we never disposed to say, practically, to ourselves—however whisperingly—that this man or that is so entirely different from myself that he never can, he never will, see Christ, His love, His redemption, as clearly and as gladly as I see it? And then perhaps the thought has already crept in, "and he never *need* do so."

This is fatalism under a veil. It makes a man's character his fate. It ignores the free and divine action of the Eternal Spirit upon men. It practically forgets the positive assurances of the Lord Jesus Christ that there is for every human soul a most urgent need that it should come to Him, and deal with Him.

This fatalism, a branch of a subtle and far-spread disease, we are helped to resist, to give the lie to, by this same wonderful record of the individualities of the Apostles. They, or at least the leaders of these leaders, were sharply and deeply differenced from each other.

And the Lord Jesus dealt with them in widely different ways. But He led them all to the same end—Himself; Himself seen and known by each as his all in all, his peace, his joy, his power, his purity, his Lord and God.

With admirable vividness this comes out in their artlessly-recorded words and deeds. How different was Thomas in mental and moral cast from John! Yet it is John who observes, who records with loving care, and so embraces, as it were, for his own the final faith of Thomas. How different was Thomas from Paul, the Galilean boatman from the marvellous youth of Cilicia trained into the Pharisaic expert in the school of Gamaliel; the rugged peasant-mind from him in whom the pride of the genius, the savant, and the zealot were, till grace changed him, all combined! And very different was their intercourse with Jesus, and with the followers of Jesus. But by "this same Jesus" they were both led into the same blessed results as regards faith in Him. "My Lord and my God," exclaims Thomas, at once adoring and appropriating, as true faith should ever do. "I live," writes Paul (Gal. i. 20), "by faith in the Son of God, who loved me, and gave Himself for me," adoring and also appropriating the same Person with the same heaven-given simplicity of faith; *his* pride also quite broken up, *his* difficulties also quite done away in the sunlight of Christ, *his* inmost heart also freely opened to learn what God would have him learn of the glory and the love of His Only Begotten.

For the present we close the Gospel again. But at least we have already gathered some fresh encouragement to patience and to faith from this first view of the story of St Thomas. May we be, for this our study, at once better able to sympathize with the differing characters and circumstances of others, and yet, all the while, more sure that, each and all, they need Christ, and the same Christ, with an absolute need. Above all, let us be sure of Him, trustful of Him, certain that He knows the way and holds the key, however impenetrable this or that mind or heart may seem to us. The more we recollect and realize these things, the better we shall, on the one hand, delight to do what we can to bear our humble witness to such a Redeemer, and the more truly, on the other hand, will our Christian witness be borne not to ourselves but to Christ Jesus our Lord.

Meanwhile, let us thank God, who commanded the light to shine out of darkness, that out of the darkness of the Apostle's doubts, and out of the darkness of the doubts of many a doubter since, He has brought forth light, the light of fresh and living evidences of the presence, the patience, the love, the glory of His dear Son. We may thankfully breathe as our own the prayer of the Church, written by the Reformers, and appointed for the memorial day of the once-perplexed disciple :

Almighty and everlasting God, who for the more confirmation of the faith didst suffer Thy holy Apostle Saint Thomas to be doubtful in Thy Son's Resurrection; Grant us so perfectly and without all doubt to believe in Thy Son Jesus Christ, that our faith in Thy sight may never be reproved. Hear us, O Lord, through the same Jesus Christ, to whom, with Thee and the Holy Ghost, be all honour and glory, now and for evermore. Amen.

VIII

THOMAS AND THE LORD.

WE began in our last chapter to study the
narrative of the doubt and the faith of Thomas,
and remarked the strong individuality of the
Apostle's character as it is indicated by St
John. It is from St John only that we get any
such information about the man; the other
Evangelists and the Acts contain mere mentions of his name. In St John it occurs seven
times, and in three cases it is given with the
translation, Didymus, Twin. Is it possible
that the Evangelist sees a moral significance in
the name, as if it suggested a certain doubleness
in the mind where love and mistrust were both
at once so strong? Not that duplicity in any
other sense is traceable in Thomas ; his was
anything but a character of guile.

In two other scenes in this Gospel, as we
remember, Thomas appears, so to speak, in

character. In xi. 16 he proposes to the others
to accompany the Lord into Judea at a dan-
gerous time : " Let us also go, that we may die
with him ; " a brief sentence, in which we see
combined a resolution almost petulant, an intense devotion to his Lord's person, *and* great
mistakes as to His nature and power. In xiv. 5
he seems to interrupt the Master in the midst
of His words about the heavenly home and His
purpose to "go and prepare" it for His followers : " Lord, we know not whither Thou
goest, and how can we know the way ? " Here
again is the mind which shapes boldly to
itself, and almost brusquely expresses, the
difficulty or doubt which it feels. One other
mention of Thomas in this Gospel must be
recalled—xxi. 2. He is there the second name
in that blessed company which met the Risen
Jesus in the early morning by the lake-side. Is
not this a beautiful and touching close to the
notices of the Apostle? He has ceased to be
the self-asserting, self-separating doubter. He
is happy now to be just a brother with his
brethren ; and so he is privileged to enjoy,
without delay, without reproof, that heavenly
interview. Of this more hereafter.

 We turn now to the narrative before us.

 Verse 24. *But Thomas, one of the Twelve,*

whose name means Twin, was not with them
when Jesus came.

"One of the *Twelve*": their, so to speak,
official title, though, alas, they were now only
eleven. This distinctive mention of the Twelve
may suggest to us that, when just above and
below the Evangelist speaks of "the disciples,"
he means the little company at large, and not
only the Apostles.

I will not repeat what was said in our last
chapter about the probable causes of Thomas'
absence, only remarking again that in his
mental frame we see, surely, the recent mental
frame of all the disciples, but expressed more
definitely and resolutely. He did but speak
out, or rather act out, what had been deep in
the hearts of all—a sense of tremendous disappointment, a deep and gloomy despondency,
with the immediate impulse to separate rather
than to combine.

Nothing can be more certain than that this
impulse to separate would have had full sway
finally, and very soon, if no magnificent antidote
to the despair of Friday had come into the
midst of them. The shame as well as pain of
having embarked in a great mistake would
have made them loth to meet and see each
other's faces for long together. And the ter-

rible act of Judas must have given them for a time a sense of mutual suspicion. If Judas had proved untrue, might not another, might not others? Those who had so often misconstrued the Master might easily suspect their fellow-servants.

In short, they were ready to disperse "every man to his own." They would have diverged, no doubt, in very different moods : some sullen, some tender, some quite silent, others seeking to explain everything. And had they done so, and had some rumours of that obscure event, the crucifixion of a religious leader in Judea, reached our day from that day, those rumours, we may rely upon it, would have been conflicting. Each section of the unhappy dispersion would have had its version of Jesus and of the Cross—without a sequel.

But they did not disperse. They reassembled, and in a spirit altogether new. Then after a while they did indeed part, but to preach one message, to confess and glorify one Lord. And the one solution of all this is—the Resurrection. Every other explanation is a violent process ; it either ignores the despair and separation of the disciples at first, or the completeness and grandeur of their moral *and mental* revolution, so prompt, decisive, and unanimous.

Verse 25. *So the other disciples began to say to him, We have seen the Lord.*

Surely they went to seek him with the news, perhaps that very night, for probably the presence of the Lord with them that evening was brief, as it seems to have been on other recorded occasions. The one Apostle who did not yet know of the mighty joy must have been an object of strong and loving interest and sympathy to his friends. If they had been tempted before to be impatient when he withdrew, they would be more than patient now ; for what can so fully calm the discords of the soul in itself, and open it out in unselfish sympathy, as the possession of a great spiritual joy? This now indeed these men had. They knew Jesus Risen ; they knew that He had given them His peace ; they knew that He had died for them, and was alive for evermore.

" He *that believeth* shall not *make haste*" (Isa. xxviii. 16). An eagerness for religious opinions, for religious truths, which is at all harsh or bitter, is not seldom due to uneasiness, not to conviction. It is one thing to be unwaveringly and entirely in earnest, another thing to be heated. Peter, John, Nathanael, and the rest would not be hard upon Thomas because he had not been with them. Full of their unspeakably glad discovery, rich in the ample possession of such a Saviour, they can only have longed with sympathetic graciousness that their friend should share it to the full.

Meanwhile, the witness would be as positive as it was kind. *We have seen the Lord;* an absolute fact. *We,* not others ; *have seen,* not guessed or dreamed ; *the Lord,* identical and immortal in His love and glory.

So they would bear witness ; lovingly, positively, and as men who were fresh from the special benediction of the Risen One. And they were persons with whom Thomas had long been familiar, and whose concurrence of witness must to him have been impressive, for they were no mere copies of each other.

Yet all this witnessing wholly, or nearly wholly, failed. It was continued, repeated ; ἔλεγον. But Thomas met it with an outspoken scepticism and refusal. Unless his own senses should assure him, *he would never believe,* οὐ μὴ πιστεύσω.

He was very, very wrong. The whole narrative, and the whole Scripture, illustrate this. In Scripture the evidence of the senses is never slighted, never said to be illusory. But it is shewn to be not the only evidence. Adequate testimony may fully take its place, even when a soul is in the question.

It was wrong; and yet who, that knows his own human heart, will say that it was unnatural? Who, that knows how violently *self*, in any of its forms, can warp reason or affection, when once self is allowed to have its way, will sit in superior judgment upon Thomas? For surely it was this subtle subjective obstacle that held him. If, as is so likely, grief had developed a certain gloomy pride of isolation, and then upon it had come in this news of the great joy found by those whom he had left in a spirit like his own, can we wonder if for the time the very thought of their certainty and happiness embittered and hardened his own resolve to doubt and to differ? A subtle sense of mortification may well have tinged the words : *Unless I see in His hands the print of the nails, and insert my finger into the print of the nails, and insert my hand into His side, I will never believe.*

Many strange but actual workings of human nature, in the absence of the peace and love of God, seem to be remarkably illustrated by the acts and words of Thomas in his gloom.

Perhaps we have in him an example of many minds among those which now doubt or reject the Gospel. Self (to use the word in the sense not of mere vanity, or shallow self-importance, but rather in that of a morbid introspection) often

stands more than the doubter suspects between
him and conviction. The proof which is really
good for another is good for him, in itself. But
it is seen distorted, for it is seen askance. We
need not live long to find out how, in the
practical affairs of common life, personal peculiarities interfere with apparently self-evidently
beneficial and just courses of action. Even so,
in the microcosm within us, reason and conscience have often to fight a hard, and often a
losing, battle with some purely irrational opposition of unregenerate self. How happy it is
when that self is subdued, as the soul of Thomas
was subdued, by the revelation of Jesus Christ
as He is; living, loving, slain and risen again,
my Lord, and my God!

Verse 26. *And after eight days again the
disciples were indoors, and Thomas with them.*

"After eight days," a full week. We are left
almost entirely uninformed as to the life of the
disciples "between times" during the Forty
Days. We see them, as it were, only under the
illumination of their Lord's presence; He goes,
and the shadow falls over them for the time.
So we do not know how that week was passed,
only that it must assuredly have been a week
of great, though private, gladness. "The fear
of the Jews" must have been strangely neutral-

ized by the consciousness of the victory and life of the Lord Jesus, while yet the disciples appear to have kept silence about it beyond their own circle—surely in consequence of a command from Him. On the other hand, their enemies seem to have been quite satisfied, so to speak, with the disappearance of the Master, and to have meditated no assault on the disciples. Whatever the mystery of the disappearance of Jesus was to Caiaphas and his fellows, *He had disappeared;* He had become at the most a spectre to them; and so manifest was the inferiority of His followers' power to move and to attract, that the Sanhedrin, it would seem, fairly dismissed the thought of them from their minds.

So the week passed, outwardly undisturbed, as far as we know or can guess. But *within* the little company, great was the stir. This obstinate doubter—this stubborn rejecter of the multifold witness to the great fact of joy—what was to be done in view of him? Again and again they would attack him with a loving siege; but the subtle influence ruled Thomas still. He would not believe.

It was a severe lesson to them all, though a lesson richly blessed, no doubt. For all their after ministry it must have taught them much;

K

it must have pressed home on them for all time the incapacity of man to set free by his own act and word his brother's soul; the weakness of mere evidences, however convincing in the abstract, to sway the heart and will without the eternal grace; the possibilities of doubt in another over what was to themselves so self-evident, and about which they were so greatly happy. Let us learn our lesson from theirs; we shall surely need it, sooner or later, if we at all attempt to bear witness for the Lord.

Meantime their words, though they had not convinced Thomas, had told upon him. Another "First Day" at length arrived, bringing back in new realization all the circumstances of the former "First Day"; and now Thomas was with them.

That week, we may be sure, had not shaken the faith of "the other disciples." Their witness to the Risen One was not less positive because their brother refused it. And even this must have told upon him. The sight of their certainty would touch, however invisibly, his convictions. The sight of their happiness must have moved his longings, even when he most freely indulged his own self-centred gloom.

They were indoors again. Thomas, in this state betwixt doubt and desire, was with them,

ready, humanly speaking, to be swayed either
way by what might happen. Can we doubt
that, if nothing had happened, or if anything
unconvincing had happened, his whole mind
would have turned to a distrust more positive
than ever? Could we suppose for a moment
so monstrous a thing as that his brethren had
devised some illusion to work on his imagination,
he was just in the mood to look it through and
through, and to be irrevocably confirmed in his
denial by the detection of the slightest unreality.

But now what happened?

Verse 26. *Jesus comes, while the doors were
fastened, and took His stand in the midst
and said, Peace be unto you. Then He says
to Thomas, Bring your finger hither, and see
My hands, and bring your hand, and insert it
into My side, and do not become unbelieving,
but believing.*

It is vain to try any elaborate " word-paint-
ing " here. The wonderful scene of mercy and
joy stands out before us. There are the disciples, perhaps in the act of some fresh effort of
reasoning and witness addressed to the stubborn
personality of the doubter, each trying his own
way; there is Thomas, perhaps more than ever, to
all appearance, argumentative, critical, resolved.
Then, on a sudden, with the same miracle of

silent entrance, the great Reasoner, the faithful Witness, Himself is there once more; JESUS, bringing the brief and mighty logic and demonstration of Himself revealed. We see Him extend His holy and deathless hands, each showing the cleft of the huge nail; we see Him move His robe, and disclose the yet wider and deeper chasm of the spear, that great wound which only St John records.

There they were displayed once more, these marks of the identity of Jesus as the Lamb that was slain. The Lord displayed them then, that we might believe on Him as such for ever. We may or may not be permitted to see them with our eyes hereafter, but to faith they are indelible; to the love which sees through tears of joy that Saviour so slain, they are in sight for evermore.

> For ever here my rest shall be,
>   Close to Thy bleeding side;
> This all my hope and all my plea,
>   For me the Saviour died.
>
> How blest are they who still abide,
>   Close shelter'd in Thy bleeding side;
> Who life and strength from thence derive,
>   And by Thee move, and in Thee live.

So there, in the lamplight, Thomas had his will. Definitely and unmistakably he there saw the Lord risen, and the marks of His slaughter. And he heard the voice of the Risen One ; it addressed him articulately and personally ; it recited with strange precision the challenge which he had made so stoutly to his brethren. He was to do the very thing ; to come close, to touch, to insert, to feel, and to believe.

Whether Thomas actually "brought thither his finger" we do not know. Probably he did, with tenderest reverence. But it is possible that he did not, so self-evidential was the *sight.* His own eyes, those unready eyes, now saw his own unmistakable Master, and the *contact* may have been almost deprecated. Certainly in the Lord's answer to the disciple's confession, only his sight is referred to.

Verse 28. *Thomas answered and said unto Him, My Lord and my God. Jesus says to him, Because you have seen Me, Thomas, you have believed; happy such as saw not and believed.*

The sequel of the interview is not recorded. As in every other Resurrection appearance, except only the incident at Emmaus, and the Ascension, we do not read any detail of the Lord's *departure.* That night He may have stayed with them, to speak of the things of the kingdom, or He may have left them as silently as He came—left them to their now completed and united joy.

But for us, as we read and think, He "goes out no more." There for ever is He, this same Jesus; and there is the subdued, happy doubter, gazing on Him, confessing Him as his Lord and his God. JESUS and Thomas are immortally present before us in that upper room, "that we, too, may believe that Jesus is the Christ, the Son of God, and that we too, believing, may have life in His name."

THOMAS is there, in his confession : *My Lord and my God.* Strange sound from those lips ! The perplexed and perplexing sceptic has come to utter a confession whose glorious fulness, and also whose personal application (" *my* Lord "), surpass even Peter's at Cæsarea Philippi, when the Father revealed to him the Son. " My GOD "—words impossible to explain away, for they were addressed obviously to Jesus direct, and they meant no less than proper Godhead, for they were uttered by an Israelite.

So Thomas confessed Him, and received Him. Doubt was gone, reserve broken, the soul quite released from the sullen wish to keep its old isolated position in sorrowful pride. He is one with his brethren now, and they shall know it ; for he has found in Jesus Risen all his desire, all his joy.

It is no unique case. How often the most positive denials have been exchanged for the very simplest faith ! St Augustine is a memorable example, not to speak of Saul of Tarsus. And many a later illustration of the same phenomenon may be quoted. Never shall I forget the authentic experience of an aged man, refined and cultured, and a resolved Socinian, who had always maintained that he had never seen Priestley really answered. Late in the long evening of his life (he died at ninety-two) his doctor one day found him, much to his surprise, dropping tears over his Bible. He had seen a new light. He had met with a Biblical phrase never noticed before, or, however, never thought of before ; *The blood of Jesus Christ His Son cleanseth us from all sin.* He too, like Thomas, after many asseverations of unbelief, reaching over many more days than eight, had seen THE LORD, and bowed before Him, in the light of the living relation between the virtue of the atoning blood and the eternal Nature of the Crucified.

And then, in this immortal chamber scene, JESUS is there. He meets the confession of His disciple—how quietly, how divinely ! There is no word of caution ; there is no " See thou do it not ; worship God." There is rather a gentle reproof that the faith so expressed had not come sooner : " Not till sight have you believed ; happy such as believe without sight." Yes, Jesus, the meek and lowly, who made Himself of no reputation, accepts this ascription of Deity as calmly as a king, born to the throne, and long upon it, accepts the ascription of loyalty from a humble subject. He only bends to His Apostle in loving censure for his past reluctance, and then gives, by anticipation, a royal blessing to—ourselves.

Happy such as saw not, and believed. Not, Happy such as believed without a reason, without a ground, but, Happy they who did not create out of themselves reasons against belief. Such, surely, is the point of this precious last Beatitude. It refers to the special difficulty of Thomas, to that obstacle to faith which individualism, which self (for this it was assuredly), had raised in the way of his accepting evidence altogether adequate. The truth had looked like a phantom to him because seen through that mist. Happy they, says the Lord, who are free from that. Happy they, oh how happy, whatever else they see or do not see, who see the witness borne to Jesus with the simplicity of a soul which seeks not self's way, but pardon, and holiness, and heaven ; which indulges no jealous comparison of self with others, and allows no restless, morbid discouragement to come from that quarter. That soul grudges no privilege, experience, freedom, power to other believers ; but, in the unspeakably happy consciousness of the reception for itself of such a Saviour on His own terms, believes indeed, rests on Him, in perfect simplicity and with perfect reason. It demands no peculiar and privileged demonstration, for it needs none. It is happy, it is assured, it loves, it obeys ; for it is emancipated from those subtle influences of the protean spirit of self which alone can make the evidence of the Gospel pages and the glad witness of already blessed believers unconvincing.

How would the released and adoring Apostle, standing free at length from self, at the feet of Jesus, exhort us, if we could hear him, to listen every day to this divine assurance of the blessedness of believing, and, for that purpose, to use every day the precious written record ; or (ver. 31) *these things have been written that we may believe that Jesus is the Christ, the Son of God, and that, believing, we may have life in His name.*

I would go from pole to pole
 To behold my risen Lord ;
But content thyself, my soul,
 Listen to thy Saviour's word :
" They who Me by faith receive,
 Without seeing who believe,
Trust My word and therein rest,
 They abundantly are blest."

Moravian Hymn-book.

IX

THE NIGHT ON THE LAKE.

WE approach the last Chapter of the Gospel according to St John. As before, we open our study with a paraphrastic version.

After these things Jesus manifested Himself again to the disciples upon (beside) the sea of Tiberias; and He manifested Himself thus. There were together Simon Peter and Thomas, whose name means Twin, and Nathanaèl, from Cana in Galilee, and the two sons of Zebedee, and other two of His disciples. Simon Peter says to them, I am going to fish. They say to him, We are coming with you too. They went out, and embarked in the boat; and that night they took nothing. But when daybreak was now come, Jesus came and stood on the beach (ἔστη εἰ τὸν αἰγιαλόν); the disciples however did not know that it is Jesus. So Jesus says to them, Children, you have not any fish? They answered Him, No. Then He said to them, Throw your

*net towards the right side of the boat, and you
will find. So they threw; and now strength
ailed them (οὐκέτι ἴσχυσαν) to draw, such was
the quantity of fish. So that disciple whom
Jesus loved said to Peter, It is the Lord. So
Simon Peter, hearing that it is the Lord, girded
on his outer coat, for he was naked, and threw
himself into the sea. The other disciples now
came with the smaller boat; for they were not
far from the land, only about two hundred
cubits off, dragging the netful of fish. So when
they had disembarked, they see a coalfire laid,
and a dish of fish set at it, and a loaf. Jesus
says to them, Bring some of the fish which you
have just taken. Simon Peter got up (into the
smaller boat), and pulled the net up on the land,
quite full of large fish, a hundred and fifty-three.
And although they were so many, the net had
not been torn.*

Verse 1. *After these things.* The interval is
not specified. It may have been now very near
the day of the Ascension. But is it not more
likely that it was not long after the confession of
Thomas—say within the first three weeks of the
Forty Days? One consideration speaks strongly
for this; I mean, that the full and solemn
restoration of Peter to the apostolic pastorate

took place on this occasion. Surely this would not be delayed long after the Resurrection.

This appearance, we observe again, is in Galilee. Here is one of the places where St John incidentally, and as it were covertly, agrees with the other Gospels. They record the command to the Apostles to meet the Lord in Galilee; he does not. But more fully than any of them John records the fact of their doing what was commanded. Now the removal of the Apostles to Galilee came almost to a certainty soon after the Resurrection, soon after the close of the Passover-time. It is unlikely that anything but Passover obligations would keep them lingering in Jerusalem at all in face of that command and promise.

There then, in Galilee, they found themselves once more. In Galilee took place this blessed interview. In Galilee, with a company of some five hundred others, they met Jesus at that unnamed mountain (was it Tabor, or was it Hermon?) where He had appointed them (Matt. xxviii. 16; 1 Cor. xv. 6). There very probably they saw Him many other times not recorded. And thence, before six weeks were over, they returned again to the city, to the upper room, and to the glorious farewell on the top of Olivet.

A partial veil, a haze of mysterious light, is

drawn across this holy and most memorable
period, the Forty Days. Notes of time here
are scarce ; intervals are wide and empty. How
different is this from the season just previous,
the Passion Week in particular, where the
diary is so full, so crowded ! Ὀπτανόμενος διὰ
ἡμερῶν τεσσαράκοντα, *Seen as by glimpses, at intervals, during forty days*, is St Luke's account
(Acts i. 3) of the Lord Jesus now. Separate
appearances are, specially by St John, recorded
with minute care ; only the *dis*appearances,
except at Emmaus and in the Ascension, are
never recorded. But the intervals are left without a conjecture, without a hint. There is no
legendary unreality about this. Rather, under
the alleged conditions, it is deeply truth-like.

At some time then undefined, but perhaps
within a fortnight of the Resurrection, we find
some at least of the disciples returned to Galilee.
Seven are mentioned ; but plainly more than
seven were near, or it would not be noticed
specially that these seven were " together."

There they were, in their old haunts, at their
old work. We cannot know for certain under
what conditions they were at that work. Had
Peter returned to his home, as home? Had
James and John rejoined their father in his
fishery ? It would seem incredible. They were

in Galilee because the Risen Lord had bid them go there ; and for the express purpose of " seeing Him." And He had already spoken words to them which showed with abundant clearness that their life's work was to be labour for the souls of sinners in His Name, and was soon to begin. With such a prospect they could not possibly go back, in the old way, to boats and nets.

So we may think of them as returned to Galilee and the Lake filled with the expectation of Jesus, but meanwhile not therefore forbidding themselves a sojourn, a lodging, under old roofs and amidst old occupations. Their Lord's company and teaching in the past, while it had always tended to disengage them from *the bond-age* of the things of time, had never for a moment tended to break their sympathy with the common life, and work, and affections of men. And they were all, in all probability, as we have already remarked, in the full vigour of young manhood, contemporaries of their Master. To await Him was blessed ; but to await Him in inaction would have been for them unnatural.

How familiar to them, and yet how strangely different too, must the scenes and the life have been ! Little more than a quarter of a year had passed since last they were there. But those few weeks were the turning-point of the history of man. A great change had come over even external conditions. There was no more the old eager and excited following about of a wonderful Leader. No longer did ever-growing Galilean multitudes throng to hear and to watch, and clamour to proclaim Him King Messiah. All this had now passed into total silence. For the time, perhaps, in the common thought of Galilee, His name had been already classed with those of Theudas and the Gaulonite Judas, exposed and ruined aspirants to the honours of Messiah. All was silent now on the mount where the Man of Nazareth had taught, and quiet in the sunny streets where He had healed the sick people, and very solitary on that eastern shore of the Lake where He had expelled the fallen spirits, and had fed the multitudes arranged in their "parterres" ($\pi\rho\alpha\sigma\iota\alpha\acute{\iota}$, Mark vi. 40) of hundreds and fifties. Many a Galilean heart which had never seen below the radiant surface of the life of Jesus must yet have felt the profound difference. Air and earth and waters were the same ; a glorious scene, glorious even now amidst comparative desertion. But the wonderful presence of the Prophet was gone, and gone (for the popular mind) into such a blank. such a gloom. Faint rumours of the

Resurrection may have reached the Galilean villages, apart from anything said by the inner circle of disciples; but even these would be mingled with the Jewish lie (Matt. xxviii. 15) which denied it. And we gather that the disciples themselves were not a little reticent about the Resurrection beyond their own company till Pentecost arrived; so reticent indeed that their witness then evidently broke as a great surprise upon the people. The thoughtful Christian may surely find in this one of the "truth-likenesses" of the Gospel narratives.

But to these disciples themselves meanwhile, in the secret soul, and in the private conversation, the familiar scenery would present another and far different change. Outwardly all was hushed, and as it were motionless; inwardly all was glowing and moving with new and glorious while infinitely solemn life. They had seen the Lord. They knew Him as alive for evermore. As yet doubtless they had taken in but little comparatively of the divine import of the Resurrection; but, at least—they knew the Lord as Risen! The mangled Victim of the Roman cross was alive, alive eternally; sure to triumph now in the great issues of His will and work, sure to be glorified, sure to save, lead, raise and glorify *them*. However reticent about it, they

L

146 JESUS AND THE RESURRECTION.

must have begun already in their old Galilee to
live the life of heaven. They were being already
transfigured from the earthly to the heavenly
mind. The glories of their native land and
air would now be to them fair parables of the
resurrection world, of an inheritance reserved
in heaven. Above all, their thoughts now would
be, as they were to be for ever, filled to over-
flowing with Jesus and His glory. The sight
of Him in His Resurrection must indeed have
been soul-possessing; the first deep draught
drawn by mortal hearts at the unfathomed
fountain of the absolute and finished redemption
from guilt, sin, death, which is, and is to come,
in Jesus Christ.

Thank God, that fountain is yet springing up
unto life eternal, that discovery is ever making.
For innumerable hearts to-day (and are not
ours among them?) earth, in all its regions and
climates, is lighted up from heaven,[1] "because
Jesus died and rose again"; "because the Son
of God is come, and hath given us an understanding, and we are in Him, the True" (1 John
v. 20).

In this Galilean scenery and sojourn, then, the
Lord again manifested Himself to the disciples
beside (ἐπί) the Tiberias Lake.

---

[1] See Appendix ii.

And He manifested Himself thus.

Verse 2. *There were together* the aforementioned seven. Four then of the Eleven were absent. We have no hint of a reason why. But both the mention of the number and the absence of anxious explanation fall perfectly in with this wonderful photograph of details by one who saw.

They were together, very probably in Capernaum, in Peter's house, waiting for their absent but promised Lord, waiting it may be for several days. And now some untold passing thing suggests, amidst the expectancy, their old occupation. The water is close by, and there lie the πλοῖον and the πλοιάριον of the house, the boat and its tender, and the sky and the lake promise well. And in the thought of embarkation there would be no discord with thoughts of Jesus. In that boat He had sate ; He had taught from its bench ; He had slept (Mark iv. 38) with His head upon its cushion.

So the men, being together, go out together to their old acts and habits, feeling very possibly, just as young men now might feel, the curious interest of returning for a while to a disused exercise of strength and skill. They take the two boats, the larger and the lesser, of which more hereafter. All probably entered the boat, and worked it together through the night; and all probably in the morning transferred themselves at last to the tender, except Peter, who had first reached the shore through the water.[1]

We watch the party which embarked : Peter, still leading with the spirit and word of enterprise ; Thomas, the self-conscious and self-asserting doubter no more, but willingly "together" with the rest ; Nathanael (no born fisherman), the guileless and genuine Israelite, the man of secret prayer ; John, the beloved, already finding it habitual to be at Peter's side ; James, his brother, first of the company to go to the Lord through death, as John the last ; and the other nameless two, whom we may, if we will, suppose to be Andrew and his fellow Bethsaidan Philip. They were indeed together ; in the house, on the water, and at length again on the other shore ; and never again in the sense of inner union were they to be apart ; working together on the world's tide with the net of souls, and sitting down at last together on the immortal strand around their glorified Lord Jesus.

It is of the essence of the Gospel to unite where it touches. It is obvious, as we saw

[1] I owe this explanation of the probable circumstances to a kind communication from Mr P. Vernon Smith.

above (p. 123), that the first disciples must
have been scattered, in shame, disgust, suspicion, if the Lord had not risen from the grave.
The Gospels show them in the act, as we
trace the walk to Emmaus, and the conduct of
Thomas. But a Saviour risen again (and HE
is the Gospel) is indeed a magnetic force to
draw round Himself, and to draw to, nay, as it
were, into one another, the utmost variety of
human souls. A personal and recognized interest in His merits, and experience of His
presence and His power, as we realize that
ours is but one harmonious instance among
countless others of the "reception of Christ
Jesus the Lord" (Col. ii. 6)—this does indeed
draw hearts together. And we may be very sure
that this sense of a blessed community will be
intensified, not chilled, by the intensity of the
individual's sense of peace and power in Christ.

Verse 3. *Simon Peter says to them, I am
going to fish.* So St John records the simple
words with which that memorable night's labour
was begun, and then he tells us how they
stepped into the boat, and then how the spring
evening and midnight were spent, as it seemed,
in vain. *That night they took nothing; and
daybreak was now come.* How brief and reserved it all is, till Jesus appears! So it is ever

in the evangelical narrative. With Jesus present, details come thick and fast—details which manifest HIM. Here, the night is recorded in one line. We should like to know all about it ; what was the look of the dark water, and the brightness of the stars above, and the stirring of the air, and the sounds on flood and shore. We should like to understand what filled the hearts of those seven men that night ; whether they were fairly bent upon their work, and so quite alive to delays and disappointments, or whether expectations of a far higher sort were strong enough to let them "ply their watery task" inattentively. The former alternative is more probable, for the record seems to show them at early morning so unexpectant of the Lord's coming to them just then that it needed the miracle to awaken them to consciousness of Him. They act, as we then see them, just like men fatigued and bewildered by long and real but fruitless effort.

But as to all details, inward and outward alike, we are left without the least certainty. Imagination shows us the two spots upon the dusky waters, under the aërial gloom of the deep midnight. It lets us hear the fishermen as they call to one another, to enquire, encourage, or direct, in the tone and phrase of Galilee.

Yet all this is mere reverie, and we do well to remember it.

But it is truth, not imagination, that bids us see in that fruitless night of toil, followed by so blessed a morrow, not only a precious narrative of real events but a living message of strength to the Christian man in the hour of trial, of delay, of seemingly unrequited labour for the Lord; and a living message, too, to the Christian Church, upon the deep dark waters of sin and time, waiting for the eternal morning, and the great ingathering, and the manifested Saviour;

> While night
> Invests the sea, and wished morn delays.

Let us lay it thankfully to heart.

X

JOY IN THE MORNING.

So the seven disciples went out for their evening's fishing, and spent that summer night in vain efforts on the lake. *And that night they took nothing.* No doubt many a well-known favourable place was tried, now the nearer now the further shore, the deeper and the shallower waters. Most of them were experienced fishermen, and they were at work where the prey was then, as now, abundant. But "that night they took nothing."

It was not an unprecedented disappointment. Some three years before they had passed a similar night (Luke v.), the night which ushered in the day when some of them received from their Friend and Teacher the call which changed their whole after-life :—"Master ('Επιστάτα), we have toiled all the night and taken nothing ; nevertheless at Thy word I will let down the net." There was *that* precedent at least to be

remembered; and perhaps there were other
occasions when they had borne the burthens
of a fruitless night, though the emphasis with
which these two experiences are recorded seems
to say that such a night was not an ordinary
incident.   It was as it were part and parcel with
the miraculously fruitful morning.

Certainly it was a providential preparation
for it.   The true Son of Man (Psa. viii. 4) ruled
the waters and their tribes all that night through.
"The fishes of the sea, and whatsoever walketh
through the paths of the sea"—of them we read
in that Messianic oracle that they are part of
His dominion.   Let us remember, as most
certainly St John means us to do, that it was
He who that night *willed* the hours of frustration
and failure.   The providence and decree of
Jesus Christ deliberately and effectually disappointed His dear disciples' hopes and efforts.
The weary hands, the aching eyes, the baffled
skill, He had to do with it all.   It was the
Lord.

It is well worth our while to bear this in
mind for our own help.   Not seldom the servant
of God is called upon to use his best skill and
strength *apparently* in vain; to labour unmistakably in vain as regards immediate successes.
Not always indeed; in many cases not very

often ; but certainly, upon the whole, not very seldom. Such experiences should always lead us to self-searching, to see what *in us* may perhaps be the reason of failure, in our spirit toward others, or towards the Lord, or in our ways and means of labour. But when, as in His presence, we may humbly believe that in these respects His will is being done in us and by us, and yet we seem to "spend our strength for nought," then let us remember the night spent on the Galilean lake, and be reassured. We shall yet find that the disappointment is, in providence, as much a blessing as the success is ; in fact, a part of the success, its prelude and preface.

Could the Seven have foreseen, however dimly, their Master's presence the next morning, and realized, however faintly, that He was in those dark hours already acting upon them and around them, would it not have lightened all the burthen indescribably? All vexation would have vanished out of the delay, simply because of their consciousness of the life, the will, the love of their Saviour and their God.

It would seem however that they had no such forecast.

Verse 4. *But when daybreak was now come, Jesus came and stood on the beach* (the eastern beach, as we gather from the evident solitude of the place); *the disciples however did not know that it is Jesus.* No; they did not know it, even John did not know it, till the miracle, the σημεῖον, was fairly done. We gather that the undefined transfiguration of our Lord's appearance, so often hinted at in the Resurrection narratives, was here also operating to delay their recognition. But we may also infer that their minds as well as eyes were at fault; they were not on the look-out to see Him; or surely the first sight of any solitary figure on the beach would have at once suggested the question, Is it not the Lord?

We can do little more than note this peculiar unconsciousness of the Apostles. Like other instances of their oblivion or "slowness" of heart, it speaks truth and fact by its very unlikelihood *à priori*, and by the perfect simplicity of the record of it. It is precisely unlike an invention. If an invention, it would be of course the invention of a later generation, when these fishermen were already viewed with the deepest reverence as the builders and rulers of the Christian community. Would an artificial picture of their conduct, drawn at such a date, have taken the line which the Gospels do take, the line of freest description and criticism of their slowness and fallibility of perception?

The thoroughly human, imperfect, provincial character and conduct attributed as a fact to the Apostles in the Gospels has thus a precious value as internal evidence of the genuineness of the record. Again and again be it said, the picture is not a composition ; it is a photograph. It is not an ideal ; it is life.

So here we have not a company of hardly human beings, seen in " the light that never was on sea or land " ; their every faculty always awake to Christ and to heaven. We have a group of men, engrossed for the time with the expectations and disappointments of common work, toiling on from hour to hour, very tired no doubt by the morning, their senses all strained and aching, bewildered and forgetting.

When it was dawn, then, in the pale rising light, where the eastward hills rise ridge over ridge towards Trachonitis, throwing their deep and misty shadows towards the water, then and there the Risen *Jesus stood upon the beach, came and stood upon the beach,* the αἰγιαλός, the pebbly or sandy margin of the crystal water. How had He spent the night? Had He walked upon the deep as long ago, though now unseen? Or had He been traversing in the quiet hours the scenes which in the days of His mortality He had frequented with His blessed presence? How total our ignorance is before such a question! The reality, the literality, of the life of the Risen One we know; blessed be the name of His Father. We know that our Redeemer lived, and liveth. But of the conditions of that life of His literal and bodily Resurrection we know, in detail, almost nothing. It is enough, however. The holy narratives lift the veil high enough to show us a Saviour present, accessible, identical, perfect God, perfect Man; alive in all His love and power, and saying to us, "Ye shall live also."

He stood upon the shore, a solitary figure, seen over "the wan water," a hundred yards or so from the boat. Peter, and John, and their fellows, could well see Him, but none of them recognized Him. Busy perhaps with some last haul of the empty net, or listless and inobservant with fatigue, *they knew not that it is Jesus.*

Verse 5. *So Jesus says to them, Children you have not any fish?* Μή τι προσφάγιον ἔχετε; The *μή* implies the supposition that they had *not* taken anything.

Παιδία, *Children.* The word is used almost as "Lads" might be used now, importing (as some similar phrases amongst our poor people do) only neighbourhood and friendliness, not

necessarily a paternal superiority. We may
observe that it is not "*My* children;" for
scarcely ever, if ever, does the Saviour—at least
in the days of His flesh—address His followers
as *His children* at all; John xiii. 33 is not an
exception.[1] They are *His brethren.* "He is
not ashamed" (hard as it sometimes is, for joy,
to believe it) "to call us brethren" (Heb. ii. 11);
His Father's children. This, however, is by the
way. The word παιδία here would be understood as merely a kindly expression on the part
of the unknown visitor.

St Chrysostom, who tends as an expositor to
a very simple and even homely explanation of
details, thinks that Jesus may have put this
question meaning to speak as *an intending
purchaser* (ὡς μέλλων τι ὠνεῖσθαι παρ' αὐτῶν). It
may be so. But the other suggestion seems to
fit more naturally into the scene—that the
question was as from a man looking with
friendly interest on what was manifestly a
moment of fruitless toil. Faint and disheart-
ened those boatmen may well have *looked*, as
they trailed the slack net. *So you have had no
success, then?*

Thus the voice came from the shore, audible

---

[1] In Heb. ii. 33 the "children" are *God's* children
entrusted to His Son. See the context.

and articulate as it always is over water. *They answered Him, No;* the brief reply of tired men.

Verse 6. *Then He said to them, Throw your net on the right side of the boat, and you will find.*

The young men acted at once upon the words. No doubt there was a spell upon them; for when JESUS speaks it is more than words. But the supernatural spell acted, as is almost always the case, through nature. Partly the non-resistance of fatigue, partly the faint hope of success by any means, partly and perhaps chiefly the thought that the stranger from his standpoint might see a cause for his confident words which they could not see—these may have been the motives. Possibly too there came over them a vague and indefinable sense (we all know what that is like) of a previous occurrence of the whole event; each step was in the footmarks of the past.

So they threw; and now strength failed them to draw, such was the quantity of fish. Here, by the way, is an incidental touch of accuracy. This inability to draw in a net which though full was not extraordinarily full (ver. 11) shows that the hands were very tired.

What the Five said and did we do not know; the narrator can think just now only of Peter and himself.

Wonderful pair of friends ! More and more, in the narrative, we find them, as we saw above (p. 18), together. Essentially different in natural character, they are now however drawn irrevocably side to side. Each has a brother who is also a chief Apostle ; but Peter and John are somehow more than brothers to each other now. We shall see yet more striking proof of this before the Gospel closes ; but let us here note the fact. And let us remember how affectingly all these records of the loving union of Peter and John, *written by John*, answer that shallow and trivial insinuation of the sceptic that this chapter was written with the poor purpose of making Peter less and John more prominent than before.

And now these two men, drawn thus together, made thus for ever one in the love of Jesus, go on to act, each in his way ; John sees, and Peter moves.

Verse 7. *So that disciple whom Jesus loved says to Peter, It is the Lord.* He saw that it was Jesus. Probably his *eyes* saw nothing new ; it was the same figure standing there, the same just visible face. But the σημεῖον, the sign-wonder, waked his soul to conscious insight with his eyes ; and he knew who it was—THE LORD.

In passing we may notice once more that title, as sweet as it is reverently solemn, which after the Resurrection seems to become the habitual designation of the Risen One, THE LORD. Let us note the word, as thus employed by the beloved one, by John ; by him who delights to tell us, with holy simplicity, that Jesus had been pleased to admit him to a peculiar personal intimacy. Yet even for John, Jesus is THE LORD. And will it not be ever thus with us also, as we grow in knowledge and in love of Him? Intimacy between sinner and sinner may often lead to diminution of respect ; intimacy between the redeemed sinner and JESUS CHRIST, the more He is known as He is, can only lead to a deeper, a more unreserved, reverence and adoration. Dost thou very dearly love Him ? Has He very wonderfully made manifest to thee His love for thee? Then surely by thee above all others He will be known and worshipped as THE LORD.

Thus John beheld Jesus. He saw the Son of God. He was conscious of His Person and Presence, which but for that insight were but the person and presence of a chance passer-by upon the lonely beach.

So Simon Peter, hearing that it is the Lord, girded on his outer coat, for he was naked, and threw himself into the lake.

He heard who it was ; he did not look, it seems, to verify the hearing. The tone of John

M

spoke for itself, and this was what, for Peter, brought the soul to look, to see the Son of God. Are we not reminded that often, very often, the calm, happy certainty shown by some beloved and trusted friend with regard to the Saviour's life, and love, and power, proves to the soul (perhaps in some hour of perplexity or bitterness) its own truthfulness? It shines out direct, an evidence of Christianity, a manifestation of Christ. "He knoweth that he saith true, that ye may believe."

Peter now acts in his own way upon the words of John. Two sides of his remarkable character come out ; an almost impetuous devotion to his Master, and a most keen consciousness of his personal unworthiness to be in his Master's presence. He was naked, γυμνός. That is to say, in all probability, as frequent usage illustrates the meaning, he was half clad, wearing nothing but an under tunic. However, he was so attired that he could not choose to appear so before "the Lord." And he wraps the outer coat around him, the ἐπενδύτης, the large overcoat for storms and cold nights. And *he girt it well round him*, διεζώσατο. It was a simple but true expression of profound reverence, the same spirit which had once (Luke v. 8) prompted him to cry, "Depart from me." But that spirit

was more enlightened now, for Peter's resistless
impulse now is—to draw near. He knew now,
not that Jesus was less awfully holy, but that
His very holiness made it necessary, and blessed,
for Peter to be quite near Him. And it is so
still. Jesus Christ would not be THE SAVIOUR
were He not infinitely holy. But He *is* the
Saviour, and being so He must be actually approached, actually touched, by the sinner who so
much wants Him. And the sinner now, like Peter
of old, as he comes and touches, will remember
both truths—that indeed His name is Holy, but
also that to come actually *to Him*, to nothing
intermediate, but to Him, is not rashness but
obedience, not presumption but salvation.

He threw himself into the lake, leaving
John, and the five others, to step, it would seem,
from the boat into the tender, anchor the boat,
and, in the tender, haul the net to shore. Peter
threw himself in, and crossed the hundred yards
of water, swimming and wading (we seem to see
the silver spray of the plunge, and the eager
passage), to find himself as soon as he can be at
the feet of the Prince of Life. Yes, he must be
as near as possible, and that as soon as possible,
to Him whom he had denied a few weeks ago,
over and over, but who had nevertheless gone
on to die for him and rise again.

Verse 8. What that first moment's interview was, we are not told. The whole group of seven were now on land. The five had assisted John to bring boats and net to the shore; and then apparently at once, without hauling *up* the net, but leaving it fast to the boat, full of its struggling prize, they had stepped out and so drew near the Lord.

Verse 9. And now, in the solitary place, beside Him, they see a meal already preparing. A fire, a coal fire, was already there; and beside its ruddy flame fish was set for eating, and the bread was ready. Manifestly there was mystery, if not miracle, in this provision, and He near whom they stood had something to teach them by it. Was it not the lesson of His independence of them, and yet care for them, and fellowship with them? It was this at least. And now He bids them add their own to His— their own, which however was His also; for what they had just caught He had by His will given them. They were to *bring it*, however.

Verse 10. *Jesus says to them, Bring some of the fish which you have just taken. Simon Peter got up* (from the beach into the tender-boat), *and*, standing there, *pulled up the net quite full of large fish.* And Peter counted the number over; we seem to hear his voice as he "tells the tale"; a distinct and definite report, no round number, *one hundred and fifty-three.* It was a large haul for that one cast-net; *and yet, although they were so many, the net had not been torn.*

So Peter's work, and his account of it, is done; and then again the solemn reticence of the Lord is broken, and He calls them to a meal around Him.

The details of ver. 12 and those which follow upon it we must consider in another chapter. All I attempt to do now, as we shut the Book once more, is to recall the reality of the blessed scene. We look on it again; the sun comes up over the hills, and turns the grey waters into gold. And there—look along the shore from where we stand—there is that group around the flame under the steep slope that borders the beach. Eight persons; seven mortal men, sitting down to their food, and in the midst of them One who is also, and supremely, Man; visible, palpable, no illusion; the risen, the ever-living Jesus.

Let us turn away thankful, if we have again indeed seen HIM; Him living then, and therefore "alive for evermore"; alive now, loving, watching, present, now. Well do I remember, though long years have passed, how at a time of great mental and spiritual trial I found, by God's great mercy, peculiar help in just this way from this very scene, as it invited me to realize afresh this mysterious but actual personal life and presence of Jesus Christ.

There, in the sight of Him, is peace. To see and know Him living, living after He had for us "poured out His soul unto death," is the solution of doubts, the banishment of fears, the conquest of passions, the strength of the soul. From amidst that group of disciples He still says, to us to-day, "Fear not; you indeed are mortal, sinful, feeble, helpless; but I am the First and the Last; I am the Living One. I was dead, but behold I am alive for ever, alive for you, with you, in you, to the endless ages."

> Jesus, such His love and power,
>   Such His presence dear,
> Everywhere and every hour
>   With His own is near;
>
> With the glorified at rest
>   Far in Paradise,
> With the pilgrim saints distress'd
>   'Neath these cloudier skies;
>
> With the ransom'd soul that flew
>   From the cross to heaven,
> With the Emmaus travellers two,
>   With the lake-borne seven.
>
> Lord, Thy promise Thou wilt keep,
>   Thine shall dwell with Thee,
> And, awaking or asleep,
>   Thus together be.

XI

THE MORNING MEAL—LOVEST THOU ME?

Jesus says to them, Come, break your fast. None of the disciples ventured to question Him, Who art Thou? knowing that it is the Lord. So Jesus comes, and takes the bread and gives it to them, and the fish in the same way. This was the now third manifestation of Jesus to His disciples, as risen from the dead.

The fishes were numbered, and Peter's work was done. And now the reticent Master speaks again; and with the word He approaches (ver. 14) the fire, evidently from a position beyond it, as the disciples looked from the beach landwards. As they sit near Him He personally dispenses the morning meal. Apparently it was a silent time. A spell was upon the Seven; a sense of awe even greater than on former occasions of interview in these blessed days. And no wonder; for at each successive time, surely, something said to them, as they looked and listened, that the Lord was nearer to His glory.

So He, none other than Himself, and by no intermediary, fed them. And He is the same still. From some points of view there is, and must be, much intermediate agency in the carrying about in the world the message and the ordinances of the Lord. Men must translate the Scriptures, and labour in their publication and exposition. Men must minister to other men the Sealing Rites of the blessed message. But in the ultimate truth of the matter nothing but Christ is the soul's aliment, and none but Christ, through the work of His Holy Spirit, is the Host, the Provider and Dispenser of Himself. "I will come in, and will sup with him, and he with Me" (Rev. iii. 20).

This then was *the third* appearance, *the third* time. The statement is meant, of course, to stand in relation to the whole of this Johannine narrative of the Resurrection period. It thus means obviously that this was the third appearance to any considerable gathering of the disciples, as on the Easter evening, and on that day week, when Thomas was brought to believe. Neither John nor the Synoptists record, for certain, any other appearance *to a company* beside these three occasions and—what surely

followed later than this—the meeting on the
Galilean mountain (Matt. xxviii.), and then the
meeting before, and at, the Ascension. This
"third time" needs notice only as an example
of the way in which Scripture expects us, if I
may say so, to use our common sense in its
explanation. Pressed literally, these words of
St John may seem to contradict other records.
Taken with remembrance of the context, which
the thoughtful reader is assumed to remember,
the agreement with the whole record is
complete.

Such, then, was that third interview. There
sate that favoured group before the Master, on
the level margin of the lake, in the stillness of
the morning, after the night of toil ; and "ate
and drank with Him after He had risen from
the dead" (Acts x. 41), and knew it was He. A
silence, as we have said, seemed to lie upon
them. It was a silence of awe, yet also of rest.
"In that hour they asked Him nothing,"because
they saw, because they knew.

Toil was over, and so also was unconsciousness of His presence, and doubt about it.
There is much in the whole fair scene to make
us believe it to be, besides its inestimable value
as a record of fact, also a picture, drawn by
the Saviour's own hand, of the eternal festival

beyond the waves of labour and strife, where "they hunger and thirst no more," and where yet "the Lamb shepherds them, and leads them to the living fountains" (Rev. vii. 16, 17). That blissful hour "is prepared as the morning." Silently as the rising of the day, but as surely too, it is coming, it will be here. Shall we not all be found there through grace, leaving the night and the deep behind us, and feeling the Sun of eternal joy rise on us, and on the Land of our desire, as we feast in and on the manifested presence of the beloved Lord?

But St John leaves the lesson, the mystery, to be drawn out by the reader, and passes on at once.

So when they had broken their fast, Jesus says to Simon Peter, Simon, son of Jonah am I dear to you more than to these? He says to Him, Yes, Lord, Thou knowest that I love Thee. He says to Him, Feed My lambs. Again He says to Him, a second time, Simon, son of Jonah, am I dear to you? He says to Him, Yes, Lord. Thou knowest that I love Thee. He says to Him, Shepherd My dear sheep (προβάτια). *He says to him the third time, Simon, son of Jonah, do you love Me? Peter was pained that He said to him the third time,*

Do you love Me?   And he said to Him, Lord,
Thou *knowest* (οἶδας) *all things;* Thou *seest*
(γινώσκεις) *that I love Thee.   Jesus says to him,*
Feed My dear sheep.

The silent meal was over then, and Jesus
speaks. He speaks so as indeed to answer fully
the unspoken question, if they had felt it stir
within them, *Who art Thou?*   He who now
speaks is indeed THE LORD.

Peter is addressed. He has been already
conspicuous in the scene ; plunging into the
lake while the others row shoreward, climbing
into the beached boat, and drawing in the net.
Now he is singled out to be for a while the one
figure, with Jesus, in our view. And this is
done (the Lord often does so still in His grace
and providence) so as to leave the disciple at
once humble and happy.

We may suppose that Peter needed both
humiliation and happiness specially just then.
His haste to reach the shore may have had in
it some slight trace of personal display of
devotion. And on the other hand there was a
deep wound in his soul, left by the denials of
that remembered and recent night of terror
In the complexities of that human heart there
was possible room for both feelings at once ;
for a yielding once more to a self-asserting

impulse, and for a sore sickness of soul in memory and conviction. Self-assertion and inmost sadness sometimes lie near together. And to both maladies the blessed Lord knows how to apply His searching, healing hand.

We are not to think that this was the first moment of Peter's restoration and acceptance. He was present on both the previous occasions when Jesus had met His disciples and had blessed them with His peace. He had enjoyed one secret interview, on the great Easter Day itself ; *the Lord appeared unto Simon* (Luke xxiv. 34) ; an appearance which assuredly conveyed to the penitent Apostle, *in private*, a blessed restoration. But very deep griefs, especially of the conscience, may well ask for more than a solitary act and word of reassurance. In his pain and exhaustion the sufferer is thankful if the message may be " doubled unto him." And besides, in this case, the secret welcome back and the general benediction could not fully take the place of a public reinstatement of the lapsed Apostle, in view of his association with his brethren and, in some sense, leadership amongst them.

So the Lord deliberately and solemnly restored him, with His own lips, and before six Apostolic witnesses. The mighty wound needed a proportionate remedy. And the remedy was to be such as also to remind him for ever of his snares and his weakness, that he might watch and stand.

Verse 15. *Simon, (son) of Jonah, am I dear to you?*

"Simon, son of Jonah." It is almost exactly the same phrase as that used in St John's first chapter (ver. 42) ; only a little briefer, by the omission of "son," as was natural in a direct appellation. The appellation occurs nowhere else in this Gospel, often as Peter is referred to in its narratives. The use of the words here is assuredly by design, and observable ; the Lord uses on purpose in this restitution of the Apostle the name which He had used at his first call. He reminds Peter thus that he must be content to start anew, to begin again as the catechumen ; not Cephas now, not Peter now, for the time, but just Simon, Jonah's son.

And the question put by the Lord is as elementary as the appellation : ἀγαπᾷς με πλεῖον τούτων ; *Do you love Me more than these others do?* It is possible, grammatically, I hardly need say, to explain the Greek either thus, or, *Do you love Me more than you love these men?* But surely of the two renderings the latter is not to the purpose of the occasion.

Nothing in the narrative suggests any special need that the Lord should, as it were, lay His hand on Peter and ask him if he could prefer Him to his Apostolic friends. But the other explanation fits exactly into the picture as we have it : " Is your love to Me warmer, stronger, higher than theirs?" The old weakness of Peter's heart was its tendency to profess a peculiar and superior love. " Though all should deny Thee, yet will not I ; I will never be offended." So he had said just before his fall ; self-assertion had gone before, close before, what had indeed seemed to be his utter ruin. He had not been willing to love, to trust, to follow, quite simply ; he must needs do so with a mind full of estimates of comparison favourable to himself : " My love, my obedience, see what they are ; admire the devoted Apostle ! " It is a mysterious possibility, the lingering of such thoughts in the same soul which at the same time in a measure feels, and utters, true love to its Redeemer. But it is as true as it is mysterious. And what shall be the antidote? Nothing but such a God-given view of Him in His beauty and glory as shall draw the soul clear off from a centre in itself to rest, not in an abstract self-oblivion, but in Him. To shake off the consciousness of our personality is the dream of the pantheist. The self-denial of the Gospel comes when the individual so sees and receives Christ that HE occupies and fills the personality with the power and peace of His living presence. Then indeed it lives; lives individually, lives with rich developments of character, yet lives purely and simply, because in and by the Lord. The more it is thus with the man the less will he be betrayed into the hollow and unhappy thought, "I love Him better than others do; I serve more, I bear more in His name, than others."

Such surely, be it said with all reverence for the blessed Apostle's sacred memory, had been the special risk for St Peter. And upon this now the Master lays His firm and loving hand, in the question : *Am I dear to you, more than to these ?*

I venture to render ἀγαπᾷς με thus : *Am I dear to you ?* It may at least remind us that there *is* a difference here in the Greek words rendered "love" in our version : ἀγαπᾶν, φιλεῖν. But it can only express imperfectly the generally recognized distinction, that ἀγαπᾶν, on the whole, denotes the more deliberate affection and φιλεῖν the warmer emotion. Archbishop Trench gives careful attention to the distinction in his *New Testament Synonyms*, a book which is often the best of commentaries on a difficult text ; and

his conclusion is as I have just said. Thus here
the Lord asks the Apostle, in His first two
queries, whether he loves Him in the clear,
exalted way of the soul's full choice and calm
satisfaction, and the Apostle, surely as owning
himself unworthy to assert so serene and sublime
an affection, feeling himself inadequate to it,
sinner that he is, replies in the other word, so
warm, so personal, but also humble; φιλῶ σε, I
love Thee with my poor heart's love. My paraphrase does but doubtfully express this, but it
can point to it. Let me only add, as regards
the study of the two words, that the distinction
is by no means to be pressed generally. The
two verbs, when either occurs apart, are apt
each to absorb something of the other's meaning. It is when placed together, as here, that
their distinction must be carefully remembered.

Simon, son of Jonah, am I dear to you? So
says the Lord Jesus twice over to His servant.
Am I dear to you? Does your heart, with a
strong, full choice of love and gladness, choose
Me? Does it rest in Me, as all its salvation and
also as all its desire? Ἀγαπᾷς με? Wonderful
question! We cannot but remark it, as we pass
on, as an instance of the mysterious, persistent
" self-assertion " of the Lord. He mentions not
the word GOD. It occurs but once in this

chapter, and then not in His utterances. It is
"*I*," "*Me*," "till *I* come," "*My* sheep," "*My*
lambs," "lovest thou *Me?*" Let us observe
this with reverent attention. It is one of the
deepest implicit proofs of the Divine Oneness of
the Father and the Son, this tone and claim of
the Son about Himself which, but for the truth
of the *Homoüsion*, the Co-essentiality, would be
nothing else than the intrusion of an alien
medium between the soul and the Maker, the
claim of a love for the creature, however exalted
a creature this might be, which is due only to
the Creator, who is blessed for ever.

"Am I dear to thee, in the dearness of this
lofty affection, this ἀγάπη?" Wonderful question, let us say it again; wonderful from this
other point of view, that it shows such a care
on HIS part for the love of such poor hearts as
ours. It is indeed lovable in JESUS CHRIST
that He loves us to love Him; that it is something to HIM that the sinful human being who
a few weeks earlier had denied acquaintance
with Him should return now, not with terror
and despair, but with love, to His blessed side.
"Give me thine *heart*" is the most searching,
as it is the most characteristic, of the demands
of the God of Revelation, of the God of Christ,
of Christ the Son of God. But it is also a

N

demand infinitely amiable. He who thus asks
for the gift of the heart has on His part a heart
to give. "Lovest thou Me? I care that thou
shouldest love Me. Read in My question the
truth, the certainty, that I loved thee, that I
love thee."

Let me quote the words of one of the greatest
of modern preachers, as he was one of the most
devoted and loving of modern believers, Adolphe
Monod ; words in his Sermon entitled, *Dieu
démandant le cœur à l'Homme:* "No other
religion presents anything which resembles this
invitation to give God the heart. Give me thy
observances, says the God of Pharisaism. Give
me thy personality, says the God of Hegel. Give
me thy reason, says the God of Kant. . . . It
remains for the God of Jesus Christ to say, Give
Me thy heart. . . . He makes it the essence
and the glory of His doctrine. With Him, to
give the heart to God is not merely an obliga-
tion of piety ; it is its root, its beginning, its
middle, and its end. It is the unmistakable
feature (*le caractère non équivoque*) of a genuine
conversion. You tell me that a man believes
the Gospel of grace ; he does well, but does he
believe it with a living faith ? You tell me that
he is in the front of every Christian effort ; ay,
but does he bring with him a Christian spirit?

But tell me that he has given his heart to God, and every other question is superfluous. Faith, works, grace, holiness, the new creation, all is there. Will you enter on the possession?"

"Am I dear to you?" Such was the question put by Jesus to Peter, on the shore, by the fire, in the presence of Peter's six listening friends. It was a strangely searching moment. The night was over, with all its movements, its excitements, its lassitude; Peter's stirring, leading spirit is for a while in check; and now, before his Master and his friends, he is faced by this question altogether of the heart, the inner heart, not of the outer act: "Am I dear to you?" Let us sit reverently down beside the Apostle, and humbly put ourselves also in the line of that question. Let us often listen for it; and not least after some hour of vivid interest, of strong exertion, of rich intercourse. Then, if ever, let us sit down before the Lord and hear Him say, "Am I dear to you?" Do not ask others whether they think you love Christ. Let Christ ask you. Friends will be very kind and indulgent in their answers for us; at least, so it will be if they are themselves humble believers. They will give us more than full credit for every work we try to do under the banner of religion, for every sacrifice we seem to make in a Christian cause. Yes, they will be kind ; and so will the Lord Jesus be. Only, He will be omniscient also, and will not for a moment mistake act for motive, hand for heart. When He puts the question, we shall have to reply with Peter, *Lord, Thou knowest all things, Thou knowest—* what shall it be?—*that I love Thee?* Why should it not be so? If you love, not worthily (that is impossible) but really, you may surely *know* it. And why not love really? Nothing can prevent it but blindness to what Jesus Christ is, oblivion of what Jesus Christ is and does for you.

Oh, sweet it is to know, most simply, that the soul loves Him ; not as it should love Him, truly, and not " more than these," with a glance of self-consciousness around ; but that indeed it does love Him—whether ἀγαπῶ or φιλῶ be its chosen word.

St Peter happily could answer at once, before his Lord and his companions, *Yes, Lord, Thou knowest that I love Thee.* Φιλῶ σε. The stress is on " I love," not on " Thee." And the φιλῶ is emphatic, as I have said above ; it indicates a certain avoidance of the other verb. " I love Thee, with such love as this poor heart can feel. I speak not of the heights of heavenly affection now. But Thou knowest, my Lord,

my Saviour, that *I do love Thee*, with most
personal devotion."

No utterance could have been more beautifully in keeping with that hour of mysterious
agitation and solemn joy. It was otherwise
with Peter in later days. In his First Epistle,
that golden document of the Gospel, he says
without reserve, of all true believers, *Him
having not seen ye love* (ἀγαπᾶτε). But here,
by the lake, what could have been more true to
all the wonderful surroundings than this φιλῶ σε ?
And we observe that the Lord, in His third
enquiry, concedes this word to the Apostle. He
meets him, He condescends to him, half-way.
" *Simon, son of Jonah, do you love Me ?*   Φιλεῖς
με? I note your chosen word ; I understand
your choice ; and now I am content to put My
question in your way. I ask you now for one
final assurance thus—φιλεῖς με ? "

Let us too hear our blessed Master put to us
His question in those terms. If indeed φιλεῖν is
in so far lower than ἀγαπᾶν that it indicates less
of insight and more of emotion, yet the word,
though lower by comparison, is in itself a
precious word. " Do you feel a loving affection
for Me ? " Do we ? Are we not somewhat too
easily content to dispense with that experience ?
In a just anxiety not to build our salvation on

our feelings (and indeed we need to be very clear upon that matter) let us not forget the other side. Let us not forget that exactly because our peace is built not on our feelings but on our most adorable and loving Lord, therefore it is for us to draw from it, in the glad necessity of a true spiritual sequence, the result of an ardent affection in the inmost heart.

> I love Thee for the glorious worth
> In Thy great Self I see ;
> I love Thee for the shameful Cross
> Thou hast endured for me.

If we believe, if we enter into the truths, let me say, of the Nicene Creed, that blessed summary of truth and love, worthy of often repetition in private, as well as before the Table of the Lord, shall not the words of our confession of His Name be inbreathed all through with the secret consciousness, strong and reverently tender, ἀγαπῶ σε, Κύριε, φιλῶ σε, Κύριε?

I have not attempted to take up *seriatim* the three questions and three answers. The *thrice-*repeated enquiry seems to carry so manifest a reference to the threefold denial, and a reference of that suppressed and implicit kind character-istic of St John's record, that it is surprising that a doubt should ever have been cast on the reference. What to my own mind makes it

certain is the whole character of the scene. It
is a solemn reinstatement of St Peter, not merely
into right relations with his Master generally,
but into Apostolic relations with Him. Certainly it was *not* a commission to him to be the
Prince of the Apostles, the universal Bishop.[1]
Were it so, Peter was most unfaithful to his
commission ; for never, by written word or
recorded deed, did he claim even the shadow of
such a power. But the Saint, though he receives
no commission here to be lord over his brethren,
does receive a threefold assurance of his full
restoration to a sacred place among his brethren.
"Be a feeder of My lambs, the weak, the young ;
be a tending watchman of My dear flock. In
all the fulness of the privilege, the labour, and
the peril, be again My own Apostle, till at the
last you are My Martyr."

I must not at present follow out further the
details of this part of the passage. I close now
with one obvious remark of application to ourselves. The Lord's questions to Peter about

---

[1] It is curious to read here in M. Lasserre's often
excellent modern French rendering of the Gospels the
significant words, *Sois* le *pasteur de mes agneaux, Sois* le
pasteur de mes brebis. The version of the Jansenist de
Saci reads simply *Paissez mes agneaux, Paissez mes
brebis.*

love to Himself are each at once followed by a command, a command to help the souls of others. From this, two reflections naturally arise, and with them we will once more withdraw for a season from that holy group on the Galilean beach.

First, the great qualification for work for Christ in the hearts of others is love to Christ in the worker's heart, real, personal love in the conscious individual experience.

Then, secondly, where that love is present, kindled by His free and wonderful love to us, there we may expect as the sure sequel that some work for Him in the hearts of others will be put by Him into our hands. He lights the holy flame. He also lays on the fuel which will draw out its life and power.

Happy the Christian who, in the path not of self-choice but of the guidance of God, finds evermore both truths exemplified ; love of the Saviour animating work for Him, work for Him giving movement, and expansion, and permanence, to the sense of love.

XII

THE MASTER AND HIS SERVANTS.

IN the previous chapter we studied the narrative of St Peter's three confessions of love to his
Master, and his Master's thrice-repeated restoration and commission of him as a shepherd of
the flock. Without returning at any length to
that scene, I notice two or three detached
points in it.

(i.) The use of the words φιλεῖν and ἀγαπᾶν.
Is this an incidental evidence that our Lord
sometimes used the Greek language in conversation with His own friends? The Aramaic
has no parallel distinction of verbs; and, on the
other hand, no one who reads St John's style
with attention can well doubt that a distinction
of verbs is intended here by him. The late Dr
A. Roberts, one of the New Testament Revisers,
in his *Discussions on the Gospels*, has made out
a very interesting case for the familiar use of
Greek in Palestine about the time of the First
Advent; and he thinks that we have here a

narrative which implies such use. Undoubtedly Aramaic was in large and frequent use. Again and again the Saviour's Aramaic words to individuals are recorded; and St Paul delivered a long address in Aramaic to the crowds in the Temple court. But are not these incidents so recorded as to suggest that the rule was, at least, very often broken? In any case, Greek *was* spoken, very much as English is spoken in Ireland. And why should not the Lord Jesus have employed it on this occasion, even if His usage were the other way, if only to bring out a sacred lesson as to different qualities of love? On the other hand, even should it be shewn beyond doubt that Aramaic was spoken that morning by the lake, we need not regard the difference of verbs in the Greek record as unimportant. I should then venture to think that the Holy Inspirer, guiding the Apostle's mind, led him to the use of words which would bring out the thought, the *animus,* of the colloquy more clearly than a verbatim record would have done, leaving out as *it* must the explanations given by the voices and manner of the speakers. But I do not think we need doubt that Greek was that language of the hour.

(ii.) As to the actual avowal by St Peter of φιλία not ἀγάπη. Bishop Wordsworth takes the view

suggested in the last chapter—that self-distrust
and a sacred sense of the Lord's glory leads St
Peter to his φιλῶ σε, and bids him shrink from
ἀγαπῶ σε, as an utterance too lofty for his
deeply humbled heart. The Bishop remarks
very beautifully (a little was said in the last
chapter in this direction) that the Saviour, while
accepting at last Peter's lower word, yet knew
that he would have grace to live the higher
word. Wonderfully is this illustrated by the
Saint's precious Epistles. Where does the New
Testament breathe a more serene and heavenly
love for the Lord than there? And yet it is a
love intense and individual too—φιλία at the
heart of ἀγάπη : "Him ye *love* (ἀγαπᾶτε) with
joy unspeakable" (1 Pet. i. 8). So let it be with
each Christian generation and each Christian
heart. The steadfast, heaven-given choice of
Christ and rest in Him must have within it also
the sacred emotion of personal and grateful
delight. Ever to the end, and beyond the end,
shall we be saying, as we look on HIM, φιλῶ σε,
Κύριε.

(iii.) The Commission to Peter : "Feed My
lambs—My sheep ; shepherd My sheep." Perhaps the word "lambs" is not, so to speak,
separative here, marking off a class different
from the "sheep." It may be just the προβάτια

from another point of view ; much as in 1 John
ii., where surely " Fathers," " Youths," " Little
ones," are terms descriptive of true disciples
from different *sides*. All the Lord's sheep are
in some respects "lambs " ; tender and adoles-
cent to the end, compared with what they shall
be hereafter. Yet it is impossible not to read
in the words at least a suggestion to the pastor
to remember specially the specially lamb-like of
the flock, the very weak and the very young.

(iv.) Let us remember too the twice-repeated
" feed," βόσκε, which is thus indicated as the
main particular in the " shepherding." Feed
them, give them provender ; that food which is
the Lord Himself, beheld, believed, received,
beloved. Let this be the Alpha and Omega of
the Christian minister's shepherding, whatever
else goes with it as assistant and subsidiary.
" The hungry sheep look up and *are not fed*,"
says Milton in a well-known passage, stigmatiz-
ing the unfaithful, unspiritual pastors of his
young days. Do not let the words be true of
the Lord's shepherds now. It is all too possible
to keep the flock of Christ in a most undesirable
sort of *fast*, both in and out of Lent ; a fast from
Christ set forth before them in His finished
sacrifice, and never-ending life, love, and power.

Would the clergy be safe from the risk of

proving, whether they know it or not, starvation preachers? Then let them every day, "with keen despatch of real hunger," be found feeding for themselves on Christ Jesus the Lord. *Unde vivo, inde dico; in quo pascor, hoc ministro.*

(v.) Lastly, observe the Lord's phrase, τά ἀρνία μου, MY lambs, MY flock, not thine. It is too easy in practice to forget it. There is a sense in which of course the man must think of class, school, parish, church, as "mine"; in the sense of personal responsibility and heart interest. But much more still must he watch and pray that he may think of them all as "Thine." And to do so will be a powerful and manifold assistance in the ministry. It will cheer, solemnize, tranquillize the pastor. It will cheer him, as reminding him that his Lord's interest in his charge is far deeper than his own can be. It will solemnize him, as reminding him of his own intensely direct relations with his Lord as His underling. It will tranquillize him, because there is nothing which more distracts us and disturbs us than self-consciousness and self-love, nothing which more settles and strengthens us than simple love to Him. Realizing that the flock, the sheep, the lambs, are HIS, we pastors shall labour for them more purely and more happily; and we shall also be more ready if it should please Him to put us and our efforts quite aside, and to hand the dear charge over to another. They are His; we are His. For the under-shepherd is himself also (blessed thought) one of the Chief Shepherd's flock.

But now without delay let us pass onward to the pregnant conclusion of the narrative.

Verse 18. The Saviour couples at once with His commission to Peter the prediction for him of a martyr's death. It comes with all the solemnity of the double *Verily. Verily, verily, I say to you, when you were a younger man, you were used to tie your own girdle, and to walk where you would; but when you have grown old, you shall stretch out your hands, and another shall tie your girdle, and carry you where you would not. Now this He said, as indicating by what sort of death he was to glorify God. And with that word He says to him, Follow Me.*

A remark or two on words and construction is called for. *When you were a younger man.* The Lord Jesus is referring to the time of Peter's life then present. Just such an act of free choice and vigorous independent motion had Peter that morning done, when he had "*girt* his upper coat upon him, and *thrown himself* into the lake." "*When you were*" is an anticipatory phrase, a prolepsis; it looks

back as if already from the time of Peter's
death. (Parallels are not unfrequent; see the
interesting one, 1 Cor. xiii. 12 : "Then shall I
know even as I *was* known," καθὼς καὶ ἐπεγ-
νώσθην). "In the days of thy youth" is the
practical meaning of the expression. There
seems to be at least a high likelihood, as we
have repeatedly noticed, that the Apostles were
very much of an age with their blessed Master.
Conventional art has usually represented them
as all, excepting St John, men of elderly years.
Far more probably they were at most thirty-five
years old ; a probability which may help us to
understand them on many occasions in their
impulses and mistakes.

In the days of thy youth, then ; the days now
fast passing, to be followed so soon by the far
different and quickly aging life of the Apostolic
evangelist and pastor. He had been used to
choose his own path in those days, in these
days. But a change should come ; he should
live to be old ; and then, on some special occasion, in some memorable way, he should choose
the path no more. He should stretch out his
hands, and another should gird him ; and the
path should be one which he did not choose, a
path against his choice, and along which he
should be *carried*.

We now well know what the Lord meant, whatever at the moment these first hearers understood in detail. St John at once applies them to his friend's death, and to that death as a special occasion of the glorification of God, and as evidently caused by man—that is, a martyr death. The future, δοξάσει, "shall glorify," does not imply (I hardly need say) that the event was still future when John wrote; it was only future when Jesus spoke. It is practically quite certain that many years before this narrative was written at Ephesus Peter had died unto the Lord : the prophecy had been fully expounded by the event. And we need not doubt that the death was by crucifixion ; indeed, the words here about the outstretched hands may assure us of this. The well-known further particulars of the martyrdom, that it was at Rome (where now stands the Church of S. Pietro in Montorio, on the far-seeing Janiculan), and that the Saint died head downwards, rest on a very different quality of evidence ; though we need not seriously doubt about Rome as the locality. As to the inverted attitude, it is Origen who first, of extant writers, speaks of it : and he wrote five generations later. It may have been.

Where you do not choose—to a death of violence and pain. Yes, let us remember this.

Peter, the saint indeed, did not choose pain as pain and death as death. That is the act of mental and spiritual aberration. What he did choose was obedience to his Lord, fidelity to his Lord, and then the Lord's glorious presence after that painful passage to it. But from *the passage* human nature shrank in Peter, even as the Lord Himself in His own true Human Nature, absolutely identical with ours, had shrunk from His own agony. I allude to this manifest fact in passing, because it is an instance of what we everywhere find in Scripture, the deeply and truly *natural* aspect in which, in it, the Christian life is presented. That life is not the extinction of nature ; it is its transfiguration, as the heart's love and the will's choice are fixed upon the supreme and all-satisfying Object. It does not make man unhuman. It is a new man, but still man. And man, as man, never can like pain, or grief, or death, for its own sake.

This obvious remark has a bearing on the value of the earliest Christian martyrdoms as a testimony to the Gospel truth. Had they been theatrical displays of unnatural courage they would have borne feeble witness to the solidity of the facts which the martyrs confessed, and for confessing which they died. The body might in that case have been given to the

O

stoning, or the steel, by a motive no better than a diseased spiritual ambition, a personal and emulous desire for a high place in the coming glory as the reward of special pain. But Stephen, James, Peter, and Paul died not so. They did not choose or court death. They chose Christ and His truth, and died rather than deny it. And here, in their calmness and spiritual sanity, in their willingness not to die if it could be avoided rightly, lies the weight and power of their *witness*, their μαρτυρία. It appears as a witness indeed; not a display of their courage so much as an indication of the strong solidity of the basis of truth beneath their feet.

We cannot but recall that one other legend of St Peter's last scenes, the *Domine, quo vadis?* Many of my readers may have pondered it with emotion near its alleged place of occurrence, just outside Rome, on the Appian Way. St Ambrose gives it to us—at the distance of three centuries from St Peter; but however uncertain in fact, it illustrates precious truths with pathetic power. The Apostle was condemned. The Roman Christians entreated and persuaded him to accept an opportunity of escape; an escape which was certainly no crime in itself. But the Lord's call to death and

glory had now come at last; and at the gate of
the City, in the grey morning, as the old man
passed out, he met a Stranger passing in; and
behold it was the Lord. "Lord, whither goest
Thou?"—"I go to be crucified in thy place."
Peter returned to his prison, and to the cross,
and by his death glorified God.

They shall carry you where you would not.
It is remarkable indeed, this solemn prophecy
of suffering, so closely connected with the joy
of love and restoration. In one way or another
it will surely be thus with every true disciple of
our beloved Saviour. To each of us without
exception He will assign some cross to bear for
Him; to each He will say, in one way or
another, "If you love Me, serve Me; and you
shall *suffer for Me.*" Only, the suffering is the
"accident," the joy the "substance." First the
pardon, the love, the gladness; then the allot-
ment of the cross, which that deep joy will make
so much better than bearable. Peter was not
to be martyred that he might win the love of
Christ, but because he had obtained it. The
order is, indeed, "first cross, then crown." But
the cross is preceded by the embrace of the
eternal arms. *Crucem porta, te portabit,* is a
beautiful motto; but let us not confuse its
meaning. The cross we carry is our cross of

trial, the cross where self is crucified. The cross which carries us is the Lord's Cross of atonement, the Cross of complete salvation. If in any sense our cross can be truly said to carry us, it can only be as it is a means to teach us how to realize better our repose on His.

So Peter received this solemn outline of his future. Strange privilege, to be permitted to know in advance just so much of " the unknown to-morrow"! Probably the whole meaning of the prediction was not at once clear to him, or to John. But at once, surely, they recognized in it a prediction, distinct and supernatural, of long service closed by violent death. Such an expectation then Peter carried with him all his life, and close to the end he refers definitely to it (2 Pet. i. 14) : "*Sudden is to be the putting off of my tabernacle, even as our Lord Jesus Christ once shewed me.*" Yet we may be sure that this knowledge of his predestined course and goal gave no unreality to his life, to his methods of work, to his precautions for safety, to his thoughts of death. Like many other divine purposes, it was indicated just so far as to reveal the infallible purpose, and yet to leave the man as consciously free as ever step by step. God knows how to make His counsel work freely in

absolute harmony with the creature's genuine
agency.

The Lord had said, *Follow Me* (ἀκολούθει μοι),
an exhortation which but for the context we
might have thought to be general (for observe
the *present* imperative) and figurative. And so
no doubt it was in great part. " If any man
serve Me, let him follow Me "—let him live near
Me, watch My will and learn My way. But the
utterance was, however, illustrated by an act.
We gather that the Lord Jesus *moved*, walking
away along the shore or towards the hill, and
bade Peter literally follow Him. The command
was not, so far as it appears, meant for the
whole party. Only Peter is addressed, and
Peter is surprised to see John following
also. The whole incident must have been
brief and symbolic. Let us translate the
verses.

Peter turning round (as he stepped forward
after his Master, evidently, and heard steps
behind him), *sees the disciple whom Jesus
loved following, the disciple who also had
leaned over at the supper to Him and said,
Lord, who is Thy betrayer? Seeing him Peter
says to Jesus, Lord, but what of him? Jesus
says to him, If I choose that he remain till I
come, how does it affect you? Do you follow*

Me. So this report went out to the brethren, that that disciple is not to die. And yet Jesus did not say to him that he was not to die, but, If I choose that he remain till I come, how does it affect you ?

This is the disciple who witnesses about these things, and who wrote these things; and we know that his witness is true.

Now there are many other things too which Jesus did, things which if they were written each in detail not even the world itself, I think, would have room for the books which would be writing.

One word, out of place, on the last two verses. Without any attempt at explicit critical discussion, I would only say that they seem to me to be written by St John himself, not added later by other hands. " *We know* " is a turn of expression quite in the Apostle's manner ; he loves to put himself as it were aside ; to speak as *ab extra* of himself. And surely, had the Ephesian Church thought it needful, or decorous, to add an *imprimatur* to an Apostle's writing, they would not have expressed themselves so simply. *The disciple* would scarcely have been in their view an adequate description for their blessed patriarch and guide, the personal friend of their Divine

Redeemer. Moreover, they would hardly have
added an attestation while John lived ; and had
they done so after his death, could they have
left the mysterious words which had prompted
the rumour of his immortality without some
further comment ?

As regards the hyperbole in which is conveyed the thought that to record all the Lord
Jesus did would be " infinite "—the phrase *is* an
hyperbole, no doubt. But if plainly intended
to be so taken, it is perfectly veracious. It most
manifestly is not a prosaic estimate of the area
which the books would cover.

Far better than any lingering over such a
verbal difficulty is an application to the heart
of what the phrase imports. It tells us that
such was the boundless wealth of the Lord's
works of love and power that even the precious
Gospel of St John is but a brief selection,
divinely ordered yet quite brief, from out of the
wealth. Let us give thanks both for the wealth
of the materials, and for the brevity of the
record—a brevity so good for the busy and
for the simple reader. Abundantly enough is
written to serve the holy purpose of the writer
—*that we may believe that Jesus is the Christ,
the Son of God, and that, believing, we may
have life in His name.*

But now to return to the narrative of verses 20—22.

We have seen, early in our study, how the hearts of Peter and John had been drawn together. Together we find the two Saints in their Passover-lodging, together at the tomb, together on the waters, together soon at the Beautiful Gate, together before the Council, together at Samaria. The last Gospel closes with this scene in which they follow their Lord together, yet in which their Lord reminds them how different at length their ways of following should be.

Peter, it would seem, had risen to follow, and then John, as he sat close to his earthly friend and to that heavenly Friend who bound them together, silently rose and followed too, while perhaps the other disciples as yet did not move. As always, John is not named ; he is described as the loved disciple, and as the man who, as he reclined at the supper, leaned nearer to the Lord, and asked Him about the traitor. Why this last detail is introduced here it is not easy to say. Peter on that occasion had been the enquirer through John. So it *may* be that the event is here mentioned as an occasion on which they had acted together. Or is it simply that the incident was an example of the near intimacy between John and his beloved Master?

So Peter turns, and sees John following. And now, full of the thought of the prediction of his own martyrdom, and instinctively connecting all that concerned himself with the concerns of his dear and ever dearer companion, he asks what *his* end shall be. Οὗτος δὲ τί; What should *he* do? Shall he also grow old, and then stretch out his hands, and be carried where he fain would not go? He is following Thee, and me, now with his steps. Shall he follow also in the manner of his life, and of his death?

I need not dwell at length on the Lord's memorable answer. At first sight at least it reads very simply, as if just a grave and gentle correction of Peter's too anxious curiosity, or at most a gentle reminder that his truest peace would be found in following personally his Redeemer in the path chosen for *him*, leaving John's path to the same choice. There may undoubtedly be a deeper meaning. It may be that the "coming" of the Son of man when the City, and Temple, and Ritual passed away—His mystical Advent in judgment and mercy then—was intended. It is at least very probable that St John was the only Apostle who survived the year 70, and that he survived it long,

living far on into the new age of the Christian
Church.

We must observe, however, that the first
disciples plainly took the "Till I come" to refer
to the great literal Second Coming, the Era of
immortality; for they reasoned from the words
that John would not die. He was to abide
till the Lord came; therefore till the Resurrection; therefore he would not sleep, but be
changed. And the old Apostle, so it seems to
me, corrects the error by calling attention to the
emphatic "*if*" (*ἐάν*) of the sentence as the Lord
spoke it, and to the "What is that to thee?"

Likely as we must feel it to be that these
solemn final words of the last Gospel should
have a deeper meaning than the literal, I cannot
think that we can be certain that it is so. The
great age reached by St John before this record
was written had very possibly given them an
emphasis and mystery among "the brethren"
which was beyond their first intention.

I love to think, though it may be too arbitrary
a thought, that the Apostle here takes pains to
correct any misconception, because, in part, of
his own deep longing to be with the Lord. He
would not linger on in an earthly immortality.
He would thankfully pass through the gate of
death, as Peter long ago had done, as yet longer

ago his Lord Himself had done, to be soon and
for ever with Him where He is.

If I will. Let us close by an act of solemn
attention to these words. Some time ago we
observed how markedly, all through this chapter,
Jesus speaks of and from Himself: *Lovest
thou Me? Feed My flock: Follow Me: Till
I come: If I will.*

Who is this who, if He speaks not blasphemy,
speaks in His own right with the voice of GOD?

If I will. "My will is to rule your future,
Peter, and John's future too." Those precious
lives, those regenerated and inspired apostolic
souls, were to accept the predestination of their
time and their labour from the mere will of
Jesus. There is no fear lest that will and His
Father's should differ, should collide; yet none
the less is His will *His will.* And that will
disposes absolutely of Peter and of John. They
love, adore, and follow. It ordains.

He wills that the one, the eager, the impetuous,
but now wonderfully chastened, the man of
strong act and word, should spend for Him
many years of heavy labour and much suffering,
and then die for Him, in a death of extreme
agony.

He wills that the other, the man of deep and
silent spiritual life and thought, the character

which we might perhaps have deemed to be "not long for this world," as the phrase is, should live on and on, working, suffering, thinking, writing, till every one of his comrades had fallen asleep, and should then die the death of all men.

The destiny of St John may remind us how deeply hidden are the details of the Lord's plans for His servants; how impossible it is for us to forecast their future by temperament or circumstance. We know a friend born and made as if for vigorous and sustained action. We know another of almost unearthly walk with God. But we know not which will be taken, and which left; or whether both will go early, or both very late. We have no hint whatever of the principles on which in these matters the Master acts. Certainly He is not capricious; but certainly also He has no such *need* of our character or labours as to allow the most laborious or the most successful Christian to say, "He cannot spare me yet."

But the great thing is to know, as we do know, that all shall be as "I WILL." There is a Will, there is a Person, above and beneath all our lives and works; and that Will, that Person, is Jesus our Lord. He and not fate, He and not chance, He and not the processes of an impersonal universe, at this hour rules and ordains our path of service, present and future ; yes, and the path too of those we love, and about whom we sometimes ask more wistfully than about ourselves, *Lord, and what shall this man do ?* Let us calmly and most thankfully recollect it. Bewildered souls try too often to find rest in absolute abject deference to the will of a poor fallen, erring man. It is the distortion into woful error of a glorious and most healthful truth. It *is* true rest to yield ourselves and our dear ones in entire simplicity, without a struggle or reserve, to the living will of the Lord Jesus Christ ; for that will is omniscient, and all-wise, and all-holy, and (let us dare to believe it now and every hour) it is a will of such love that it does not for a minute forget, in the light of the glory of God, the true interests and true joy of the feeblest and most halting of the disciples.

Then let us, not so much think about Him as go direct to Him, to learn the secret which made Peter and John quite happy in their several paths ; happy to work together, happy to work asunder. Their secret was, " It is the Lord ; Thou hast loved me ; Thou knowest that I love Thee."

So the one lived on till he had written, " Be sober, and hope to the end, for the grace that is to be brought unto you at the revelation of Jesus Christ."

So the other lived on, utterly alone at length in a new generation, a new world, but happy and sanctified to the end in the eternal truth, and able to write this about it : " Now are we the sons of God ; and it doth not yet appear what we shall be, but we know that, when He shall appear, we shall be like Him, for we shall see Him as He is."

THE END.

APPENDICES.

I.

THE MESSAGE OF THE MAGDALENE
(p. 75).

" So from that happy grove,
From the still precincts of the Sepulchre,
She pass'd, obedient.   Through the city streets
'Mid the first footfalls of the morn she went
Seeking the scatter'd brethren, and to each
With glad reiteration still in turn
Delivering the same story ;—she had seen
The Lord, and He had spoken thus to her.
   " Blest herald of redemption ! first to bear
Into these dying scenes of guilt and care
The tidings of that Sepulchre unseal'd ;
The marvel, the simplicity divine,
The nameless joy not dream'd of but reveal'd,
The eternal light we had not taught to shine,
Kindled by JESUS.   She with one calm word
That she had seen arisen her buried Lord,
And from His lips had heard in that glad hour,
For those who left Him in His pain alone,
News not of wrath but of His rising power

And session for them on His Father's throne ;
She first awoke the never-ending voice,
Redeemer, of Thy Gospel ; the new song
In which innumerable souls rejoice,
Who, though in seeming triumph oft and long
Death wounds them, spoiling from their love's
    embrace
Its fondest treasures, and themselves meanwhile,
Claiming his prey, yet in Thy living grace
Find more than resignation—with a smile
Of strange delight discovering for their own
Thy sacrifice and resurrection-crown.

  " She first, all happy Magdalena, bore
From Joseph's Grot the bliss unheard before,
And still her tidings was the broken tomb ;
    And still, though ages roll,
    That message from the soul,
And that alone, must chase the enfolding gloom :
    Here still the worn and wandering mind
    Her true repose must find ;
    Here learn the secret that can save ;
    Beside, within, that Grave.

  " Here still the heart can feel, and only here,
A tide of joy that brings no mingled fear
Of ebbing languor soon to fleet amain ;—
    The soon exhausted life
    In faint and flagging strife
Seeking its vanish'd gladness to regain ;—
    Not here from Fancy's haunted well
    Uncertain waters swell,
    But pour descending, never dry,
    From Truth's own fount on high.

" Yes, Truth indeed is here ; the Event divine,
O Saviour Lord, the Work that all is Thine ;
Once, once for all, with all its sequel, done ;
    Not in ourselves but Thee
    The almighty Cause we see
Which endless through its vast effects must run :
    Here we may trust to Thee the scope
      Of our undying hope ;
    Here we may know our doubts are vain ;
    For Thou art risen again.

" We by no far-drawn reasonings, brilliant length
But fragile, hold our Heaven.   For us the strength
Of demonstration is the Risen One still ;
    Our wisdom, science, all,
    Is at Thy feet to fall ;
Thou art our thought profound, our logic skill ;
    Our evidence of deathless bliss,
      Our earnest, still is this,
    That Thou hast shewn, from death restored,
    Thy face, beloved Lord.

" So let us tune, beneath the upkindling sphere,
Where stars on stars, Thy handiwork, appear,
Now gathering thick, our parting sound of praise ;
    Here midst the twinkling gloom,
    Here by this long-loved tomb,
Through Thee we antedate the eternal lays :
    'Tis here, above this precious dust,
      We sing Thee, as is just ;
    For by Thy Sepulchre this hour
    We overcome death's power.

" Thy Resurrection stands, and thence is cast
The smile of heaven o'er future, present, past ;
                P

The Past is with Thy death-wrought victory
   bright;
      And though awhile we weep
      The silence and the sleep,
Year after year, of those beyond our sight,
     Yet not by drear misgivings torn
       Those buried loves we mourn;
     Seasons and times we count in vain,
      But Thou art risen again.

"Then from that Truth an endless Future
   springs,
Spiritual, real, throng'd with glorious things,
Peace, Resurrection, Heaven, for all Thine own;
     With death we cheerly deal;
     In thankful joy we kneel
Where shall be dress'd so soon our turf and stone:
   JESUS our Lord, the First and Last,
      Thy rising work is past;
     Then present is our strength and rest,
      And all our future, blest."
               H. C. G. M.,
   God's Acre (Christianus and other Poems).

II.

"EARTH LIGHTED UP FROM HEAVEN"

(p. 146).

   "Though what if Earth
Be but the shadow of Heaven?"
     MILTON, *Paradise Lost*, v. 574.

"Acquaint thyself with God, if thou wouldst taste
His works. Admitted once to His embrace
Thou shalt perceive that thou wast blind before:...

[Well for] the mind that has been touch'd from
    Heaven,
And in the school of sacred wisdom taught
To read His wonders in whose thought the world,
Fair as it is, existed ere it was."
              Cowper, *The Task,* Book V.

    " With Him for guide
Tracing the Paschal road (as oft we traced)
Along rich Ephraim's pastoral hills, I felt
Old Paradise restored ; in every field,
And mount, and lonely tree, a light of joy
Mingled of earth and heaven. The gleaming shores
Of my Gennesareth . . . shone with a charm
Unutterable, as if the curse indeed
Were cancell'd, and an earth beloved on high
Were made by only saints."
    H. C. G. M., *The Beloved Disciple, a Poem.*

    " Heaven above is softer blue,
        Earth around is sweeter green ;
    Something lives in every hue
        Christless eyes have never seen ;
    Birds with gladder songs o'erflow,
        Flowers with deeper beauty shine,
    Since I know, as now I know,
        I am His and He is mine."
        Wade Robinson,
        Hymns of Consecration, No. 260.

" The Christians, as men who know God, ask from
Him petitions which are proper for Him to give and
for them to receive. . . And because they acknowledge
the goodnesses of God towards them, lo, on account

of them there flows forth the beauty that is in the world."

> ARISTIDES, *Apology for the Christians, addressed to the Emperor Hadrian,* ch. xvi.

III.

MR RUSKIN ON THE INCIDENT OF JOHN XXI.

To introduce a severe critique of the splendid *conventionalism* of Raphael's "cartoon" of the scene, Mr Ruskin thus paints it :

" I SUPPOSE there is no event in the whole life of Christ to which, in hours of doubt or fear, men turn with more anxious thirst to know the close facts of it, or with more earnest and passionate dwelling upon every syllable of its recorded narrative, than Christ's showing Himself to His disciples at the Lake of Galilee. There is something pre-eminently open, natural, full fronting our disbelief, in this manifestation. The others, recorded after the Resurrection, were sudden, phantom-like, occurring to men in profound sorrow and wearied agitation of heart ; not, it might seem, safe judges of what they saw.[1] But the agitation was now over. They had gone back to their daily work, thinking still their business lay net-wards, unmeshed from the literal rope and drag. 'Simon Peter saith unto them, I go a-fishing. They say unto him, We also go with thee.' True words enough, and having far echo beyond those Galilean hills. That night they caught nothing ; but when the morn-

---

[1] This sentence must be taken with great reserve. It does not cover all the facts of Luke xxiv. and John xx.—H. C. G. M.

ing came, in the clear light of it, behold! a figure stood on the shore. They were not thinking of anything but their fruitless hauls. They had no guess who it was. It asked them simply if they had caught anything. They say, No; and it tells them to cast again. And John shades his eyes from the morning sun with his hands to look who it is; and though the glistening of the sea, too, dazzles him, he makes out who it is at last; and poor Simon, not to be outrun this time, tightens his fisher's-coat about him, and dashes in over the nets. One would have liked to see him swim those hundred yards, and stagger to his knees upon the beach.

"Well, the others get to the beach, too, in time, in such slow way as men in general do get in this world to its true shore, much impeded by that wonderful 'dragging the net with fishes'; but they get there—seven of them in all; first the Denier, and then the slowest believer, and then the quickest believer, and then the two throne-seekers, and two more, we know not who.

"They sit down on the shore, face to face with Him, and eat their broiled fish as He bids. And then to Peter, all dripping still, shivering, and amazed, staring at Christ in the sun, on the other side of the coal-fire,—thinking a little perhaps of what happened by another coal-fire, when it was colder, and having had no word changed with him by his Master since that look of His—to him so amazed, comes the question, 'Simon, lovest thou Me?' Try to feel that a little; and think of it till it is true to you."

Modern Painters; Part iv., ch. iv., § 16.
(Extracted also in *Frondes Agrestes*, p. 152.

THE RESURRECTION
OF JESUS

by

JAMES ORR, M.A., D.D.

Late Professor of Apologetics and Systematic Theology,
United Free Church College, Glasgow

Foreword by
Dr. Cyril J. Barber

Klock & Klock Christian Publishers, Inc.

2527 GIRARD AVE. N.

MINNEAPOLIS, MINNESOTA 55411

Originally published by
Charles Scribner's Sons
New York, n.d.

Copy from the personal library of
Dr. Cyril J. Barber

ISBN: 0-86524-062-0

Printed by Klock & Klock in the U.S.A.
1980 Reprint

FOREWORD

Dr. Philip Schaff, a noted evangelical of a generation past, was for many years widely regarded as the "dean" of American church historians. On one occasion he made the following remark about the life, ministry, and continuing legacy of Jesus Christ.

Without money and arms, [He] conquered more millions than Alexander, Caesar, Mohammed and Napoleon; without science and learning, He shed more light on things human and divine than all the philosophers and scholars combined; without eloquence of the school, He spoke words of life such as were never spoken before, nor since, and produced effects which lie beyond the reach of orator or poet. Without writing a single line, He has set more pens in motion and furnished themes for more sermons, orations, discussions, works of art, learned volumes, and sweet songs of praise than the whole army of great men of ancient and modern times. Born in a manger and crucified a malefactor, He now controls the destinies of the civilized world and rules a spiritual empire which embraces one-third of the inhabitants of the globe.

All of this is true because of His bodily resurrection from among the dead. The Apostle Paul affirmed this in Romans 4:25.

In recent years it has become fashionable to riducule and then reject the Bible's teaching of Christ's resurrection. Recently the *Los Angeles Times* featured an article under the title "Did Jesus Rise Bodily? Most Scholars Say 'No'." After having interviewed many of the Catholic and Protestant theologians on the faculty of the Graduate Theological Union in Berkeley, one New Testament professor stated that he "did not know of one school there in which a significant part of the faculty would accept statements that Jesus rose physically from the dead or that Jesus was a divine being."

It therefore becomes necessary for each evangelical Bible-believing Christian to be "ready to make a defense to every one who asks of him a reason for the hope that is in him" (I Peter 3:15). In offering such a defense, however, he does not stand alone for, in contrast to the statement made by the Berkeley professor just quoted, the Christian church has had many able defenders of the faith, not the least of which was James Orr (1844-1913).

James Orr was born and died in Glasgow, Scotland. He studied in the Theological Hall of the United Presbyterian Church and Glasgow University, receiving successively the M.A. (in philosophy), B.D., and D.D. degrees. Following graduation, Dr. Orr was appointed Examiner for the university's degrees in philosophy, and later became Professor of Church History in the Theological College of the United Presbyterian Church. A capable apologist, Dr. Orr was invited to lecture in the universities of Edinburgh (1891), Chicago (1895), Allegheny and Auburn (1897), and Princeton (1903).

Professor Orr's published writings include *The Christian View of God and the World* (1893), *The Supernatural in Christianity* (1894), *The Ritschlian Theology and the Evangelical Faith* (1897), *Neglected Factors in the Study of the Early Progress of Christianity* (1899), *The Progress of Dogma* (1902), *The Image of God in Man* (1905), *The Problem of the Old Testament* (1905), *The Virgin Birth of Christ* (1907), *The Resurrection of Jesus* (1908), *Sidelights in Christian Doctrine* (1909), *Revelation and Inspiration* (1910), etc.

Written after many years of reflection and debate, James Orr's *The Resurrection of Jesus* provided the reader with an analysis of the historic witness to and theological implications of the bodily resurrection of Christ for both believers and unbelievers. His discussion of the issues is at once objective, biblical, and consistent. It is a pleasure to recommend the reprinting of this fine work.

Cyril J. Barber
Author, *The Minister's Library*

CONTENTS

I

II

III

IV

V

THE PRESENT STATE OF THE QUESTION

I

THE PRESENT STATE OF THE QUESTION

A RESTATEMENT of the grounds of belief in the great fact of the Lord's Resurrection seems called for in view of the changed forms of assault on this article of the Christian faith in recent years. It is difficult, indeed, to isolate this particular fact, outstanding as it is, from its context in the Gospel history taken as a whole, every point in which is made subject to a like minute and searching criticism. On the other hand, the consideration of the evidence for the Resurrection may furnish a vantage ground for forming a better estimate of the value of the methods by which much of the hostile criticism of the Gospels is at present carried on.

As preliminary to the inquiry, it is desirable that a survey should be taken of the changed lights in which the question appears in past and in contemporary thought.

Time was, not so far removed, when the Resurrection of Jesus was regarded as an immovable corner-stone of Christianity. A scholar and historian like the late Dr. Arnold, of Rugby, summed up a general belief when he wrote : " I have been used for many years to study the history of other times, and to examine and weigh the evidence of those who have written about them ; and I know of no fact in the history of mankind which is proved by better and fuller evidence of every sort, to the understanding of a fair inquirer, than the great sign which God has given us, that Christ died and rose again from the dead." [1]   It will be recognized by any one familiar with the signs of the times that this language could not be employed about the state of belief to-day.

It was not that this article of Christian belief had not been long enough and violently enough assailed. The Resurrection of Jesus has been a subject of controversy in all ages. The story which St. Matthew tells us was in circulation among the Jews " until this day " [2]—that the disciples had *stolen* the body of Jesus—was still spread abroad in the days of Justin Martyr.[3] It reappears in that grotesque mediæval concoction, the *Toledoth Jeschu.*[4] Celsus, whom Origen combats, ridicules the Christian belief, and, with modern acuteness, urges the contradictions in the Gospel narratives.[5]

[1] Sermon on the Sign of the Prophet Jonas.
[2] Matt. xxviii. 15.   [3] *Dial. with Trypho*, 108.
[4] With some difference, in both the Wagenseil (1681) and the Huldreich (1705) recensions.
[5] Origen, *Against Celsus*, ii. 56–63 ; v. 56, 58.

Deistical writers, as Woolston and Chubb, made the Resurrection a chief object of their attacks.[1] On the Continent, from Reimarus to Strauss, the stream of destructive or evasive [2] criticism was kept up. Strauss must be regarded as the most trenchant and remorseless of the assailants even to the present hour.[3] What escaped his notice in criticism of the narratives is not likely to have much force now. If, therefore, faith in the Resurrection till recently remained unshaken, it was not because the belief was not contested, but because of the confident conviction that the attack all along the line had failed. Other elements in the Gospel tradition might be doubtful, but here, it was supposed, was a rock on which the most timorous might plant his feet without fear. Details in the Resurrection narratives themselves might be, probably were, inaccurate ; but the central facts—the empty grave, the message to the women, the appearances to the disciples, sustained as these were by the independent witness of Paul in 1 Corinthians xv. 7, the belief of the whole Apostolic

---

[1] Replied to by Sherlock, West, Paley, etc.

[2] Several writers in this period advocated the theory that Christ's death was only a case of swoon or suspended animation (thus Paulus, Schleiermacher, Hase, etc.). Strauss may be credited with having given this theory its death-blow. See his *New Life of Jesus* (E.T.), i. pp. 13–33 ; 408–12.

[3] For the full strength of Strauss's criticism the original *Life of Jesus* (1835) should be consulted.

church—stood secure. This temper of certainty is excellently reflected in the Apologetic textbooks of the most recent period. In these the discussion travels along fixed and familiar lines—theories of imposture, of swoon, of subjective hallucination or visions, of objective but *spiritual* manifestations, all triumphantly refuted, and leaving the way open for the only remaining hypothesis, viz., that the event in dispute actually happened.

It is not suggested that Apologetic, up to this recent point, had failed in its main object, or that its confidence in the soundness of its grounds for belief in the Resurrection was misplaced. It is not implied, even, that the evidence which sufficed then is not adequate to sustain faith now. It may turn out that it is, and that in the *essence* of both attack and defence less is really changed than the modern man supposes. Still even the casual observer cannot fail to perceive that, in important respects, the state of the controversy is very different to-day from what it was, say, fifteen or twenty years ago. Forces which were then only gathering strength, or beginning to make themselves felt, have now come to a head, and the old grounds for belief, and the old answers to objections, are no longer allowed to pass unchallenged. The evidence for the Resurrection may be much what it has been for the last nineteen centuries, but the temper of the age in dealing with that evidence has undeniably altered. The subject is approached from new sides, with new presuppositions, with new critical methods and apparatus, with a wider outlook on the religious history of mankind, and a better understanding, derived from comparative study, of the growth of religious myths ; and, in the light of this new knowledge, it is confidently affirmed that the old defences are obsolete, and that it is no longer open to the instructed intelligence—" the modern mind," as it is named—to entertain even the possibility of the bodily Resurrection of Christ from the grave. The believer in this divine fact, accordingly, is anew put on his defence, and must speak to purpose, if he does not wish to see the ground taken away from beneath his feet.

It has already been hinted, and will subsequently become more fully apparent, that the consideration of Christ's Resurrection cannot be dissociated from the view taken of the facts which make up the Gospel history as a whole. This should be frankly acknowledged on both sides at the outset. Christ is not divided. The Gospel story cannot be dealt with piecemeal. The Resurrection brings its powerful attestation to the claims made by Jesus in His earthly Ministry ; [1] but the claim to Messiahship and divine Sonship, on the other hand, with all the evidence in the Gospels that supports it, must be taken into account when we

[1] Rom. i. 4.

are judging of the reasonableness and probability of the Resurrection. No one can, even if he would, approach this subject without some prepossessions on the character, claims, and religious significance of Jesus, derived from the previous study of the records of His life, or, going deeper, from the pre-suppositions which have governed even that study. The believer's presupposition is Christ. If Christ was what His Church has hitherto believed Him to be—the divine Son and Saviour of the world—there is no antecedent presumption against His Resurrection; rather it is incredible that He should have remained the prey of death.[1] If a lower estimate is taken of Christ, the historical evidence for the Resurrection will assume a different aspect. It will then remain to be seen which estimate of Christ most entirely fits in with the totality of the facts. On that basis the question may safely be brought to an issue.

This leads to the remark that it is really this question of *the admissibility of the supernatural* in the form of miracle which lies at the bottom of the whole investigation. The repugnance to miracle which is so marked a characteristic of the " modern " criticism of the Gospels can hardly, without an ignoring of the course of discussion for at least the last century and a half, be spoken of as a " new " thing. It underlay the rationalism

[1] Acts ii. 24.

of the older period, and some of the most stinging words in Strauss's *Life of Jesus* are directed against the abortive attempts of well-meaning mediating theologians to evade this fundamental issue. Strauss's own position is made clear beyond possibility of mistake, and anticipates everything the " modern " man has to urge on the subject. " Our modern world," he says, " after many centuries of tedious research, has attained a conviction that all things are linked together by a chain of causes and effects, which suffers no interruption. . . . The totality of things forms a vast circle, which, except that it owes its existence and laws to a superior power, suffers no intrusion from without. This conviction is so much a habit of thought with the modern world, that in actual life the belief in a supernatural manifestation, an immediate divine agency, is at once attributed to ignorance and imposture." [1] Strauss at this stage is persuaded that " the essence of the Christian faith is perfectly independent of his criticism " ; that " the supernatural birth of Christ, His miracles, His resurrection and ascension, remain eternal truths, whatever doubts may be cast on their reality as historical facts " ; and that " the dogmatic significance of the life of Jesus remains inviolate." [2] At a later period, in his book on *The*

---

[1] The words are from the fourth edition (1840) of the (older) *Life of Jesus* (E.T.) i. p. 71.   [2] Ibid. Pref. p. xi.

Old and the New Faith, he reached the true gravitation level of his speculations, and in answer to the question, "Are we still Christians?" boldly answered "No."[1]

The "modern" man has thus no reason to plume himself on his denial of miracle as a brand-new product of the scientific temper of the age in which he lives. His "modernity" goes back a long way in its negations. What is to be admitted is that the magnificent advance of the sciences during the past century has accentuated and reinforced this temper of distrust (or positive denial) of the miraculous; has given it greater precision and wider diffusion; has furnished it with new and plausible reasons, and made it more formidable as a practical force to be encountered. There is no doubt, in any case, that this spirit rules in a large proportion of the works recently issued on the Gospels and on the life of Christ, and is the concealed or avowed premiss of their treatment of the miraculous element in Christ's history, and notably of His Resurrection.[2] The same temper has insensibly spread through a large part of the Christian community. Dr. Sanday

[1] In 1872.
[2] One may name almost at random such writers as A. Sabatier, Harnack, Pfleiderer, Wernle, Weinel, Wrede, Wellhausen, Schmiedel, Bousset, Neumann, O. Holtzmann, E. Carpenter, Percy Gardner, G. B. Foster (Chicago), N. Schmidt, K. Lake, etc.

truly enough describes " the attitude of many a loyal Christian " when he says that " he [the Christian] accepts the narratives of miracles and of the miraculous as they stand, but with a note of interrogation." [1] Others frankly reject them altogether. A chief difficulty in dealing with this widely-spread tendency is that it is, in most cases, less the result of reasoning than, as just said, a " temper," due to what Mr. Balfour would call " a psychological climate," [2] or Lecky would describe as " the general intellectual condition " of the time.[3] Still, it is only by fair reasoning, and the adducing of considerations which set things in a different light, that it can be legitimately met ; apart, that is, from a change in the " climate " itself, a thing continually happening. When this is done, it is remarkable how little, in the end, it is able to say in justification of its sweeping assumptions.

It is not only, however, in the general temper of the time that a change has taken place in the treatment of our subject ; the new spirit has

---

[1] *The Life of Christ in Recent Research*, p. 103.

[2] " A psychological ' atmosphere ' or ' climate ' favourable to the life of certain modes of belief, unfavourable. and even fatal, to the life of others."—*Foundations of Belief*, fourth edition, p. 218.

[3] See the " Introduction " to Lecky's *History of Rationalism in Europe*, and his interesting summary of the causes of " The Declining Sense of the Miraculous " in the close of chap. ii. of that work.

armed itself with new weapons, and, first of all, with those supplied to it in the methods and results of the *later textual and historical criticism.* Even the tyro cannot be unaware of the almost revolutionary changes wrought in the forms and methods of New Testament criticism—following in the wake of Old Testament criticism [1]—within the last generation. There is, to begin with, an enormous increase in the materials of criticism, with its results in greater specialization and increased urgency in the demand for a many-sided equipment in the textual critic, commentator, and historical writer.[2] Then, with extension of knowledge, has come a sharpening of intelligence and increased stringency of method—a painstakingness in research, an attention to detail, aptitude in seizing points of relation and contrast, skill in disentangling difficulties, fertility in suggestion—above all, a boldness and enterprise in speculation [3]—which leave the older and more cautious scholarship far in the rear. Doubtless, if the Resurrection be truth, the application of these

[1] It is a sign of the times that Old Testament scholars like Wellhausen and Gunkel are now transferring their attentions to the New Testament.

[2] See the remarkable catalogue of qualifications for the commentator set forth in the Preface to Mr. W. C. Allen's new commentary on St. Matthew (*Intern. Crit. Com.*).

[3] Dr. Sanday notes this as a characteristic of recent work on the Gospels. See his *Life of Christ in Recent Research*, p. 41.

stricter methods should only make the truth the more apparent. But it is obvious also that, for those who care to use them in that way, the methods furnish ready aids for the disintegration of the text and evaporation of its historical contents. If a passage for any reason is distasteful, the resources in the critical arsenal are boundless for getting it out of the way. There is slight textual variation, some MS. or version omits or alters, the Evangelists conflict, it is unsuitable to the speaker or the context, if otherwise unchallengeable, it is late and unreliable tradition. Wellhausen's *Introduction to the First Three Gospels* is an illustration of how nearly everything which has hitherto been of interest and value in the Gospels—Sermon on the Mount and parables included—disappears under this kind of treatment.[1] Schmiedel's article on the "Gospels" in the *Encyclopædia Biblica* is a yet more extreme example. The application of the method to our immediate subject is admirably seen in Professor Lake's recent book on *The Historical Evidence for the Resurrection of Jesus Christ*. A painfully minute and unsparing verbal criticism of the Gospel narratives and of the references in Paul results naturally in the conclusion that there is *no* evidence of any value—except, perhaps, for the general fact of "appearances"

[1] See his *Einleitung*, pp. 52–57, 68–72, 86–87, 90–93, etc.

to the disciples. No fibre of the history is left standing as it was. Material assistance is afforded to this type of criticism by the theory of the relations of the Gospels which is at present the prevailing one—what Mr. Allen believes to be " the one solid result of literary criticism," [1] viz., the dependence of the first and third Gospels, in their narrative portions, on the " prior " Gospel of St. Mark. It is temptingly easy, on this theory, to regard everything in these other Gospels which is not found in, or varies from, St. Mark, as a wilful " writing up " or embellishment of the original simpler story ; as something, therefore, to be at once set aside as unhistorical.[2]

These which have been named are dogmatic and literary assaults ; but now, from yet another side, a formidable attack is seen developing on the historicity of the narratives of the Resurrection—namely, from the side of *comparative religion and mythology*. It is in itself nothing new to draw comparisons between the Resurrection of Jesus and the stories of death and resurrection in pagan religions. Celsus of old made a beginning in this direction.[3] The myths, too, on which

[1] *St. Matthew*, Pref. p. vii. It is not to be assumed that this judgment, on which more will be said after, is acquiesced in by every one. Cf. chap. iii.

[2] This is pretty much Wellhausen's method, except that Wellhausen attaches little or no historical value even to St. Mark. Prof. Lake follows in the same track.

[3] Origen, *Against Celsus*, ii. 55–58.

reliance is placed in these comparisons are, in many cases, really there,[1] and frequently collections have been made of them for the purpose of discrediting the Christian belief. The subject may now be said to have entered on its scientific phase in the study of comparative mythology—for instance, in such a work as Dr. J. G. Frazer's *Golden Bough* [2]—and as the result of the long train of discoveries throwing light on the religious beliefs and mythological conceptions of the most ancient peoples—Babylonian, Egyptian, Arabian, Persian, and others. In its newest form—sometimes called the " Pan-Babylonian," though there is yet great diversity of standpoint, and no little division of opinion, among the writers to whom the name is applied—the movement has already attained to imposing proportions, and has given birth to an important literature. Among its best-known representatives on the Continent, of different types, are H. Winckler, A. Jeremias, H. Gunkel, P. Jensen ; Dr. Cheyne may speak for it here. A chief characteristic of the school is that, declining to look at any people or religion in isolation from general history, it aims at explaining any given religion from the circumstances of its environ-

---

[1] Myths of death and resurrection are prominent in the ancient Mysteries. This phase of the subject will be discussed after.

[2] Cf. also L. R. Farnell's book, *The Evolution of Religion.*

ment, and from analogies and parallels drawn from other religions. Conceptions derived ultimately from Babylonia were spread through the whole East, and these, entering through many channels, had a powerful influence in moulding, first the Israelitish, then the Christian religions. Winckler boldly applied his theory to the religious ideas and history of the Old Testament; Gunkel and the others named [1] extend it to the New. " Conservative theologians," writes Dr. Cheyne, " will have to admit that the New Testament now has to be studied from the point of view of mythology as well as from that of philological exegesis and Church-history. . . . For that harmonious combination of points of view which is necessary for the due comprehension of the New Testament, it is essential that the help of mythology, treated of course by strictly critical methods, should be invoked. In short, there are parts of the New Testament—in the Gospels, in the Epistles, and in the Apocalypse—which can only be accounted for by the newly-discovered fact of Oriental syncretism, which began early and continued late. And the leading factor in this is Babylonian." [2]

The story of the Resurrection is naturally one

---

[1] Cf. Gunkel's *Zum Religionsgeschichtlichen Verständniss des neuen Testaments.* Jeremias is an exception to the general position in so far that, while accepting the analogies, he does not deny the New Testament facts. See his *Babylonisches im N.T.*   [2] *Bible Problems*, pp. 18, 19.

of the "legends" on the rise of which the new
Babylonian theory is supposed to be able to cast
special light, and Dr. Cheyne gratefully accepts
its help.[1] Professor Lake regards it as a theory
which, while not proved, " one has seriously to
reckon with." [2] Even Dr. Cheyne, however, is
outdone, and is stirred to active protest, by the
astonishing lengths to which the theory is carried
by Professor Jensen in his recent massive work,
The Gilgamesh Epic in World Literature,[3] which
literally transforms the Gospel history into a
version of the story of that mythical Babylonian
hero ! It is the saving fact in theories of this
kind that they speedily run themselves into excesses
which deprive them of influence to right-thinking
minds.[4]

Yet another point of view is reached (though
it may be combined with the preceding), when
the attempt is made to show that *the idea and
spiritual virtue* of Christ's Resurrection can be
conserved, while the belief in a bodily rising from
the tomb is surrendered. This is the tendency
which manifests itself especially in a section of
the school of theologians denominated Ritschlian.
It connects itself naturally with the disposition
in this school to seek the ground of faith in an

[1] *Bible Problems*, pp. 21, 115 ff.   [2] *Ut supra*, p. 263.
[3] *Das Gilgamesch-Epos in der Weltliteratur*, Bd. I.
[4] The general theory is discussed in Chap. ix.

immediate religious impression—in something verifiable on its own account—and to dissociate faith from doubtful questions of criticism and uncertainties of historical inquiry. Ritschl himself left his relation to the historical fact of the Resurrection in great obscurity. Of those usually reckoned as his followers, some accept and defend the fact,[1] but the greater number sit loose to the idea of a bodily Resurrection, claiming that it cannot be established by historical evidence, and in any case is not an essential element of faith.[2] Most *reject* the bodily rising as inconsistent with an order of nature. The certainty to which the Christian holds fast is that Christ, his Lord, still lives and rules, but this is, as Herrmann would say, a " thought of faith "—a conviction of Christ's abiding life, based on the estimate of His religious worth, and not affected by any view that may be held as to His physical resuscitation. There can be no doubt that the feeling which this line of argument represents is very widely spread.

The name which most readily occurs in connexion with the view of the Resurrection now indicated is that of Professor Harnack, whose Berlin lectures, translated under the title, *What*

---

[1] E.g., Kaftan, Loofs, Häring.

[2] Among those who take this position may be named Herrmann, J. Weiss, Wendt, Lobstein, Reischle, etc. Some of these admit supernatural impressions. See below, chap. viii.

is Christianity ? [1] have helped not a little to popu-
larize it. Harnack had earlier unambiguously
stated his position in his *History of Dogma.* " Faith,"
it is there contended, " has by no means to do
with the knowledge of the form in which Jesus
lives, but only with the conviction that He is
the living Lord." " We do not need to have
faith in a fact, and that which requires religious
belief, that is, trust in God, can never be a fact
which would hold good apart from that belief.
The historical question and the question of faith
must, therefore, be clearly distinguished here."
He seeks to show the weakness of the historical
evidence—" even the empty grave on the third
day can by no means be regarded as a certain
historical fact "—and declares : " (1) that every
conception which represents the Resurrection of
Christ as a simple reanimation of His mortal body
[no one affirms that it is] is far from the original
conception, and (2) that the question generally as
to whether Christ has risen can have no existence
for any one who looks at it apart from the contents
and worth of the Person of Jesus." [2] Quite to
the same effect, if in warmer language, Harnack
distinguishes in his Berlin lectures between what
he calls " the Easter message " and " the Easter
faith "—the former telling us of " that wonderful

---

[1] *Das Wesen des Christentums.*
[2] Eng. trans. i. pp. 85–86.

event in Joseph of Arimathæa's garden, which, however, no eye saw"; the latter being "the conviction that the Crucified One still lives; that God is just and powerful; that He who is the firstborn among many brethren still lives." The former, the historical foundation, faith "must abandon altogether, and with it the miraculous appeal to our senses." Nevertheless, "Whatever may have happened at the grave and in the manner of the appearances, one thing is certain : this grave was the birthplace of the indestructible belief that death is vanquished, that there is a life eternal." [1] The logic is not very easy to follow, but this is not the place to criticise it. Enough if it is made clear how this mode of conceiving of the Resurrection of Christ, which imports a new element into the discussion, presents itself to the minds that hold it.

The "appearances" to the disciples, however, still are there, variously and well attested, as by St. Paul's famous list in I Corinthians xv. 4–8, as to which even Strauss says : "There is no occasion to doubt that the Apostle Paul heard this from Peter, James, and perhaps from others concerned (cf. Gal. i. 18 ff., ii. 9), and that all of these, even the five hundred, were firmly convinced that they had seen Jesus who had been dead and was alive again." [2]

[1] *What is Christianity?* E.T., 1900, pp. 161-2.
[2] *New Life of Jesus*, i. p. 400.

What is the explanation ? Were they simply, as Strauss thought, visions, hallucinations, delusions ? Here is a new dividing-line, even among those who reject the reality of the Lord's bodily Resurrection. The appearances were too real and persistent, they feel, to be explained as the mere work of the imagination. Phantasy has its laws, and it does not operate in this strange way. There were appearances, but may they not have been *appearances of the spiritually risen* Christ, manifestations from the life beyond the grave by one whose body was still sleeping in the tomb ? So thought Keim, who argued powerfully against the subjective visionary theory [1]—so thinks even Professor Lake.[2]

The idea is not wholly a new one,[3] but Keim brought new support to it in his *Jesus of Nazara*, and since then it has commended itself to many minds, who have found in it a *via media* between complete denial of the Resurrection and acceptance of the physical miracle of the bodily rising. It has obtained the adhesion of not a few of the members of the Ritschlian school.[4]

All this belongs to the older stage of the controversy. It perhaps would not have sufficed to bring

[1] *Jesus of Nazara* (E.T.), **vi.** pp. 323 ff.
[2] *Ut supra*, pp. 271-6.
[3] It appears in Schenkel, Weisse, Schweitzer, and others.
[4] Among these Bornemann, Reischle, and others, leave the question open : J. Weiss argues for supernatural impressions, etc.

about a revival of the theory but for the new turn
given to speculation on appearances of the dead by
the investigations and reports of the Society of
Psychical Research. It is to "the type of phenomena collected" by this Society, "and specially
by the late Mr. F. W. H. Myers," that Professor
Lake attaches himself in his hypothetical explanation.[1] His position, as stated by himself, is a curious
inversion of the older one. Formerly, the Resurrection of Jesus was thought to be a guarantee of the
future life—of immortality. Now, it appears, the
future life "remains merely a hypothesis until it
can be shown that personal life does endure beyond
death, is neither extinguished nor suspended, and
is capable of manifesting its existence to us."[2]
Professor Lake has not the sanguineness of Professor
Harnack. He thinks that "some evidence" has
been produced by men of high scientific standing connected with the above Society, but "we
must wait until the experts have sufficiently sifted
the arguments for alternative explanations of the
phenomena before they can actually be used as
reliable evidence for the survival of personality
after death."[3] The belief in the Resurrection of
Christ even in the *spiritual* sense—that is, as survival
of personality—depends on the success of these
same experiments of the Psychical Research Society.

[1] *Ut supra*, p. 272. [2] Ibid. p. 245. [3] Ibid.

This theory, it will naturally occur, is not a theory of " Resurrection," in the New Testament sense of that word at all ; but we have to do here with the fact that some people believe that it is, or, at least, that it represents the reality which lies behind the narratives of Resurrection in the Gospels. Mr. Myers himself identifies the two things, and, as illustrating this phase of speculation, which has assumed, in an age of unbelief in the supernatural, a semi-scientific aspect, it may be useful, in closing, to quote his own words :—

" I venture now," he says, " on a bold saying : for I predict that, in consequence of the new evidence, all reasonable men, a century hence, will believe the Resurrection of Christ, whereas, in default of the new evidence, no reasonable men, a century hence, would have believed it. The ground of the forecast is plain enough. Our ever-growing recognition of the continuity, the uniformity of cosmic law has gradually made of the alleged uniqueness of any incident its almost inevitable refutation. . . . And especially as to that central claim, of the soul's life manifested after the body's death, it is plain that this can less and less be supported by remote tradition alone ; that it must more and more be tested by modern experience and inquiry. . . . Had the results (in short) of ' psychical research ' been purely negative, would not Christian evidence—I do not say Christian *emotion*, but Christian *evidence*—have received an overwhelming blow ?

" As a matter of fact—or, if you prefer the phrase, in my own personal opinion—our research has led us to results of a quite different type. They have not been negative only, but largely positive. We have shown that, amid much deception and self-deception, fraud and illusion, veritable manifestations do reach us from beyond the grave. The central claim of Christianity is thus confirmed, as never before. . . . There is nothing to hinder the conviction that, though we be all ' the children of the Highest,' He came nearer than we, by some space by us immeasurable, to that which is infinitely far. There is nothing to hinder the devout conviction that He of His own act ' took upon Him the form of a servant,' and was made flesh for our salvation, foreseeing the earthly travail and the eternal crown." [1]

[1] *Human Personality and its Survival,* II., pp. 288–9.

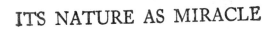

ITS NATURE AS MIRACLE

II

ITS NATURE AS MIRACLE

It is granted on all sides that the Christian Church
was founded on, or in connexion with, an energetic
preaching of the Lord's Resurrection from the dead.
The *fact* may be questioned : the *belief* will be
admitted.

" In the faith of the disciples," Baur says, " the
Resurrection of Jesus Christ came to be regarded as a
solid and unquestionable fact. It was in this fact
that Christianity acquired a firm basis for its historical development." [1]

Strauss speaks of " the crowning miracle of the
Resurrection—that touchstone, as I may well call
it, not of Lives of Jesus only, but of Christianity
itself," and allows that it " touches Christianity to
the quick," and is " decisive for the whole view of
Christianity." [2]

" The Resurrection," says Wellhausen, " was the
foundation of the Christian faith, the heavenly
Christ, the living and present Head of the disciples." [3]

[1] *History of the First Three Centuries* (E. T.) i. p. 42.
[2] *New Life of Jesus*, i. pp. 41, 397.
[3] *Einleitung in die Drei Ersten Evangelien,*p. 96.

" For any one who studies the marvellous story
of the rise of the Church," writes Dr. Percy Gardner,
" it soon becomes clear that that rise was conditioned—perhaps was made possible—by the conviction that the Founde was not born, like other
men, of an earthly father, and that His body did
not rest like those of other men in the grave. . . ." [1]

" The Resurrection of the Lord Jesus Christ,"
says Canon Henson, " has always been regarded as
the corner-stone of the fabric of Christian belief ;
and it certainly has from the first been offered by
the missionaries of Christianity as the supreme demonstration of the truth which in that capacity
they are charged to proclaim." [2]

" There is no doubt," affirms Mr. F. C. Burkitt,
" that the Church of the Apostles believed in the
Resurrection of their Lord." [3]

All which simply re-echoes what the Apostle Paul
states of the general belief of the Church of his time.
" For I delivered unto you first of all that which also
I received : that Christ died for our sins according
to the Scriptures ; and that He was buried : and
that He hath been raised on the third day according
to the Scriptures." [4]

Here then, is a conceded point—*the belief of the
Apostolic Church in the Resurrection of the Lord.* It

[1] *A Historic View of the New Testament,* Lect. v., Sect. 5.
[2] *The Value of the Bible and Other Sermons,* p. 201.
[3] *The Gospel History and its Transmission,* p. 74.
[4] I Cor. xv. 3, 4.

is well to begin with this point, and to inquire what the *nature* of the belief of the earliest Church was. Was it belief in visionary or spiritualistic appearances ? Belief in the survival of the *soul* of Jesus ? Belief that somehow or somewhere Jesus lived with God, while His body saw corruption in the tomb ? Or was it belief that Jesus had actually risen in the body from the grave ? That He had been truly dead, and was as truly alive again ?

If the latter was the case, then beyond all question the belief in the Resurrection of Jesus was belief in a true *miracle*, and there is no getting away from the alternative with which this account of the origin of Christianity confronts us. Strauss states that alternative for us with his usual frankness. " Here then," he says, " we stand on that decisive point where, in the presence of the accounts of the miraculous Resurrection of Jesus, we either acknowledge the inadmissibility of the natural and historical view of the life of Jesus, and must consequently retract all that precedes, and so give up our whole undertaking, or pledge ourselves to make out the possibility of the result of these accounts, i.e., the origin of the belief in the Resurrection of Jesus, without any corresponding miraculous fact." [1]

Now, that the belief of the Apostles and first disciples was really belief in a *true physical Resurrection* in other words, a Resurrection of the body of Jesus

[1] *Ut supra*, i. p. 397.

from the grave, it seems impossible, in face of the evidence, to doubt. Few of the writers above cited *do* doubt it, whatever view they may take of the reality lying behind the belief. We are happily not here dependent on the results of a minute criticism of the Gospels or of other New Testament texts. We are dealing with a belief which interweaves itself, directly or indirectly, with the whole body of teaching in the New Testament. If Harnack makes a distinction between the Easter " message " and the Easter " faith," it is certain that the first Christians made no such distinction. This admits of ample proof.

Take first the narratives in the Synoptics. There are three of these, in St. Matthew, St. Mark, and St. Luke, and the cardinal feature in each is the empty tomb, and the message to the women, and through them to the disciples, that the Lord had risen. " He is not here, He is risen." [1] The body had left the sepulchre. It is not otherwise in St. John. The Magdalene, and after her Peter and John, whom she brings to the spot, find the tomb empty.[2] It is to be remembered that there are several other miracles of resurrection in the Gospels,[3] and these

---

[1] Matt. xxviii. 6 ; Mark xvi. 6 ; Luke xxiv. 6, 22, 24.
[2] John xx. 2–13.
[3] Matt. ix. 18, 23–25 ; Mark v. 33–43 ; Luke vii. 11–15, viii. 49–56 ; John xi. ; cf. Matt. xi. 5, and Christ's repudiation of the Sadduccan denial of the resurrection, Matt. xxii. 29–32.

throw light on what was understood by Resurrection in the case of the Master. They were all bodily resurrections. The professed fear of the authorities that the disciples might steal away the body of Jesus, and say, " He is risen from the dead," points in the same direction.[1]

With this belief in the bodily Resurrection correspond the narratives of the appearance of the Risen One to His disciples. It is not the truth of the narratives that is being discussed at this stage, though indirectly that is involved, but the nature of their testimony to the Apostolic belief, and on this point their witness can leave little doubt upon the mind. The appearances to the women,[2] to the Apostles,[3] to the two disciples on the road to Emmaus,[4] to the disciples in Galilee,[5] all speak to a person who has risen in the body—not to an incorporeal spirit or phantom. The conditions of existence of the body were, indeed, in some respects supernaturally altered,[6] as befitted the new state on which it had entered, and was yet more fully to enter. But it was still a body which could be seen, touched, handled ; which evinced its identity with the body that had been crucified, by the print of the nails

---

[1] Matt. xxvii. 64.
[2] Matt. xxviii. 9, 10 ; John xx. 14–18 ; cf. Mark xvi. 9.
[3] Luke xxiv. 36–43 ; John xx. 19–29 ; cf. Mark xvi. 14.
[4] Luke xxiv. 13–32.
[5] Matt. xxviii. 16 and 17 ; John xxi.
[6] This is touched on below, pp. 53–4 ; cf. chap. vii.

and the spear-mark in the side.[1] These marks of
His passion, it is implied, Jesus bears with Him even
in the body of his glory.[2] He walked with His
disciples, conversed with them, ate with them:
" shewed Himself alive," as Luke says, " after His
passion by many proofs." [3] If any tangible evidence could be afforded of the real Resurrection
of the Lord from the grave, it was surely furnished
in that wonderful period of intercourse with His
disciples, prior to the final Ascension to His
Father.

What the Gospels attest as the belief of the Apostolic Church on the nature of the Resurrection is
amply corroborated by the witness of St. Paul. It is,
indeed, frequently argued that since St. Paul, in the
words, " He appeared ($\overset{\text{\'{}}}{\omega}\phi\theta\eta$) to me also," puts the
appearance of the Lord to himself at his conversion
in the same category with the appearances to the
disciples after the Resurrection,[4] he must have regarded these as, like his own, visionary.[5] Canon
Henson repeats this objection. " The Apostle, in

[1] Luke xxiv. 39–40 ; John xx. 24–28.
[2] Cf. Rev. v. and vi. [3] Acts i. 3.
[4] I Cor. xv. 3–9.
[5] Thus, e.g., Weizsäcker (*Apostolic Age*, E. T. i. pp. 8, 9),
Pfleiderer (*Christian Origins*, E. T., pp. 136–137, 160–161).
Weizsäcker says : " There is absolutely no proof that Paul
presupposed a physical Christophany in the case of the
older Apostles. Had he done so he could not have put
his own experience on a level with theirs. But since he
does so we must conclude that he looked upon the visions
of his predecessors in the same light as his own."

classing his own ' vision ' of the risen Saviour on
the road to Damascus with the other Christo-
phanies, allows us to conclude that in all the appearances there was nothing of the nature of a resuscitated body, which could be touched, held, handled,
and could certify its frankly physical character by
eating and drinking."[1] This, however, is to miss the
very point of the Apostle's enumeration. St. Paul's
object in his use of " appeared " is not to suggest
that the earlier appearances were visionary, but
conversely to imply that the appearance vouchsafed
to himself on the road to Damascus was as real
as those granted to the others. He, too, had verit-
ably " seen Jesus our Lord." [2] That St. Paul conceived of the Resurrection as an actual reanimation
and coming forth of Christ's body from the tomb
follows, not only from his introduction of the clause,
" and that He was buried," [3] but from the whole
argument of the chapter in Corinthians, and from
numerous statements elsewhere in his Epistles.

In 1 Corinthians xv. St. Paul is rebutting the contention of the adversaries in that Church that there
is no resurrection from the dead for believers, and
he does this by appealing to the Resurrection of
Christ. The latter fact does not seem to have been
disputed. If there is no resurrection from the dead,
St. Paul argues, then Christ has not risen ; if Christ
has risen, His Resurrection is a pledge of that of

[1] *Ut supra*, p. 204.   [2] 1 Cor. ix. 1.   [3] 1 Cor. xv. 4.

His people.[1] It is perfectly certain that the sceptics
of Corinth were not denying a merely *spiritual*
resurrection ; they evidently believed that death was
the extinction of the individual life.[2] As little is
St. Paul contending in his reply for a merely spiritual
resurrection. He contends for a resurrection of
the *body*, though in a transformed and spiritualized
condition.[3] Professor Lake will concede as much as
this. " There can be clearly no doubt," he says,
" that he [Paul] believed in the complete personal
identity of that which rose with that which had
died and been buried." [4] As respects Christ, " He
believed that at the Resurrection of Jesus His body
was changed from one of flesh and blood to one which
was spiritual, incorruptible, and immortal, in such a
way that there was no trace left of the corruptible
body of flesh and blood which had been laid in the
grave." [5] This, however, need not imply, as Professor Lake supposes it to do,[6] that the transformation was effected all at once, nor exclude such appearances as the Gospels record between the Resurrection
and Ascension.

[1] 1 Cor. xv. 12–23.   [2] xv. 32.   [3] xv. 33–57.
[4] *Historical Evidence for the Resurrection of Jesus Christ,*
p. 20.
[5] Ibid. p. 23.
[6] Ibid. pp. 27 and 35. Canon Henson argues in the
Hibbert Journal, 1903–4, pp. 476–93, that there is a contradiction between St. Paul and St. Luke in their conceptions of
Christ's Resurrection body. Cf. below, p. 182.

The Apostle's view of the bodily Resurrection of Jesus is unambiguously implied in the various statements of his other Epistles. Thus, in Romans viii. 11 we have the declaration : " But if the Spirit of Him that raised up Jesus from the dead dwelleth in you, He that raised up Christ Jesus from the dead shall give life also to your mortal bodies through His Spirit that dwelleth in you." Here plainly it is the " mortal body " which is the subject of the quickening. Later, in verse 23 of the same chapter, we have : " Waiting for our adoption, to wit, the redemption of our body." In Ephesians i. 19, 20, " the exceeding greatness of [God's] power to usward who believe," is measured by " that working of the strength of His might which He wrought in Christ, when He raised Him from the dead." In Philippians iii. 10, 11, 21, the hope held out is that the Lord Jesus Christ, awaited from heaven, " shall fashion anew the body of our humiliation that it may be conformed to the body of His glory." The like implication of a bodily Resurrection is found in 1 Thessalonians iv. 13–17, and many more passages.

It seems unnecessary to accumulate evidence to the same effect from the remaining New Testament writings. No one will dispute that this is the conception in St. Peter's address in Acts ii. 24–32, and the statements in 1 Peter i. 3, 21, iii. 21, are hardly less explicit. The Apocalypse emphasizes the fact that Jesus is " the firstborn of the

dead." [1] " I am the first and the last, and the
Living One; and I was dead, and behold, I am
alive for evermore." [2] " These things saith the first
and the last, who was dead, and lived again." [3]

On a fair view of the evidence, therefore, it seems
plain that the belief of the Apostolic Church was
belief in a true bodily Resurrection of Jesus Christ,
and it is as little open to doubt that, if such an event
took place, it was a *miracle*, i.e., a true supernatural
intervention of God, in the strictest sense of the
word. Whether that of itself suffices to debar the
" modern " mind from accepting the Resurrection
as an historical fact is matter for discussion, but
there should be no hesitation in conceding that
a question of miracle is involved.

The only possible alternative to this is to assume
that Jesus at His burial was *not really dead*—that
His supposed death from crucifixion was in reality
a " swoon," and that, having revived in the " cool
air " of the tomb, and issued forth, He was believed
by His disciples to have been raised from the dead.
This naturalistic explanation, although numbering
among its supporters no less great a name than
Schleiermacher's, [4] is now hopelessly discredited. It

[1] Rev. i. 5.   [2] i. 17, 18.   [3] ii. 8.

[4] It is doubtful how far Schleiermacher himself remained
satisfied with this explanation given in his *Leben Jesu*
(posthumously published). In his *Der christliche Glaube*
(sect. 99), he takes up a more positive attitude, allowing,
if not a direct, still a mediate connexion with the doctrine

was previously mentioned that Strauss practically gave the swoon theory its death-blow, and little has been heard of it since his time. " It is evident," Strauss well says, " that this view of the Resurrection of Jesus, apart from the difficulties in which it is involved, does not even solve the problem which is here under consideration—the origin, that is, of the Christian Church by faith in the miraculous Resurrection of a Messiah. It is impossible that a being who had stolen half-dead out of the sepulchre, who crept about weak and ill, wanting medical treatment, who required bandaging, strengthening, and indulgence, and who still at last yielded to His sufferings, could have given to the disciples the impression that He was a Conqueror over death and the grave, the Prince of Life, an impression which lay at the bottom of their future ministry." [1] The hypothesis, in fact, cannot help passing over into one of fraud, for, while proclaiming Jesus as the Risen Lord, who had ascended to heavenly glory, the Apostles must have known the real state of the case, and have closely kept the secret that their Master was in concealment or had died.

Miracle, therefore, in the Resurrection of Jesus cannot be escaped from, and it is well that this, the most fundamental objection to belief in the

of Christ's Person, inasmuch as anything that reflects on the Apostles reflects back on Christ who chose them.

[1] *Ut supra*, i. p. 412.

Resurrection, should be grappled with at once. It is, as before said, not the Resurrection alone that is involved in this objection, but the whole picture of Christ in the Gospels. That picture, as critics are coming to admit, is the picture of a supernatural Personage throughout.[1] It is at least something to have it recognized that the Resurrection does not stand as an isolated fact, but is congruous with the rest of the Gospel history.

It is, however, precisely this element of the miraculous which, it is boldly declared, the " modern " mind cannot admit. The scientific doctrine of " the uniformity of nature " stands in the way. Nature, it is contended, subsists in an unbroken connexion of causes and effects, determined by immutable laws, and the admission of a breach in this predetermined order, even in a single instance, would be the subversion of the postulate on which the whole of science rests. For the scientific man to admit the possibility of miracles would be to involve himself in intellectual confusion. Apart, therefore, from the difficulty of proof, which, in face of our experience of the regularity of nature, and of the notorious fallibility of human testimony to

[1] Cf. Bousset, *Was wissen wir von Jesus ?* pp. 54, 57. " Even the oldest Gospel," this writer says, " is written from the standpoint of faith ; already for Mark, Jesus is not only the Messiah of the Jewish people, but the miraculous eternal son of God, whose glory shone in this world."

extraordinary events,[1] is held to present another insuperable obstacle to the acceptance of miracle, the very idea of a miraculous occurrence is thought to be precluded. Even Dr. Sanday writes in his latest work, *The Life of Christ in Recent Research :* " We are modern men, and we cannot divest ourselves of our modernity. . . . I would not ask any one to divest himself of those ideas which we all naturally bring with us—I mean our ideas as to the uniformity of the ordinary course of nature." [2]   As an illustration from a different quarter, a sentence or two may be quoted from the biographer of St. Francis of Assisi, P. Sabatier, who expresses the feeling entertained by some in as concise a way as any. " If by miracle," he says, " we understand either the suspension or subversion of the laws of nature, or the intervention of the First Cause in certain particular cases, I could not concede it. In this negation physical and logical reasons are secondary ; the true reason—let no one be surprised —is entirely religious ; the miracle is immoral. The equality of all before God is one of the postulates of the religious consciousness, and the miracle, that good pleasure of God, only degrades Him to the level of the capricious tyrants of the earth." [3]

[1] Hume's famous argument against miracles turns in substance on the contrast between our unalterable experience of nature and the fallibility of human testimony to wonderful events.
[2] I . 204.   [3] *Life of St. Francis,* p. 433.

The application of this axiom to the life of Christ
in the Gospels, and specially to such a fact as the
Resurrection, naturally lays the history, as we
possess it, in ruins.[1] There is no need, really,
for investigation of evidence ; the question is
decided before the evidence is looked at. Professor Lake quotes from Dr. Rashdall with reference to the reanimation or sudden transformation
of a really dead body, in " violation of the best
ascertained laws of physics, chemistry, and physi-
ology " : " Were the testimony fifty times stronger
than it is, any hypothesis would be more possible
than that."[2]

A word may here be said on the mediating attempts which have frequently been made, and
still are made, to bridge the gulf between this
modern view of the uniformity of nature and
the older conception of the supernatural as direct
interference of God with the order of nature, through
the hypothesis of " unknown laws." This is what
Dr. Sanday in the above-mentioned work calls
" making both ends meet,"[3] and it commends
itself to him and to others as a possible means

---

[1] Cf., on the other hand, Kaftan's vigorous protest
against this modern view of the world in his pamphlet
Jesus und Paulus, pp. 4, 5, 9, 72. "I am no lover," he
says, " of the modern view of the world ; rather I find it
astonishing that so many thinking men should be led
astray by this bugbear " (*Popanz*).

[2] *Ut supra*, p. 267.   [3] P. 203.

of reconciliation between miracle and science. The hypothesis has its legitimate place in a general philosophy of miracles; for it is certainly not an essential part of the Biblical idea of miracle that natural forces should not be utilized. Even assuming that miracle were confined to the wielding, directing, modifying, combining or otherwise using, the forces inherent in nature, it is impossible to say how much, in the hands of an omniscient, omnipotent Being, this might cover. Still, when all this has been admitted, the real difficulty is not removed. There is a class of miracles in the Gospel—the Virgin Birth and the Resurrection may safely be placed among them, though they are not the only examples—which is not amenable to this species of treatment; miracles which, if accepted at all, unquestionably imply direct action of the Creative Cause. We have no reason whatever to believe—the Society for Psychical Research does not help us here—that hitherto unknown laws or secret forces of nature will ever prove adequate to the instantaneous healing of a leper, or the restoring of life to the dead. It is with regard to this class of miracles that the scientist takes up his ground. Assume what you will, he will say, of wonderful and inexplicable facts due to unknown natural causes: what cannot be admitted is the occurrence of events due to direct Divine intervention; what Hume would speak of as the effects of " particular volitions," [1] or Renan, of " private volitions." [2] These, in his judgment, are cases of the interpolation into nature of a force which breaks through, rends, disrupts, the natural sequence, and can hardly be conceived of otherwise than as a disturbance of the total system. It is this objection the believer in the miracle of the Resurrection has to meet.

But can it not be met ?   It is granted, of course, that there are views of the universe which exclude miracle absolutely. The atheist, the Spinozist, the materialist, the monist like Haeckel, the absolutist, to whom the universe is the logical unfolding of an eternal Idea—all systems, in short, which exclude a Living Personal God as the Author and Upholder of the world—have no alternative but to deny miracle. Miracle on such a conception of the world is rightly called impossible. But that, we must hold, is not the true conception of the relation of God to His world, and the question is not—Is miracle possible on an atheistic, or materialistic, or pantheistic conception of the world ? but, Is it possible and credible on a theistic view—on the view of God as at once immanent in the world, yet subsisting in His transcendent and eternally

[1] *Natural Religion*, Pt. XI.
[2] *Philosophical Dialogues*, E. T., pp. 6 ff.   " Two things appear to me quite certain . . . we find no trace of the action of definite beings higher than man, acting, as Malbranche says, by private volitions."

complete life above it—All-Powerful, All-Wise, All-Holy, All-Good ? It is here, e.g., that a writer like Professor G. B. Foster, in his *Finality of the Christian Religion*, seems utterly inconsistent with himself in his uncompromising polemic against miracles.[1] He would be consistent if he took up Spinoza's position of the identity of God with nature. But he claims to hold by the Father-God of Jesus Christ, and expressly finds fault with " naturalism " because it denies ends, purposes, ruling ideas, the providence of a just and holy God. But by what right, on such a basis, is the supernatural ruled out of the history of revelation, and especially out of the history of Christ ? Once postulate a God who, as said, has a being above the world as well as in it, a Being of fatherly love, free, self-determined, purposeful, who has moral aims, and overrules causes and events for their realization, and it is hard to see why, for high ends of revelation and redemption, a supernatural economy should not be engrafted on the natural, achieving ends which could not be naturally attained, and why the evidence for such an economy should on *a priori* grounds be ruled out of consideration. To speak of miracle, with P. Sabatier, from the religious point of view, as " immoral," is simply absurd.

[1] He goes so far as to say that " an intelligent man who now affirms his faith in such stories as actual facts can hardly know what *intellectual* honesty means " (p. 132).

On such a genuinely theistic conception of the
relation of God to the world and to man, the scientific
objection to miracle drawn from " the uniformity
of Nature," while plausible as an abstract statement, is seen, on deeper probing, to have really very
little force. Professor Huxley and J. S. Mill are
probably as good authorities on science as most,
and both tell us that there is no scientific impossibility in miracle—it is purely and solely a question
of evidence.[1] What, in the first place, is a " law
of nature " ? Simply our registered observation
of the order in which we find causes and effects
ordinarily linked together. That they are so linked
together no one disputes. To quote Mr. W. C. D.
Whetham, in his interesting book on *The Recent
Developments of Physical Science :* " Many brave
things have been written, and many capital letters
expended, in describing the Reign of Law. The
laws of Nature, however, when the mode of their
discovery is analyzed, are seen to be merely the
most convenient way of stating the results of experience in a form suitable for future reference.
. . . We thus look on natural laws merely as convenient shorthand statements of the organized
information that at present is at our disposal." [2]
Next, what do we mean by " uniformity " in this

---

[1] Huxley, *Controverted Questions*, pp. 258, 269 ; Mill,
Logic, Bk. III. chap. xxv.
[2] Pp. 31, 37.

connexion ? Simply that, given like causes operating under like conditions, like effects will follow.
No one denies this either. Every one will concede
to Dr. Sanday " the uniformity of the *ordinary*
course of nature." If it were otherwise, we should
have no world in which we could live at all. The
question is not, Do natural causes operate uni-
formly ? but, Are natural causes the only causes
that exist or operate ? For miracle, as has frequently been pointed out, is precisely the assertion
of the interposition of a *new* cause ; one, besides,
which the theist must admit to be a *vera causa*.[1]

Not to dwell unduly on these considerations, it
need only further be remarked that it misrepresents
the nature of such a miracle as the Resurrection
of Christ—or of the Gospel miracles generally—to
speak of miracles, with Dr. Rashdall, as " completely isolated exceptions to the laws of nature," [2]
or as arbitrary, capricious breaks in the natural
order, " violations " of nature's laws. Miracles
may well be parts of a system, and belong to a higher
order of causation—though not necessarily a mechani-
cal one. Professor A. B. Bruce, in this connexion,
refers to Bushnell's view of miracles as " wrought
in accordance with a purpose," what he calls " the
law of one's end," and to the phrase used by Bishop
Butler for the same purpose, " general laws of

---

[1] Thus J. S. Mill.   [2] See Lake, *ut supra*, p. 268.

wisdom." [1] And is it not the case that, in any worthy theistic view, God must be regarded as Himself the ultimate law of all connexion of phenomena in the universe, and the immanent cause of its changes? This means that a free, holy Will is the ultimate fact to be reckoned with in the interpretation of nature. The ultimate Cause of things has certainly not so bound Himself by secondary laws that He cannot act at will beyond, or in transcendence of them. [2]

The following may be quoted from Professor A. T. Ormond's *Concepts of Philosophy*, as one of the latest utterances from the side of philosophy. Professor Ormond says : " As to the miracle, in any case where it is real, it is either intended in the divine purpose, or it is not. If not, then it has no religious significance. If, however, it be intended in the divine purpose, it then has a place in the world-scheme which evolution itself is working out.

---

[1] *The Miraculous Element in the Gospels*, pp. 65–6 ; cf. Bushnell, *Nature and the Supernatural*, pp. 264–9 ; Butler, *Analogy*, Pt. II. chap. iv. sect. 3.

[2] There are at least three cases in which direct creative action seems to be no " violation " of natural order, but rather to be called for in the interests of that order : (*a*) In the initial act of creation *establishing* the order ; (*b*) in the founding of a *higher* order or kingdom in nature, e.g at the introduction of life (organic nature), (*c*) where the exercise of creative energy is *remedial* or redemptive. In this last case the creative act is not disturbance or destruction of nature, but the restoration of an order already disturbed (Christ's miracles of healing, etc.).

How could a genuine miracle contradict evolution unless we conceive evolution as being absolute? It is not evolution but the form of naturalism we have been criticising, that is inconsistent with any genuine divine happenings." [1]

It is granted, then, that, in the Resurrection of Jesus Christ from the dead, we are in presence of a miracle—a miracle, however, congruous with the character, personal dignity, and claims of Him whose triumph over death is asserted—and there is no evading the issue with which this confronts us, of an actual, miraculous economy of revelation in history. This assuredly was no exception—a single hole drilled in the ordinary uniform course of nature, without antecedents in what had gone before, and consequents in what was to follow. It belongs to a divine system in which miracles must be conceived as interwoven from the beginning. The Resurrection was a demonstration of God's mighty power ("the strength of His might" [2]); but was an act in which the Son Himself shared, re-taking to Himself the life He had voluntarily laid down. It is in the light of this miraculous character of the Resurrection we have to consider the phenomena of the appearances of the risen Lord, which otherwise may seem to present features difficult to reconcile. It is an error of Harnack's

[1] *Op. cit.* p. 603.
[2] Eph. i. 19.

to speak of the ordinary conception of the Resurrection as that of " a simple reanimation of His mortal body." [1] No one will think of it in that light who studies the narratives of the Gospels. They show that while Jesus was truly risen in the body, He had entered, even bodily, on a new phase of existence, in which some at least of the ordinary natural limitations of body were transcended.[2] The discussion of these, however, belongs properly to another stage, and may here be deferred.   Enough that the central fact be held fast that Jesus truly manifested Himself in the body in which He was crucified as Victor over death.

[1] *History of Dogma*, E. T. i. pp. 85–6.

[2] Cf. the remarks on this subject in Dr. Forrest's *The Christ of History and Experience*, pp. 146 ff., and in Milligan, *The Resurrection of Our Lord*, pp. 12 ff.   Dr. Forrest says : " These contradictory aspects, instead of casting a suspicion on the appearances, are of the essence of the problem which they were intended to solve. Christ hovers, as it were, or the border-line of two different worlds, and partakes of the characteristics of both, just because He is revealing the one to the other. . . .   During the forty days His body was in a transition state, and had to undergo a further transformation in entering into the spiritual sphere, its true home " (pp. 150, 152).   Preludings of these changes are seen in the Transfiguration, the Walking on the Sea, etc.

THE GOSPEL NARRATIVES AND CRITI-
CAL SOLVENTS

III

THE GOSPEL NARRATIVES AND CRITICAL SOLVENTS

IT was before stated that a change in the treatment of the evidence for the Resurrection is necessitated by the new and more stringent methods of criticism applied to the narratives of the Gospels, and especially by the theory, now the prevalent one, of the dependence of the first and third Gospels, in their narrative parts, on the second—that of St. Mark. It is desirable, before proceeding further, to give attention to these new critical methods and their results, in their bearings on the subject in hand. It is, of course, too much to ask, even if one had the competency for the task, that a full discussion of the Synoptical problem should precede all examination of the narratives of the Resurrection, or that the Johannine question should be exhaustively handled before one is entitled to adduce a testimony from the Fourth Gospel. On the other hand, it seems imperative that something should be said on the critical aspect of the subject—enough at least to indicate the writer's own position, and some of the grounds that are believed to justify it—still always with a strict eye on the special point under investigation.

It will prepare the way for this critical inquiry if a glance be taken first at the range of the New Testament material here falling to be dealt with. The narratives of the Resurrection go together with the narratives of the burial and of the post-Resurrection appearances of Jesus, and form an inseparable whole with them. Supplementary to the Gospel narratives are certain passages in the Book of Acts and in Paul.

The distribution of the subject-matter may be thus exhibited :—

St. Matthew : Burial, xxvii. 57–66 ; Resurrection, xxviii. 1–8 ; Appearances, xxviii. 9–20.

St. Mark : Burial, xv. 42–47 ; Resurrection. xvi. 1–8. *App. to St. Mark :* Appearances, xvi. 9–20.

St. Luke : Burial, xxiii. 50–56 ; Resurrection, xxiv. 1–12 ; cf. vers. 22–24 ; Appearances, xxiv. 12–53.

St. John : Burial, xix. 38–42 ; Resurrection, xx. 1–13 ; Appearances, xx. 14–29 ; xxi.

Acts : Appearances, i. 3–11.

St. Paul : Burial and Resurrection, 1 Cor. xv. 4 ; Appearances, 1 Cor. xv. 5–8.

The narratives thus tabulated contain the historical witness to the Lord's Resurrection, so far as that witness has been preserved to us. On them,

accordingly, the whole force of critical enginery
has been directed, with the aim of discrediting their
testimony. The narratives are held to be put out
of court (1) On the ground of their manifest discrepancies ; (2) Through the application of critical
methods to the text ; (3) Through the presence of
legendary elements in their accounts.

The consideration of the alleged discrepancies
can stand over, save as they prove to be involved
in the general discussion. Even if all are admitted,
they hardly touch the *main* facts of the combined
witness—especially the testimony to the central
fact of the empty tomb and the Lord's Resurrection
on the third day. " No difficulty of weaving the
separate incidents," says Dr. Sanday, " into an
orderly and well-compacted narrative can impugn
the unanimous belief of the Church which lies behind
them, that the Lord Jesus rose from the dead on the
third day and appeared to the disciples." [1] " There
are many variations and discrepancies," writes
Mr. F. C. Burkitt, " but all the Gospels agree in the
main facts." [2] Strauss' statement of these discrepancies, which he discovers in every particular of
the accounts, still remains the fullest and best, and
the use he makes of them is not one to the liking of
the newer criticism. " Hence," he says, " nothing

---

[1] *Outlines of the Life of Christ*, p. 180 : cf. Alford, *Greek
Testament*, i. Prol. p. 20.
[2] *The Gospel History and its Transmission*, p. 223.

but wilful blindness can prevent the perception that no one of the narrators knew and presupposed what another records." [1]

As previously indicated, the critical attack on the narratives of the Resurrection connects itself with the criticism of the Gospels as a whole. The newer criticism is principally distinguished from the older by a different attitude of mind to the Gospel material, and it proceeds by bolder and more assumptive methods. It starts rightly with a painstaking and exhaustive induction of the phenomena to be interpreted; [2] its peculiarity comes to light in the more daring, and often extremely arbitrary way in which it goes about the interpretation. It is no longer held to be enough to determine and explain a text. The newer criticism must get behind the text and show its genesis; must show by comparison with related texts its probable " genealogy; " [3] must take it to pieces, and discover what motive or tendency is at work in it, how it is coloured by environment and modified by later conditions—in brief, how it " grew ": this generally with the assumption that the saying or fact must originally have been something very different from what the text

[1] *Life of Jesus*, iii. p. 344.

[2] Illustrations are furnished in the analysis of the linguistic phenomena of the Gospels in Sir John Hawkins' *Horae Synopticae*, Plummer's *St. Luke*, Introd., Harnack's *Lukas der Arzt* (St. Luke and Acts), etc.

[3] Cf. Lake. *Res. of Jesus Christ*, pp. 167-8.

represents it to be. Such a method, no doubt, may open the way to brilliant discoveries, but it may also, and this more frequently, lead to the criticism losing itself in fanciful conjectures. Abundant illustration will be afforded when we come to the examination of the Resurrection narratives.

One question of no small importance is that of the relation of the Synoptical Gospels to each other. It has already been pointed out that the current theory on this subject—what Mr. W. C. Allen and Mr. Burkitt regard as "the one solid result" of the literary criticism of the Gospels—is that St. Matthew and St. Luke, as respects their narrative parts,[1] are based on St. Mark.[2] It is desirable to keep this question in its right place. It would manifestly be a suicidal procedure to base the defence of the Resurrection on the acceptance or rejection of any given solution of the Synoptical problem, especially on the challenge of a theory which has obtained the assent of so many distinguished scholars. Assume it to be finally proved

[1] The supposed *Logia* source does not come into consideration here.

[2] Allen, *St. Matthew*, Pref. p. vii. : "Assuming what I believe to be the one solid result of literary criticism, viz. the priority of the second Gospel to the other two synoptic Gospels." Burkitt, *The Gospel History*, p. 37 : "the one solid contribution," etc. "We are bound to conclude that Mark contains the whole of a document which Matthew and Luke have independently used, and, further, that Mark contains very little besides."

that St. Matthew and St. Luke used St. Mark as a chief " source," the limits of the evidence for the Resurrection would be sensibly narrowed, but its intrinsic force would not be greatly weakened. St. Mark, after all, is not inventing. He is embody- ing in his Gospel the common Apostolic tradition of his time—a tradition which goes back to the Apostles themselves, and rests on their combined witness. There is no reason for believing that St. Mark took the liberties with the tradition, in alter- ing and " doctoring " it, which some learned writers suppose. If the other Evangelists, whose Gospels, on any showing, are closely related to St. Mark's, adopted the latter as one of their sources, it can only be because they recognized in that Gospel a form of the genuine tradition. Their adoption of it, and working of it up with their own materials, but set an additional imprimatur on its contents. At the same time, it is not to be gain- said that, in practice, the attack on the credit of the Gospels has been greatly aided by the preva- lence of this theory of the dependence of the other Synoptics on St. Mark. As before indicated, it affords leverage for treating the narratives of the first and third Gospels as a simple " writing up " and embellishing of St. Mark's stories, and for re- jecting any details not found in the latter as unhis- torical and legendary. The *modus operandi* is expounded by Professor Lake. " When, therefore,"

he says, " we find a narrative which is given in all
three Gospels, we have no right to say that we have
three separate accounts of the same incident ; but
we must take the account in Mark as presumably
the basis of the other two, and ask whether their
variations cannot be explained as due to obscuri-
ties or ambiguities in their sources, which they tried
to clear up. . . . Since Matthew and Luke, so far
as they are dealing with the Marcan source, are not
first-hand evidence, but rather the two earliest
attempts to comment on and explain Mark, we are
by no means bound to follow the explanations given
by either." [1]

This leads to the question—Is the theory true ?
Despite its existing prestige, this may be gravely
questioned. Detailed discussion would be out of
place, but the bearing of the theory on the Resurrection narratives—which will be found to afford
some of the most striking disproofs of it—is so
direct, that a little attention must be given to it.

The grounds on which the Marcan theory rests
are stated with admirable succinctness by Mr.
Burkitt. " In the parts common to Mark, Matthew
and Luke," he says, " there is a good deal in which
all verbally agree ; there is also much common to
Mark and Matthew, and much common to Mark
and Luke, but hardly anything common to Matthew
and Luke which Mark does not share also. There

[1] *Ut supra*, p. 45.

is very little of Mark which is not more or less adequately represented either in Matthew or in Luke. Moreover, the common order is Mark's order. Matthew and Luke never agree against Mark in transposing a narrative. Luke sometimes deserts the order of Mark, and Matthew often does so ; but in these cases Mark is always supported by the remaining Gospel." [1]

With little qualification this may be accepted as a correct description of the facts, and it admirably proves that there existed what Dr. E. A. Abbott calls an " Original Tradition," to which St. Mark, of the three Evangelists, most closely adhered, giving little else, while St. Matthew and St. Luke borrowed parts of it, [2] combining it with material drawn from other funds of information. But does this prove the kind of *literary* dependence of the first and third Gospels on St. Mark which the current theory supposes ? Or, if dependence exists in any degree, is this the form of theory which most adequately satisfies the conditions ? It is not a question of the *facts*, but one rather of the *interpretation* of the facts. A few reasons may be offered for leaning to a negative answer to the above queries.

---

[1] *Ut supra*, p. 36.
[2] Cf. Abbott, *The Common Tradition of the Synoptic Gospels*, Introd., pp. vi., vii. " To speak more accurately, it is believed that the Gospel of St. Mark contains a closer approximation to the Original Tradition than is contained in the other Synoptics."

1. The impression undeniably produced by agreement in the character and order of the sections in the Gospels is seriously weakened when account is taken of the *widely divergent phraseology* in large parts of the resembling narratives. The divergence is so marked, and so often apparently without motive, that, notwithstanding frequent assonances in words and clauses, a direct borrowing of one Evangelist from another seems next to incredible. The narratives of the Resurrection are a palmary example,[1] but the same thing is observable throughout. Mr. Burkitt has been heard on the agreements ; let Alford state the facts that make for literary independence. " Let any passage," he says, " common to the three Evangelists be put to the test. The phenomena presented will be much as follows : first, perhaps, we shall have three, five, or more words *identical ;* then as many *wholly distinct ;* then two clauses or more expressed in the same words but *differing order ;* then a clause contained in one or two, and *not in the third ;* then *several words identical ;* then a clause or two not only *wholly distinct* but *apparently inconsistent ;* and so forth ; with recurrences of the same arbitrary and anomalous alterations, coincidences, and transpositions."[2] A simple way of testing this state-

[1] See the words of Strauss quoted earlier (pp. 59–60)
[2] *Greek Testament*, i. Prol. p. 5.

ment is to take such a book as Dr. Abbott's *The Common Tradition of the Synoptic Gospels*, where the narratives are arranged in parallel columns, and verbal agreements of the *three* Evangelists (the so-called "Triple Tradition"; the "Double Tradition," can be obtained by underlining in pencil) are indicated in black type, and note the proportion of agreement to divergence in the different sections. The proportion varies, but in most cases the amount of divergence will be found to be very considerable. Dr. Abbott himself goes so far as to say: "Closely though the Synoptists in some passages agree, yet the independence of their testimony requires in these days [as recently as 1884] no proof. Few reasonable sceptics now assert . . . that any of the three first Evangelists had before him the work of the other two. Proof, if proof were needed, might easily be derived from a perusal of the pages of the following Harmony, which would show a number of divergences, half-agreements, incomplete statements, omissions, incompatible, as a whole, with the hypothesis of borrowing."[1]

It cannot be said that the difficulties created by these remarkable phenomena have, up to the present time, been successfully overcome by the advocates of the dependence theory. Dr. A. Wright, in contending for an original "oral" Mark,

[1] *Ut supra*, Introd. p. vi.

thinks they have not yet been removed.[1] Sir
John Hawkins, though he argues for a use of St.
Mark, yet draws attention to a large series of phenomena which he declares to be, " on the whole, and
when taken together, inexplicable on any exclu-
sively or mainly documentary theory." " Copying
from documents," he says, " does not seem to
account for them : but it is not at all difficult to
see how they might have arisen in the course of oral
transmission."[2] To bring the phenomena into
harmony with the theory of literary dependence
on St. Mark there is needed the assumption of a
freedom in the use of sources by St. Matthew and
St. Luke which passes all reasonable bounds, and
commonly admits of no satisfactory explanation.
" The Evangelists," says Mr. Burkitt, " altered
freely the earlier sources which they used as the

---

[1] Cf. his *Synopsis of the Gospels in Greek*, Introd. p. x.
" At present the hypothesis of a Ur-Markus having been
discredited and practically abandoned, the supporters of
documents insist—in spite (as I think) of the very serious
difficulties which they have not yet removed—that St.
Mark's Gospel was used by St. Matthew and St. Luke."
He points out elsewhere the difficulties of supposing that
St. Luke used St. Mark (p. xvi.).   Dr. Wright's own theory
of a proto-, deutero-, and trito-Mark is loaded with many
difficulties.

[2] *Horae Synopticae*, p. 52.   The instances given in Pt.
iv., sects. ii., iii., include variations in the reports of the
sayings of Jesus, the attribution of the same, or similar
words, to different speakers, the use of the same, or similar
words, as parts of a speech, and as part of the Evangelist's
narrative, transpositions, etc.

basis of their narratives." [1]   This freedom of theirs
is then used as proof that "literary piety is a
quality. . . which hardly makes its appearance in
Christendom before 150 A.D." [2] With doubtful
consistency the same writer declares that, if the
Evangelists had worked on a " fixed oral tradition,"
he "cannot imagine how they dared to take such
liberties with it " ! [3]   That is, a "fixed tradition"
is sacred, and dare not be tampered with, but a
document *embodying* this tradition, even though
by a writer like St. Mark, is liable to the freest
literary manipulation ! It is to be remembered
that the proof of the alleged lack of "literary
piety" is mainly the assumption itself that St.
Mark *was* used by the other Evangelists.

2. Assuming, however, some degree of dependence
in the relations of the Gospels, the question is still
pertinent—Is the theory of dependence on St.
Mark *that which alone, or best, satisfies the conditions ?*
It has not always been thought that it is, and very
competent scholars, on grounds that seem cogent,
take the liberty of doubting it still.   It is almost
with amused interest that one, in these days, reads
the lengthy and learned argumentation of a Baur,
a Strauss, a Dr. S. Davidson,[4] to demonstrate from

[1] *Ut supra*, p. 18.   [2] P. 15.
[3] P. 35.   Elsewhere he bases an argument on St. Luke's
"literary good faith " (p. 118).
[4] Cf. Strauss, *New Life of Jesus*, i. pp. 169–83 ;   S.
Davidson, *Introd. to New Testament*, i. pp. 278 ff., etc.

the textual phenomena that St. Mark was the *latest* of the three Gospels, and depended on St. Matthew and St. Luke, not they on St. Mark.[1] The very phenomena now relied on to prove the originality of St. Mark, e.g., his picturesqueness, are turned by these writers into an argument against him. The argument from verbal coincidences is reversed, and St. Mark is made out to be based on the others because in numerous instances St. Mark's text agrees partly with St. Matthew and partly with St. Luke. And, assuredly, if dependence is assumed, lists can easily be furnished in which the secondary character of the text of St. Mark can as plausibly be maintained. But the Tübingen theory of St. Mark's dependence is by no means the only alternative to the prevailing view. The learned Professor Zahn, e.g., strikes out on a different line, and supposes a dependence of St. Mark on the *Aramaic* St. Matthew, but, conversely, a partial dependence of the *Greek* St. Matthew on

---

[1] More recently, the dependence of St. Mark on St. Matt. and St. Luke is upheld by an able scholar, Dr. Colin Campbell, whose work, *The First Three Gospels in Greek, arranged in Parallel Columns* (second edition, 1899), is designed to support this thesis. In a recent communication Dr. C. writes : " I have seen nothing yet to alter my conviction as to the substantial truth [of this hypothesis] . . . Every detail I have accumulated—and I have a large mass of material—convinces me that the prevalent view is wrong. . . . There are multitudes of expressions in Mark which are best understood if we presuppose his use of Matthew and Luke." (Pages of instances are given.)

the canonical St. Mark.[1] It is, in short, yet too
early to take the dependence on St. Mark as a fixed
result.

3. A strong argument against the current theory
seems to the present writer to arise from *St.
Luke's Prologue,*[2] in which the principles which guided
the Evangelist in the composition of his Gospel
are explicitly laid down. It is to be noted that,
in this Preface, St. Luke assumes that the chief
matters he is about to relate are already well known
—fully established (πεπληροφορημένων)—in the
churches ; that they had been received from those
who " from the beginning were eye-witnesses
(αὐτόπται) and ministers of the word " ; that they
had been the subject of careful catechetical instruction (κατηχήθης) ; that many attempts had already
been made to draw up written narratives of these
things. For himself St. Luke claims that he has
" traced the course of all things accurately from
the first," and his object in writing, as he says,
" in order " (καθεξῆς), is that Theophilus may
" fully know " (ἐπιγνῷς) the " certainty " (ἀσφά-
λειαν) of those things concerning which he had
already been orally instructed. Does this, it may
be asked, suggest such a process of composition

[1] *Einleitung,* ii. pp. 322 ff.
[2] Luke i. 1–4 ; cf. on this point Dr. A. Wright, *St.
Luke's Gospel in Greek,* pp. xiv., xv. ; *Synopsis of Gospels
in Greek,* p. xviii.

as the current theory supposes ? St. Luke speaks, indeed, of " many " who had taken in hand to draw up written narratives. He alludes to these earlier attempts, not disparagingly, but evidently as implying that they were unauthoritative, lacked order, and generally were unfitted for the purpose his own Gospel was intended to serve. He himself, in contrast with the " many," goes back to first-hand sources, and writes " in order." He is not appropriating the work of others, but drawing from his own researches.[1] How does this tally with the hypothesis now in vogue ? On this hypothesis another principal Gospel not only existed, but was known to St. Luke, and was used by him as a main basis of his own. This Gospel was the work of John Mark, son of Mary of Jerusalem, companion of St. Peter ; therefore may be presumed to have been of high authority. St. Luke sets such value on St. Mark's Gospel that he takes up fully two-thirds of its contents into his own—draws from it, in fact, nearly all his narrative material. He relies so much on its " order " that in only one or two instances does he venture to deviate from it. Does this harmonize with the account he himself

[1] Dr. Wright says : " His authorities were not written documents, but partly eye-witnesses, partly professional catechists " (*ut supra*). Dr. Plummer says : " That [the reference to ' eye-witnesses '] would at once exclude Matthew, whose Gospel Luke does not appear to have known. It is doubtful whether Mark is included in the πολλοί."

gives ? The linguistic phenomena in St. Luke, which show a far wider divergence from the Marcan type than in the first Gospel, again present diffi-culties.[1] On the other hand, the " order," which appears to belong to the form which the narratives had come to assume before any Gospel was written,[2] cannot alone be relied on to prove dependence, and singular *omissions* remain to be accounted for.[3]

On the whole, therefore, it appears safer not to allow a theory of dependence to rule the treatment, or to create an initial prejudice against one Gospel in comparison with another. St. Matthew and St. Luke may be heard without assuming that either Gospel, in its narrative portions, is a simple echo of St. Mark.

It is impossible here to enter on the grounds which, it is believed, justify the view that the Fourth Gospel is a genuine work of the Apostle

[1] Cf. Wright, *Synopsis*, p. xvi.

[2] In all the Synoptics certain groups or chains of events are linked together in the same way, evidently as the result of traditional connexion. E.g., the Cure of the Paralytic, the Call and Feast of Matthew, Questionings of Pharisees and of John's Disciples ; again, the Plucking of the Ears of Corn, the Cure of the Man with the Withered Hand (Sabbath Stories). St. Matthew frequently trans-poses, in the interests of his own plan—chiefly, however, in the *earlier* part of his Gospel.

[3] Cf. Burkitt, p. 130 : " He freely omits large portions of Mark," etc. One important series in St. Matthew (xiv., 22–xvi. 12) and St. Mark (vi. 45–viii. 26) is, for no obvious reason, wholly omitted in St. Luke.

John,[1] containing authentic reminiscences of that
Apostle of the Lord's doings and teachings, especially in Judæa, and in His more intimate intercourse
with His disciples, thus filling up the outline of the
other Evangelists in places which they had left
blank.[2] The difficulty which weighs so strongly
with Mr. Burkitt of finding a place in the frame-
work of St. Mark for the Raising of Lazarus is
certainly not insuperable ; [3] while his own view of
the free invention of this and other incidents and
discourses by the Evangelist [4] deprives the Gospel
of even the slightest claim to historical credit.
But the whole tone of the Gospel suggests a writer
who has minute and accurate knowledge of the
matters about which he writes—down even to
small personal details—and who *means* to be taken
as a faithful witness.[5]   As such he is accepted here.

[1] Reference may simply be made to the works of Principal Drummond and Dr. Sanday on the Fourth Gospel.
Mr. Burkitt is hard driven when he relies on the late and
untrustworthy references to Papias to overturn the unanimous early tradition of St. John's residence in Ephesus
(p. 252).

[2] Mr. Burkitt doubts if our Synoptic Gospels contain
stories from more than forty separate days of our Lord's
life (p. 20).   [3] Cf. pp. 222–3, and Pref. to second edition.

[4] " If [Mark] did not know of it [The Raising of Lazarus],
can we believe that, as a matter of fact, it ever occurred ? "
Cf. pp. 225–6, 237, etc.

[5] The interesting treatment of "The Historical Problems of the Fourth Gospel," from a lay point of view,
in R. H. Hutton's *Theological Essays*, well deserves attention at the present time.

The way is now open for the consideration of the application of these critical theories to the narratives of the Resurrection, and attention may first be given to certain features in the accounts of the Resurrection itself.

At first sight, nothing might seem plainer than that the narratives of the first three Gospels, while necessarily related, are yet *independent*, in the sense that no one of them is copied from, or based on, the others. As already hinted, the difficulties of a theory of dependence are here at their maximum. In scarcely any particular—time, names and number of women, events at the grave, number, appearance and position of angels, etc.—do their accounts exactly agree. This is indeed the stronghold of the argument from " discrepancies " of which so much is made. The theory, however, is, that the narratives in St. Matthew and St. Luke are derived from the simpler story of St. Mark ; and in carrying through this theory the advocates of dependence are driven to the most arbitrary and complicated hypotheses to explain how the divergences arose. It will be interesting to watch the process of dissolving the credit of the narratives by the aid of this assumption in the skilled hands of a writer like Professor Lake—though the result may rather appear as a *reductio ad absurdum* of the theory itself.

To begin with, certain cases of omission of details

by St. Matthew and St. Luke are proposed to be solved by the hypothesis of an " original Mark " (*Ur-Markus*), from which these details were absent. Professor Lake, while not committing himself to the theory, which Dr. Wright tells us is now " discredited and practically abandoned," [1] yet so far inclines to it that he thinks—the reader will note the *simplicity* of the hypothesis—" there is something to be said for the view that the original Marcan document did not give any names in Mark xv. 47, and that this form was used by Luke ; [2] that a later edition, used by Matthew, identified the women as Mary Magdalene and the other Mary ; and that another editor produced the text which is found in the canonical Mark." [3]

More serious, however, is the difficulty that the narratives are frequently divergent in phraseology and circumstance in what they *do* relate. How is this to be explained ? To take a leading example, St. Mark narrates of the women that " entering into the tomb, they saw a young man sitting on the right side, arrayed in a white robe." [4] St. Matthew has an independent story of a great earthquake, and represents an angel as rolling away the stone and sitting upon it.[5] St. Luke records that,

---

[1] *Synopsis*, p. x.

[2] It is a difficulty that St. Luke so often omits the proper names in St. Mark. Cf. Wright, *ut supra.*

[3] Lake, *ut supra*, p. 54.

[4] Mark. xvi. 5.   [5] Matt. xxviii. 2–5.

when they had entered the tomb, " two men stood by them in dazzling apparel." [1] No divergence could be greater, on the principle that " the two other Gospels, Matthew and Luke, are closely based on the Marcan narrative." [2] But Professor Lake is not discouraged. Accepting St. Mark's narrative as the original, " the others," he thinks, " all fall into place on an intelligible though complicated system of development under the influence of known causes." [3] " Complicated " indeed—and unreal—as will be seen by glancing at it.

First, there is a slight (infinitesimal) possibility that the Marcan text may originally have read, " came to the tomb " (instead of " entered into "),[4] and this left it doubtful whether the " young man " of the story was seen " on the right side " inside or outside the tomb.[5] In " elucidating " the point left in ambiguity, St. Luke took it the one way and St. Matthew the other—hence their variation. Only, if this is not the correct reading, the explanation falls.

Next, the " young man " in St. Mark " appears without any explanation of his identity or mission." [6] He was really, on Professor Lake's theory, as will be seen later, a youth at the spot who tried to persuade the women that they had come to the

[1] Luke xxiv. 3–5. [2] Ut supra, p. 63.
[3] P. 62–3. [4] The Vat MS. reads ἐλθοῦσαι.
[5] Ut supra, pp. 62–3. [6] P. 184.

wrong tomb.[1] Naturally, however, attempts were
soon made to identify him. " The most obvious
view for that generation, in which angelology was
so powerful a force, was that he was an angel.
This view is adopted in Matthew."[2] " Still a
further step is to be found in the doubling of the
angel, again strictly in accordance with Jewish
thought." This in St. Luke, St. John, and the
Gospel of Peter.[3] " Why are there two men in
Luke instead of one ? The answer is not quite
plain, but it seems probable that there was a general
belief in Jewish and possibly other circles that two
angels were specially connected with the messages
of God."[4] Elsewhere the probability is conceded
that St. Luke is here following a different tradition
from St. Mark's.[5] But why, then, not all through ?

We are not done yet, however, with this " young
man " of St. Mark's narrative. An attempt is
made " to bring together and trace the development of the various forms in which the original
' young man ' is represented in various books."[6]
" Two hypotheses," we are told, " naturally presented themselves : one that the young man was
an angel ; the other that he was the Risen Lord
Himself."[7] St. Matthew, after his manner, adopted
both views. The angel sitting on the stone is one
form : the appearance of Jesus to the women as

[1] Cf. pp. 251–2.   [2] P. 185.   [3] P. 185.
[4] P. 67.   [5] Pp. 67, 92.   [6] P. 67.   [7] P. 85

they went [1] is the other. This appearance of
Jesus recorded by St. Matthew is held to be a
" doublet " of St. Mark's young man story. So
is St. John's account of the appearance of the Lord
to Mary Magdalene.[2]

If attention has been given to this incident in
some detail, it is because, in its far-fetched conjectures and hypothetical ingenuities, it represents
so characteristically the processes by which it is
sought to dissipate the credibility of the Gospel
narratives, and the methods by which the Marcan
theory is applied to this end. The real effect of
its forced combinations and toppling structure " of
possibles " and " perhapses " is to cast doubt on
the theory with which it starts, and lend strength
to the view of the independence of the narratives.
After all, why should St. Luke, whose narrative is
so very divergent, be supposed to be dependent on
St. Mark in his account of the Resurrection ? Professor Lake has been heard admitting that it is
possible that St. Luke followed a different tradition.
Going a stage further back, we find Mr. Burkitt
allowing that St. Luke in the Passion " deserts
Mark to follow another story of the last scenes." [3]
At the other end, St. Luke is admittedly original
in his account of the *post*-Resurrection appearances.

---

[1] P. 85, Matt. xxviii. 9.
[2] P. 186, John xx. 14, 15.
[3] *Ut supra*, p. 130.

Why then should he not be so in the narrative of the Resurrection itself ? The same question may be asked regarding St. Matthew. The harmonistic expedients censured in commentators are mild in comparison with the violence needed to evolve the narratives of either of the other Evangelists out of that of St. Mark.

The detailed examination of the narratives next to be undertaken will further illustrate the untenableness of the new critical constructions, and provide the basis of a positive argument for the reality of the Resurrection.

THE CREDIBILITY OF THE WITNESS—
THE BURIAL

IV

THE CREDIBILITY OF THE WITNESS—THE BURIAL

ONE of the most touching scenes in Goethe's *Faust* is where the heart-sick sceptic, about to drain the poison-goblet, is turned from his purpose by hearing the ringing of the Easter bells, and the choral hymns, proclaiming that the Lord is risen. " I hear your message," is his first comment, " but I have not faith.   Miracle is faith's favourite child." [1] In this we hear the voice of to-day.   But the sweet sounds, with their tidings of victory and joy for the world, melt and conquer—for the time.

> Sing ye on, sweet songs that are of heaven !
> Tears come, Earth has her child again.

It is this " Easter Message," fraught with such infinite consolation for mankind, which is again placed in question.   The mood of the sceptic is resumed.   Faith may, if it will, believe that Jesus lives with God ; that He has not in spirit succumbed to death.   But the historical fact on which the Church has hitherto reposed its confidence in His

[1] " Das Wunder ist des Glaubens liebstes Kind."

83

victory over death—His Resurrection in the body
from the grave—is negatived as incredible, and
the evidence on which the belief rests is declared
to be valueless as proof of so great a wonder. A
little has already been said of the methods by which
the breaking down of the evidence is attempted on
the part of historical criticism. Much is made of
the secondary character of the narratives, of their
contradictions, of the mythical and legendary
elements alleged to be apparent in them. The
accounts are pitted against each other, are picked
to pieces, and attacked in their separate details
(" divide and conquer.").[1] Their larger coherences,
the connexion with the life of Christ as a whole,
their antecedents and consequents in revelation
and history—all this is left out of view or minimized. It is time to come to closer quarters with
this bold challenge of the evidence, and to ask how
far the denial rests on satisfactory grounds.

One or two general remarks are pertinent at the
outset.

It is customary to urge as decisive against the
narratives of the Gospels that not any of the writers
are first-hand witnesses. This, however, as already
hinted, is to take much too narrow a view. If the

---

[1] Cf., amongst recent works, *Die Auferstehung Christi*,
by Arnold Meyer (1905), and the work of Prof. Lake repeatedly referred to, *The Historical Evidence for the Resurrection of Jesus Christ*. (Now Abbé Loisy's *Les Évangiles
Synoptiques*.)

Fourth Gospel, as is here presumed, and as indications in its Resurrection narratives themselves
tend to show, is a genuine work of the Apostle John,
we have one witness of foremost rank who *was* an
eye-witness. St. Mark, according to a tradition
which there seems no reason to doubt, was the
" interpreter " of St. Peter [1]—another primary
witness. St. Luke lays stress upon the fact that
the things which he relates rested primarily on the
testimony of those " which from the beginning
were eye-witnesses and ministers of the word." [2]
The Gospel of St. Matthew, if not directly the work
of that Apostle, must have been written by one in
such close intimacy with the Apostle—another
first-hand witness—that his Gospel ever after passed
as St. Matthew's own.[3] St Paul's appeal is to
eye-witnesses.[4]

But there is more than this. It is never to be
forgotten that, as the words of St. Luke above cited
imply, the writers of. the Synoptical Gospels, like
Confucius in China, were not " originators " but
" transmitters." Their business was not to create,
but simply to record, as faithfully as they could,

[1] Papias, in Eusebius, *Ecc. Hist.* iii. 39, and generally
in the ancient Church. Cf. Meyer, Weiss, Westcott, Sal-
mon, Zahn, etc.

[2] Luke i. 2.

[3] Cf. Zahn, *Einleitung*, ii. 259. All early writers agree
in accepting the Greek Gospel as St. Matthew's, even
while declaring that he wrote in Aramaic.

[4] 1 Cor. xv. 5–8.

a tradition already existing and well established in the Church—a tradition derived originally from Apostles, circulating in oral and written form, and well preserved by careful catechetical teaching. It is to be remembered that the Apostles, with numerous other eye-witnesses, lived for years together at Jerusalem, continuously engaged in the work of instruction ; that during this period they were in constant communication with each other, with their converts, and with the Churches which they founded ; that the witness which they bore necessarily acquired a fixed and familiar form ; and that the deposit of the common tradition which we have in the Gospels has behind it, in its main features, all the weight of this consentient testimony—is, therefore, of the highest value as evidence. If it is not the testimony of this or that single eye-witness, it may be something better.

Next, as to the " contradictions." These, it will be seen immediately, are greatly exaggerated. But even on the points which present undeniable difficulties, certain things, in fairness, are to be borne in mind. We see how minute, faithful, and life-like are the narratives of the Lord's Crucifixion. The events of the Resurrection morning could not be less well known. The Apostles were, above all things else, witnesses to the Resurrection.[1] Within a few weeks of the Crucifixion they were proclaim-

[1] Acts. i. 22, ii. 32, iii. 15, iv. 33 ; 1 Cor. xv. 15.

ing the Resurrection of Jesus in the streets of Jerusalem, and making multitudes of converts by their preaching.[1] The facts must have been constantly talked about, narrated in preaching, experiences compared, particular incidents connected with this or that person or group of persons, either as original informants, or as prominent persons in the story. It is further to be remembered that the Resurrection day was necessarily one of great excitement. Events and experiences, as the tale was told, would be mingled, blended, grouped, in a way which no one who was not an eye-witness, like St. John, would be able afterwards clearly to disentangle. Yet the essential facts, and even the chief details of the story, would stand out beyond all reasonable question. This is what we would expect in the narratives of the Gospels, and what, in fact, we find. No one of the Evangelists professes to give a complete account of everything that happened on that wonderful Easter morning and day. Each selects and combines from his own point of view ; gives outstanding names and facts, without disputing or denying that others may have something else to tell ; in default of more exact knowledge, sometimes generalizes. It is here that St. John, with his more precise and consecutive narration, affords valuable aid,[2] as he

[1] Acts ii.–iv.
[2] It is possible to agree with Renan here. " In all that

does so frequently in matters of chronology in the Gospels.

In narratives of this description, however credible in origin and substance, it is clearly as hopeless as it is unfair to adopt the methods of a pettifogging attorney, bent at all costs on tripping the witness up on small details. No two of the Evangelists, e.g., agree precisely in the terms they employ as to the time of the visit of the women to the tomb.[1] Yet in all four it is plainly implied that the visit took place in early morning, when dawn was merging into day, and that it was full daylight before the visit was completed. One Evangelist names certain women ; others add a name or two more —names familiar in all the accounts. How small such points are as the basis of a charge of irreconcilable contradictions ! How few statements of public events, even where stricter accuracy of expression is aimed at, could endure to have such methods applied to them ![2]

concerns the narrative of the Resurrection and the appearances," he says, " the Fourth Gospel maintains that superiority which it has for all the rest of the Life of Jesus. If we wish to find a consecutive logical narrative, which allows that which is hidden behind the allusions to be conjectured, it is there that we must look for it " (*Les Apôtres*, p. ix.). Attention may again be drawn to R. H. Hutton's essay on " The Historical Problems of the Fourth Gospel " (*Theol. Essays*, No. vii.).

[1] On this and the next example, see after.

[2] Critics are always girding at the doctrine of " verbal inspiration." Yet their own objections rest on the postu-

Two examples may illustrate.

Professor Huxley was a man of scientific mind, from whom accurate statement in an ordinary narrative of fact might justly be expected. It happens, however, that in Huxley's *Darwiniana* the scientist makes two references in different papers to the origin of the breed of Ancon sheep. It is instructive to put the two passages side by side.

Here is the first :—

With the 'cuteness characteristic of their nation, the neighbours of the Massachusetts farmer imagined that it would be an excellent thing if all his sheep were imbued with the stay-at-home tendencies enforced by Nature on the newly-arrived ram, and they advised Wright to kill the old patriarch of his fold, and instal the Ancon ram in his place. The result justified their sagacious anticipations.[1]

Here is the other :—

It occurred to Seth Wright, who was, like his successors, more or less 'cute, that if he could get a stock of sheep like those with the bandy legs, they would not be able to jump over the fences so readily ; and he acted upon that idea.[2]

Here, manifestly, are " discrepancies " which, on critical principles, should discredit the whole story. In the latter narrative we have Seth Wright alone ; in the former, neighbours ; [" the second

late of the narrowest view of verbal inspiration, and lose their force on any other hypothesis.

[1] *Darwiniana*, pp. 38–9.   [2] P. 409.

narrative," we might say in the usual style, " knows nothing of neighbours ; " the longer version is plainly a later expansion]. In the latter, the idea is Seth Wright's very own—the product of his own 'cuteness ; in the other, the 'cuteness is wholly in the neighbours, and Seth Wright only acts on their advice. Yet how contemptuously would any sensible person scout such hypercriticism !

A second instructive example is furnished in a recent issue of the *Bibliotheca Sacra*.[1] A class in history was studying the French Revolution, and the pupils were asked to look the matter up, and report next day by what vote Louis XVI was condemned. Nearly half the class reported that the vote was unanimous. A considerable number protested that he was condemned by a majority of one. A few gave the majority as 145 in a vote of 721. " How utterly irreconcilable these reports seemed ! Yet for each the authority of reputable historians could be given. In fact, all were true, and the full truth was a combination of all three." On the first vote as to the king's guilt there was no contrary voice. Some tell only of this. The vote on the penalty was given individually, with reasons, and a majority of 145 declared for the death penalty, at once or after peace was made with Austria, or after confirmation by the people. The votes for

---

[1] Oct., 1907, pp. 768–9.

immediate death were only 361 as against 360. History abounds with similar illustrations.[1]

It helps, further, to set this question in its right light, if it is kept in mind that the Gospel narratives take for granted the Resurrection of Jesus as a fact universally accepted, on Apostolic testimony, and aim primarily, not at proof of the fact, but at telling how the event came about, and was brought on that Easter morning to the knowledge of the disciples, with the surprising consequences. It is not evidence led in a court of law, but information concerning an event which everybody already knew and believed in, which they furnish. This explains, in part, their naïve and informal character. It reminds us also that, while the value of these narratives, as contributing to the evidence of the fact, cannot be exaggerated, the certainty of the fact itself rests on a prior and much broader basis— the unfaltering Apostolic witness.[2] The origin of

[1] As an example of another kind, reference may be made to Rev. R. J. Campbell's volume of *Sermons Addressed to Individuals*, where, on pp. 145-6 and pp. 181–2 the same story of a Brighton man is told with affecting dramatic details. The story is no doubt true in substance; but for "discrepancies"—let the reader compare them, and never speak more (or Mr. Campbell either) of the Gospels!

[2] As shown in a previous paper, the *belief* in the Resurrection is admitted on all hands. R. Otto, in his *Leben und Wirken Jesu*, says: "It can be firmly maintained: no fact in history is better attested than, not indeed the Resurrection, but certainly the rock-fast conviction of the

the Christian Church, it will hereafter be argued, can simply not be explained except on the assumption of the reality of the fact. Meanwhile it is to be inquired what credit attaches to the Gospel relation of the circumstances of this astonishing event which has changed the whole outlook of the generations of mankind upon the future.

Let the chief points be taken in order, and their credibility examined. The force of the objections of a destructive historical criticism can then be tested.

A first fact attested by all the witnesses is that *Jesus died and was buried*. St. Paul sums up the unanimous belief of the early Church on this point in the words : " That Christ died for our sins according to the Scriptures, and that He was buried." [1] The reality of Christ's death, as against the swoon theories, was touched on before, and need not be re-argued. No one now holds that Jesus did *not* die !

" He was buried," St. Paul says. How He was buried is told by the Evangelists. The **facts** must have been perfectly well known to the primitive community, and the accounts in all four Gospels, as might be expected, are in singular agreement. [2]

first community of the Resurrection of Christ " (p. 49). It is here contended that the belief is inexplicable, under the conditions, without the fact.

[1] I Cor. xv. 3, 4. ;

[2] Matt. xxvii. 57–61 ; Mark xv. 42–7 ; Luke xxiii. 50–6 ; John xix. 38–42.

Combining their statements, we learn that Joseph
of Arimathæa, an honourable councillor (Mark and
John), and secret disciple of Jesus (Matthew, John),
a " rich man " (Matthew), one " looking for the
kingdom of God " (Mark, Luke), " a good man and
a righteous " (Luke), begged from Pilate the body
of Jesus (all four), and, wrapping it in a linen cloth
(all), buried it in a new (Matthew, Luke, John)
rock-tomb (all) belonging to himself (Matthew, cf.
John), in the vicinity of the place of crucifixion (in
" a garden," John says), and closed the entrance
with a great (Matthew, Mark, implied in the others)
stone. St. John further informs us that Nicodemus
assisted in the burial, bringing with him costly
spices. Phraseology differs in the accounts, and
slight particulars furnished by one Evangelist are
lacking or unnoticed in the others. St. Mark alone,
e.g., tells of Pilate's hesitation in granting Joseph's
request, and alone relates that Joseph " bought "
a linen cloth. Yet the story, on the face of it, is
harmonious throughout, and what any Evangelist
fails to state the rest of his narrative generally
implies. St. Luke and St. John do not even mention the rolling of the stone to the door of the tomb
(the fact was one so well known that it could be
omitted). But it is told how the stone was found
removed on the Resurrection morning.[1]

What has historical criticism to say to this story ?

[1] Luke xxiv. 2 ; John xx. 1.

One method is simply to deny or ignore it, and to
aver, in teeth of the evidence, that the body of
Jesus was probably cast by the Jews to the dung-
hill,[1] or otherwise disposed of. This, however, is
generally felt to be too drastic a procedure, and the
tendency in recent criticism has been to accept the
main fact of Joseph's interment of the body of
Jesus,[2] but usually with qualifications and explanations which deprive the act of the character it has
in the Gospels. Professor Lake's book may again
serve to illustrate the process. According to this
writer, the narrative which, to the ordinary eye,
reads so harmoniously is honeycombed with contradictions. The variations and omissions in the
accounts form, indeed, a difficulty in the way of the
Marcan theory—e.g., the omission of St. Mark's
mention of the hesitation of Pilate (Matthew, Luke),
or of the names of the women at the tomb (Luke)
—but this is got over, or minimized, by the suggestion of an " Ur-Markus." [3] Then the path is open
to assume that St. Matthew's " rich man," and St.

---

[1] Thus Strauss, Réville, etc. Réville, quoted by Godet,
says the Jews perhaps cast the body of Jesus on the dust-
heap, and adds, " as was generally done with the bodies
of executed criminals." Godet points out that " such a
custom was not in conformity with Jewish or Roman
law " (*Defence of the Christian Faith*, E. T., p. 106).

[2] Thus Renan, H. J. Holtzmann, O. Holtzmann, Prof.
Lake, etc. Strauss allows that Roman law permitted
the handing over of the body to friends (*Ulpian*, xlviii. 24).

[3] *Res. of Jesus Christ*, pp. 52–4.

Luke's " good man and righteous," are but varying
interpretations (" paraphrases ") of St. Mark's " a
councillor of honourable estate " ; [1] that the discipleship of St. Matthew, said to be unknown to,
and in contradiction with, St. Mark, is an attempt
to find a " motive " for the burial ; [2] that St. Luke,
by the use of the term " hewn in stone " (λαξευτῷ
contradicts the description of the tomb in the other
Synoptics ; [3] while St. John goes still further astray
in regarding the tomb as " a kind of mausoleum," [4]
etc. " The discipleship ascribed to Joseph in John
[as in Matthew] is not really to be reconciled with
the Marcan account." [5] The probable truth is
held to be that Joseph, a member of the Sanhedrim,
and acting as its representative,[6] was moved to do
what he did solely by regard for the precept in
Deuteronomy xxi. 22 ff. : that the body of a criminal
hanged on a tree should be buried before sunset.[7]

But how far-fetched and distorted is all this
theorizing ! The contradictions in the narratives

[1] Pp. 50–1.   [2] Pp. 46, 50, 61, 173, etc.
[3] P. 51. "In Mark we have an ordinary rock-tomb ;
in Luke, a tomb of hewn stone ; in John, a mausoleum
with a place for the body in the centre " (p. 176).
[4] Pp. 172–3.   [5] Pp. 172.
[6] Pp. 177, 182. Mr. Burkitt, on the other hand, seems
to question that βουλήτης means a member of the Sanhedrim, and hints that St. Luke has here again mistaken
St. Mark (Gospel History, p. 56). There is no reason to
doubt St. Luke's accuracy in his understanding of the word.
[7] Pp. 130, 182.

hunted out with such painstaking zeal simply do not exist. To take first the question of discipleship. If the *word* " disciple " is not used by St. Mark and St. Luke, is not the *fact* of discipleship to the degree intended—a secret sympathy now coming to avowal—written across their narratives as plainly as across those of St. Matthew and St. John ? What else but discipleship of this kind could move a member of the Sanhedrim (" he had not," St. Luke tells us, " consented to their counsel and deed." [1]), on the very day of Christ's crucifixion, to come boldly forward (" having dared," St. Mark says [2]), to ask from Pilate the body of the Crucified ; then, having bought linen, to wrap it therein and give it reverent burial in a rock-tomb (according to St. Matthew, his own ; [3] according to St. Matthew, St. Luke, St. John,[4] new) ? Indeed, does not the very expression used by St. Mark and St. Luke, " looking for the kingdom of God," imply, *for them*, a measure of discipleship ?

Is it probable, Professor Lake asks, that a disciple would have been a member of the Sanhedrim, or

---

[1] Luke xxiii. 51.   [2] Mark xv. 43.   [3] Matt. xxvii. 60.
[4] Matt. xvii. 60 ;   Luke xxiii. 53 ; John xix. 41.   " In the first Gospel," says Strauss, " Joseph is a disciple of Jesus—and such must have been the man who, under circumstances so unfavourable, did not hesitate to take charge of His body " (*Life of Jesus*, iii. p. 297). Renan follows the narratives without hesitation, including the anointing (*Vie de Jésus*, chap. xxvi.).

have omitted the anointing ? [1] " If Joseph was
not a disciple, he probably did not anoint the body,
if he was, he probably did." [2] Then the absence of
the mention of the anointing in St. Mark is taken
as a proof that Joseph was not a disciple. But
in St. Matthew's narrative, where the discipleship
is asserted, there is no anointing either. On Professor Lake's showing, it should nevertheless be
presupposed. [3] " Mark says that Joseph was a
member of the Sanhedrim, and that he did not
anoint the body." [4] St. Mark makes no such statement. What Professor Lake converts into this
assertion is an inference of his own from a later
part of the narrative, where St. Mark speaks of the
purchase of spices by the women with a view to
their anointing on the first day of the week. [5]

The attempt to make out a discrepancy about the
tomb is even less successful. In the adjective λαξευτῷ
in St. Luke Professor Lake seems to have discovered
a signification unknown to most students of the
language. One asks, by what right does he impose
on this word, occurring here alone in the New Testament, a sense contrary to that of the corresponding

---

[1] *Ut supra*, p. 171.   [2] P. 173.

[3] In another place he says, " He [Matthew] had given
an explanation of the burial by Joseph of Arimathæa—
discipleship—which rendered it improbable that the latter
had omitted the usual last kindnesses to a dead friend's
body " (p. 61).   St. Matthew should at least be cleared
of contradiction to St. John.

[4] P. 171.   [5] Mark xvi. 1.

word in the other Gospels? In the one case in which it occurs in the LXX (Deut. iv. 49), it cannot well mean aught else than hewn out of the rock. Meyer appears to give the meaning correctly, " hewn in stone, therefore neither dug nor built." [1] But the tomb, it is objected, was not necessarily Joseph's own, as St. Matthew affirms. Surely, however, the very use of it for the burial of the Lord's body, which all the Evangelists attest, is the strongest of proofs that it was. The tomb was evidently one of some distinction. Three witnesses describe it as " new," " where never man had yet lain" (Matthew, Luke, and John), and it was situated in " a garden." [2] Can those who write thus have thought of it as other than the property of the councillor who used it. Or was it the custom in Judaea for people simply to appropriate any one's rock-tomb that pleased them? [3] Professor Lake finds

---

[1] *Com. in loc.* On Jewish tombs and burial customs, cf. Latham, *The Risen Master*, pp. 33–6, 87–8, and plates.

[2] John xix. 41.

[3] Cf. Ebrard, *Gospel History*, E. T., p. 446 ; Godet, *Com. on St. John*, E. T., iii. p. 282. O. Holtzmann's theory of the Resurrection, as will be seen later, turns on the very point that the tomb was Joseph's (*Leben Jesu*, p. 392). A. Meyer's conjecture (*Die Auferstehung*, p. 123) that the tomb was a chance, deserted one, not only contradicts the evidence but is out of harmony with St. Mark's narrative of the loving care shown in Christ's burial. The circumstance that St. John gives the proximity of the tomb as a reason for the burial (xix. 42) in no way contradicts the ownership by Joseph.

a discrepancy even in St. Luke's omitting to mention the closing of the door with a stone ! But he adds in a footnote : " But the stone is implied in Luke xxii. 2. Either St. Luke forgot his previous omission or the latter was, after all, accidental ! " [1]

The futility of the counter-explanation offered of Joseph of Arimathæa's action hardly needs elaboration. Is it credible that any member of the Sanhedrim, without living sympathy with Jesus —still more the Sanhedrim as a body or their representative—should behave in the manner recorded from the simple motive of securing that a criminal who had undergone execution should be buried before sunset ? The answer may be left to the reader's own reflections.

Connected with the burial is the story of *the guard at the tomb*, narrated only by St. Matthew [2]—therefore lacking the breadth of attestation of the main history. It is not, on that account, as is very frequently assumed, to be dismissed as legendary. If it has behind it the authority of St. Matthew, it is certainly not legendary ; even if not his, it may come from some first-hand and quite authentic source. It will fall to be considered again in connexion with the events of the Resurrection. Meanwhile it need only be remarked that its credibility is at least not shaken by many of the objections

[1] *Ut supra*, p. 51.
[2] Matt. xxvii. 62–9 ; cf. xxviii. 4, 11–15.

which have been urged against it.[1] If the Gospel
narratives are to be believed, the action, teaching,
and miracles of Jesus—including the Resurrection
of Lazarus [2]—had made a deep impression on the
authorities. Especially had the events of the past
week stirred them to the depths.[3] Had they not
on the previous night condemned Jesus for a blas-
phemous claim to Messiahship ? Had not mysterious
words of His about the building of the temple in
three days been quoted against Him ? [4] Had the
betrayer dropped no hints of sayings of Jesus in
which, repeatedly, He had spoken of His being put
to death and rising again the third day ? [5] If
such things came to the ears of the chief priests and
Pharisees, as it is implied they did, do they not
furnish sufficient motive for what followed ? Herod's
conscience-stricken thought about Jesus, that He
was John the Baptist risen from the dead,[6] shows
that such ideas as Resurrection were not far to
seek. Even if the guilty consciences of those re-
sponsible for Christ's crucifixion prompted no such
fears, was not the fact that the body had been com-

---

[1] See these in Meyer's *Com. on Matthew, in loc.*
[2] Cf. John xi. 47–57.
[3] Matt. xxi. 12–16, xxiii., xxvi. 3–5, etc.
[4] Matt. xxvi. 6–1 ; Mark xiv. 58 ; cf. John ii. 18–22.
[5] Matt. xvi. 21 ; xvii. 22, 23 ; xx. 16, 19 (so Mark, Luke).
O. Holtzmann accepts and builds upon the genuineness
of these sayings (*Leben Jesu*, p. 388). So earlier, Renan,
in part (*Les Apôtres*, ch. i.).
[6] Matt. xiv. 2 ; Mark vi. 14–61 ; Luke ix. 7–9.

mitted to Christ's friends enough to create the apprehension that His disciples might remove it and afterwards pretend that He had risen ? It was with this plea that they went to Pilate and obtained the watch they sought. To make security doubly sure, they sealed the tomb with the official seal. The sole result, under providence, was to afford new evidence for the reality of the Resurrection.

The events of the Resurrection morning itself now claim our attention. But a minor point already alluded to, connecting the Resurrection narratives with those just considered, viz., the *purpose* attributed to the holy women by two of the Evangelists [1] *of anointing the body of Jesus*, may first be touched on. In regard to it several difficulties (" contradictions ") have been raised.

There is first the supposed inconsistency between this intention of the women of Galilee and the fact recorded by St. John alone,[2] that the anointing had already been done by Joseph and Nicodemus, with lavish munificence, at the time of burial. The women were present at that scene.[3] Why then should they contemplate a repetition of the function ? Then contradictions are pointed out in the narratives of the Synoptics themselves, inasmuch as St. Matthew, from a motive which Professor Lake

[1] Mark xvi. 1 ; Luke xxiii. 56 ; xxiv. 1.
[2] John xix. 39, 40. Strauss elaborates this objection. Renan finds no difficulty.
[3] Matt. xxvii. 61 ; Mark xv. 49 ; Luke xxiii. 55.

thinks he can divine,[1] omits this feature altogether, while St. Mark places the purchase of the spices on the Saturday (" when the Sabbath was past "),[2] and St. Luke on the Friday [3] evening. Are these difficulties really formidable? In a fair judgment it is hard to believe it. The difficulty is rather with those who suppose that St. Matthew, with St. Mark's Gospel before him, designedly omitted or changed this particular, or that St. Matthew and St. Luke, both copying from St. Mark, fell into contradiction with each other,[4] and with their source. Grant independent narration, and the difficulties mostly vanish.

With reference to the first point, it should be observed that, in strictness, St. John, in his narrative of the burial, says nothing of " anointing." The " mixture of myrrh and aloes " need not have been an ointment, and the language of the Gospel, "bound it [the body] in linen cloths with the spices,"[5]

---

[1] *Ut supra*, p. 61. The motive, as stated above, is that St. Matthew presupposes an anointing by Joseph. He has also a guard at the tomb. A. Meyer (*Die Auferstehung*, pp. 108, 111) contents himself with the guard.

[2] Mark xvi. 1.   [3] Luke xxiii. 56.

[4] St. Luke is thought to have been ignorant of, or to have momentarily forgotten, the Jewish method of reckoning days—a likely supposition (p. 59). Is it not St. Luke himself who tells us in verse 54 : " And the Sabbath drew on (Greek, " began to dawn ") ?

[5] John xix. 40. Luthardt comments : " Probably of pulverized gum, myrrh and aloe-wood, that was strewn between the bandages " (*Com. in loc.*). St. Luke distin-

suggests that it was not.[1] But not to press this
point, the circumstances have to be considered.
The burial by Joseph of Arimathæa was extremely
hurried. The permission of Pilate had to be obtained, the body taken down, linen and spices
bought, the body prepared for burial and interred,
all within the space of two or three hours—possibly
less.[2] It was probably cleansed, and enswathed
within the linen sheet or bandages with the spices,
without more being attempted. There was plainly
room here for the more loving and complete anointing which the devotion of the women would suggest.[3] Probably this was intended from the first.
It is not, at least, surprising that their affection
should contemplate such an act, and that steps
should immediately be taken, perhaps a beginning
of purchases made, to carry out their purpose.

Next, with respect to the alleged Synoptic inconsistencies, Professor Lake being witness, St. Matthew's text, albeit silent, does not exclude, but

guishes, as a physician would, between " spices " and
" ointments " (xxiii. 56).

[1] Cf. Latham, *The Risen Master*, pp. 9 (quoting Elli-
cott), 36–7.

[2] The haste was due to the nearness of the Sabbath
(Mark and Luke).

[3] If, in modern custom, wreaths were placed on the
grave of a friend in a hurried burial, would this preclude
the desire of other mourners, who had not earlier opportunity, to bring *their* wreaths ? or would they carefully
reckon up whether enough had not already been done ?
Cf. Ebrard, *Gospel History*, p. 446.

presupposes, such an anointing—if anointing it was—as that described by St. John.[1] Much less, surely, can it be held to exclude the intention, recorded in St. Mark and St. Luke, of the women to anoint—a circumstance probably left unnoticed because never carried into effect,[2] or because soon overshadowed by greater events. The point is very immaterial as to when precisely the purchases of spices were made. The " internal probability," as Professor Lake would say, is that the purchases were commenced in the short space that remained before the Sabbath began, and were completed after the Sabbath ended. Most likely some women made purchases at one time, others at another. In stating, however, that " they returned, and prepared spices and ointments,"[3] St. Luke is probably not intending to fix any precise time : perhaps had not the means of doing it. The next verse ["And on the Sabbath they rested, according to the commandment "] as the μέν shows, and the R.V. correctly indicates, begins a new paragraph.

With the narratives of the wonderful events of the Easter morning, which are next to be considered,

[1] *Ut supra*, p. 61.
[2] The reasons assigned by the critics are quite gratuitous. St. Matthew has in view, like the others, an anointing for burial (cf. the story of Mary of Bethany, chap. xxvi. 13. Strauss makes adroit use of this incident for his own purpose, *New Life of Jesus*, i. pp. 397–8).
[3] Luke xxiii. 56.

the core of the subject is reached. It is conceded on all hands that the Resurrection narratives present problems of exceptional interest and difficulty. It is not simply the so-called " discrepancies " in the narratives which create the problems. These, as said before, may prove to be of minor account. What are they all compared with the tremendous agreement in the testimony which Strauss himself thus formulates : " According to all the Gospels, Jesus, after having been buried on the Friday evening, and lain during the Sabbath in the grave, came out of it restored to life at daybreak on Sunday " ? [1] The problems arise from the fact that now, in the historical inquiry, an unequivocal step is taken into the region of the supernatural. Naturalism or supernaturalism— there is no escape from the alternative presented. There are consequently two, and only two, possible avenues of approach to these narratives, and according as the one or the other is adopted, the light in which they appear will be different. If they are approached, as they are by most " moderns," with the fixed persuasion that there is, and can be, no resurrection of the dead, it is impossible to avoid seeing in them only a farrago of contradictions and incredibilities. For it is undeniably a supernatural fact which they record—the revivification of the Son of God, the supreme act of triumph

[1] *New Life of Jesus,* i. p. 397.

by which the Redeemer of the world, through the might of the Father, resumed the life He had voluntarily laid down.[1] The element in which they move is the supernatural—the earthquake which opens a path from the tomb and scatters the guards ; angelic appearances and messages ; manifestations of the Risen Lord Himself. If nothing of this can be accepted, the narratives, with the faith which they embody, and the effects of that faith in history, remain an enigma, incapable, as the attempts at the reading of their riddle show, of solution.[2]

Here, then, a choice must be made. If Strauss's dictum, " Every historian should possess philosophy enough to be able to deny miracles here as well as elsewhere,"[3] is accepted, it becomes an insult to intelligence to speak of the narratives as evidence of anything. If, on the other hand, with scope for the discussion of details, the presence of the supernatural in the heart of the narratives is frankly acknowledged, harmony speedily begins to manifest itself where before there was irreconcilable confusion. As R. H. Hutton, a man of no

---

[1] John x. 17, 18 ; cf. Matt. xx. 28, etc.

[2] Justly has Prof. F. Loofs said : " He who has never felt that, with the message, ' Christ is risen,' something quite extraordinary, all but incomprehensible to natural experience, has entered into the history of the world, has not yet rightly understood what it is to preach the Risen One " (*Die Auferstehungsberichte*, p. 7).

[3] Quoted by Godet. *Com. on St. John*, iii. p. 323.

narrow intellect and a cultured judge of historical evidence, puts it : " The whole incredibility which has been felt in relation to this statement [the Lord's Resurrection] arises, I imagine, entirely from its supernatural and miraculous character. . . . A short statement of how the matter really stands will prove, I think, that, were the fact *not* supernatural, the various inconsistencies in the evidence adduced of it would not weigh a jot with any reasonable mind against accepting it." [1]

It is in this spirit that the discussion of the Resurrection narratives will be approached in the succeeding chapters. The evidence will be taken as it is given—not with the *a priori* demand for some other kind of evidence, but with the aim of ascertaining the value of that actually possessed. It will be fully recognized that, as before allowed, the narratives are fragmentary, condensed, often generalized,[2] are different in points of view, difficult in

[1] *Theol. Essays*, third edition, p. 131. The whole essay should be consulted.

[2] In illustration of what is meant by " generalizing," the following may be adapted from Ebrard (*Gospel History*, pp. 450–1). A friend is at the point of death. On returning from a journey, I am met in succession by different persons, one of whom tells me of his illness, two others inform me of his death, while a fourth gives me a parting message. In writing later to an acquaintance, I state briefly that on my way home I had met four friends, who had given me the particulars of his illness and death, and conveyed to me his last dying words. Of what interest would it be to the recipient of the letter to know whether

some respects to fit into each other, yet generally, with patient inspection, furnishing a key to the solution of their own difficulties—receiving also no small elucidation from the better-ordered story of St. John. In contrast with the extraordinary treatment accorded to them by the newer school, the study, it is hoped, will do something to create or strengthen confidence in their credibility.

all the friends came together, or separately, which came first and which brought the message ? In the same way, it mattered little to the readers of the Synoptic Gospels to know whether the women all went together to the grave, or whether one went before the rest, etc. Yet in this lies most of the difficulty.

CREDIBILITY *continued*—" THE EASTER MESSAGE "

V

CREDIBILITY *continued*—" THE EASTER MESSAGE "

PROFESSOR HARNACK, in his lectures on Christianity, bids us hold by " the Easter faith " that " Jesus Christ has passed through death, that God has awakened Him to life and glory," but warns us against basing this faith on " the Easter message of the empty grave, and the appearances of Jesus to His disciples." [1]   On what, then, one asks, is the faith to be based which connects it peculiarly with Easter ? Or on what did the Apostles and the whole primitive Church base it, except on their conviction that, in St. Paul's words,[2] Jesus " was buried, and that He hath been raised on the third day according to the Scriptures ; and that He appeared to Cephas," and to the others named ? But in all these " stories told by Paul and the Evangelists," Professor Harnack reminds us, " there is no tradition of single events which is quite trustworthy." [3]

[1] *What is Christianity ?* pp. 160–3.
[2] 1 Cor. xv. 4–6.   [3] P. 162.

111

It is this assertion of the insecurity of the Easter message of the Resurrection as a basis for faith which is now to be tested. Attention will be given first to the points which are more central and essential. It is, of course, easy to spirit away every part of the evidence by sufficiently bold denials, and by constructions which betray their weakness in the fact that hardly two of them agree together. It will be seen as the inquiry proceeds that the contradictions imputed to the Evangelists are trifles compared with those of the critics among themselves in seeking to amend the history. Agreeing only in rejecting the evidence of the Gospels as to what actually happened, they lose themselves in a maze of contradictory conjectures.

A few examples may be of service.

Weizsäcker, like Pfleiderer, is certain that St. Paul knew nothing of the women's visit to the grave. "The only possible explanation," he says, "is that the Apostle was ignorant of its existence."[1] "Paul," says Pfleiderer, "knows nothing of the women's discovery of the empty grave."[2] Professor Lake, on the other hand, thinks that St. Paul *did* know of it, and accounts in this way for his mention of "the third day."[3]

Further, as "Paul's knowledge of these things

[1] *Apost. Age,* E. T., i. p. 5.
[2] *Christian Origins,* p. 134.
[3] *Res. of Jesus Christ,* pp. 191–6.

must have come from the heads of the primitive Church," Weizsäcker deduces that " it is the primitive Church itself that was ignorant of any such tradition." [1] The visit of the women must therefore be dismissed as baseless legend. Keim agrees.[2] But Renan,[3] Réville, H. J. Holtzmann,[4] O. Holtzmann, Professor Lake—indeed most—accept the fact as historical.

Another crucial point is the empty tomb. Strauss, Keim, and, more recently, A. Meyer [5] treat the empty grave as an inference from belief in the Resurrection. But a " hundred voices," Keim acknowledges, are raised in protest, and " many critics, not only of the Right, but even of the Left, are able to regard it [the empty grave] as certain and incontrovertible." [6] " There is no reason to doubt," says O. Holtzmann, " that the women did not carry out their intention of anointing, because they found the grave empty." [7] Renan does not dream of questioning the fact.

Many critics, including Professor Lake,[8] think it impossible that Jesus should have spoken of His death and Resurrection on the third day. Others, as A. Meyer [9] and O. Holtzmann,[10] find in such say-

[1] *Ut supra.*   [2] *Jesus of Nazara,* E. T., vi. p. 296.
[3] *Les Apôtres,* ch. i.   [4] *Die Synoptiker,* p. 105.
[5] *Die Auferstehung Christi,* pp. 120–25.
[6] *Ut supra,* pp. 297–8.   [7] *Leben Jesu,* p. 391.
[8] *Ut supra,* pp. 255–9.
[9] *Ut supra,* pp. 181–2.   [10] *Ut supra,* p. 388.

ings of Jesus an important element in the development of belief in the Resurrection.

A favourite view, shared by Strauss, Weizsäcker, Keim, Pfleiderer, A. Meyer, Professor Lake, is that the disciples, immediately after the Crucifixion, fled to Galilee, there, and not at Jerusalem, receiving the visions which convinced them that the Lord had risen.[1] On this hypothesis, the women, even if they visited the tomb, had no share in the origin of the belief in the Resurrection.[2] Most, on the other hand, who, like Renan [3] and H. J. Holtzmann,[4] accept the visit to the tomb, hold that the Apostles were still in Jerusalem on the Easter morning.

To return to the positive investigation. It has already been seen that no doubt can rest on the cardinal fact that Jesus *did* die, and was buried ; and Harnack will allow a connexion of the Easter message with " that wonderful event in Joseph of Arimathæa's Garden," which, however, he says, " no eye saw." [5] What was the nature of that connexion ?

1. It is the uncontradicted testimony of all the witnesses that it *was* the *Easter morning*, or, as the Evangelists call it, " the first day of the week,"

[1] Weizsäcker, i. pp. 2, 3 ; Keim, vi. pp. 281 ff. ; A. Meyer, pp. 121, 127–30, etc.
[2] A Meyer, p. 124 ; Lake, p. 195.
[3] *Les Apôtres*, ch. i.
[4] *Ut supra*, p. 105.   [5] *Ut supra*, p. 161.

or *third day* after the Crucifixion, on which the
event known as the Resurrection happened ; in
other words, that Jesus rose from the dead *on the
third day*. The four Evangelists, whatever their
other divergences, are agreed about this.[1] The
Apostle Paul, who had conversed with the original
witnesses only eight or nine years after the event,[2]
confirms the statement, and declares it to be the
general belief of the Church.[3] Not a ripple of
dubiety can be shown to rest on the belief. " There
is no doubt," Professor Lake allows, " that from
the beginning the Resurrection was believed to
have taken place on the third day.[4]

Here, then, it might seem, is an unchallengeable
basis from which to start, for a whole Christian
Church can hardly be conceived of as mistaken
about an elementary fact connected with its own
origin. But the fact is not unchallenged. Nothing in this history is. Strauss long ago set the
example in endeavouring to show how the belief
might have originated from Old Testament hints.[5]

[1] Matthew xxviii. 1 ; Mark xvi. 2 ; Luke xxiv. 1 ;
John xx. 1. The predictions of Jesus of His rising on the
third day may be added, if only as evidence of the belief.
[2] Galatians i. 18, 19 ; ii. 1, 9. Strauss says " There is
no occasion to doubt that the Apostle Paul had heard this
from Peter, James, and others concerned." (*New Life
of Jesus*, i. p. 400.)
[3] 1 Corinthians xv. 3.
[4] *Ut supra*, p. 253 ; cf. p. 264.
[5] *Ut supra*, i. pp. 438-9.

Professor Lake, who thinks it rests " on theological rather than historical grounds," [1] devotes some twenty-five pages of his book, in different places, to weaken its foundations.[2] A new Babylonian school derives it from pagan myths.[3] A writer like A. Meyer combines all the standpoints, and would explain it from Old Testament passages, predictions of Jesus, and Greek, Persian, and Babylonian analogies.[4]

It is difficult to know what to make of a criticism of this kind, which so boldly sets aside existing evidence to launch out on assertions for which no proof can be given. It is the more difficult in Professor Lake's case, that in the end he accepts the Marcan tradition of the visit of the women to the tomb—or what they took to be the tomb—on the morning of the third day after the Crucifixion, for the purpose of anointing.[5] If they did—and who can reasonably doubt it ?—why all this pother in seeking an explanation from Old Testament suggestions, Babylonian mythology, and other obscure quarters ? It is argued, to be sure, that even the experience of the women was not a proof that the Resurrection did not take place on the

[1] *Ut supra*, p. 264.
[2] Cf. pp. 27–33, 191–3, 196–9, 253–65.
[3] Cf. Cheyne, *Bible Problems*, pp. 110 ff. ; Lake, pp. 197–8, 261.
[4] *Ut supra*, pp. 178–85.
[5] *Ut supra*, pp. 182, 196, 246, etc.

second day rather than on the *third*, and mythology is called in to help to fix the day.[1] One reads even : " It is never stated, but only implied in Mark that the Resurrection was on the third day." [2] As if, in St. Mark's time, a single soul in the Church had a doubt on that subject !

The treatment of St. Paul's testimony to " the third day " is not less arbitrary. The attempt is made by Professor Lake to separate St. Paul's mention of the third day from his witness to the appearances ; " the strongest evidence for the alternative [negative] view " being, that it requires that St. Paul should have said, " and was seen on the third day," not " and was raised on the third day." [3] One asks, Could Jesus have been seen until He was raised ? It is granted that St. Paul was acquainted with the Jerusalem tradition which embraced this fact.[4] Yet several pages discuss, with indecisive result, whether " the third day " was not " merely a deduction from Scripture." [5] The conclusion is that, whatever St. Paul's reason (it is allowed later on that it is " not impossible " that his reference may be to the experience of the women),[6] " we can only be almost certain that it cannot have been anything which he was able to rank as first-hand evidence of the Resurrection." [7]

---

[1] Pp. 254, 259–63.   [2] P. 198.   [3] Pp. 27–8.
[4] P. 41.   [5] Pp. 29–32.   [6] P. 196.
[7] P. 32.

Is not the unreality of such reasoning itself a power-ful corroboration of the historicity of the Gospel and Pauline statements?

2. The next important element in the witness, in part implied in the preceding, is *the visit of the women to the tomb of Jesus* at early morning on the third day.[1] Here, again, with some variation, we have a substantial nucleus of agreement. The differences will be looked at immediately; but how little they touch the main matter is ap-parent from the circumstance that, even among the extremer sceptics, the greater number admit that the women—the same named in the Gospels—*did* go to visit the tomb of Jesus on that memorable morning. Strauss can hardly admit it, for he throws doubt on the previous fact of the burial. But most who allow that Jesus was laid in the (or *a*) rock-tomb admit that the sorrowing women who had followed Him from Galilee, and had wit-nessed the Crucifixion and entombment,[2] or mem-bers of their company, did, as was most natural, come to the tomb on the morning after the close of the Sabbath, as day was breaking, for the pur-pose of anointing the body. Professor Lake ad-mits this; the two Holtzmanns admit it; even

1 Matthew xxviii. 1 ; Mark xvi. 1, 2 ; Luke xxiv. 1, 10 ; cf. xxiii. 55 ; John xx. 1.
2 Cf. Matthew xxvii. 55, 56 ; Mark xv. 40, 41 ; Luke xxiii. 49 ; John xix. 25.

A. Meyer, although, without the least ground, he disconnects the incident from the third day, concedes that visits were made.[1] Renan gives a summary of the facts, yet with a touch of inconsistency with his previous statements which, in the Evangelists, would be called " contradiction," he tells, e.g., of " the Galilean women who on the Friday evening had hastily embalmed the body," [2] forgetful that earlier he had correctly described the embalming as performed by Joseph and Nicodemus.[3]

The essential point being thus conceded, long time need not be spent on the alleged discrepancies with regard to (i) the *names and number* of the women. St. John's account in this connexion will be considered by itself. Meanwhile what must strike every careful reader is, that the names of all, or most, of the women concerned are, if not directly in the narratives of the Resurrection, yet in the related accounts of the closing scenes, given by each of the Evangelists. It is St. Mark, the supposed source, that tells how, at the Crucifixion, " there were also women beholding from afar : among whom were both Mary Magdalene, and Mary the mother of James the less, and of Joses, and Salome, who, when He was in Galilee, followed Him and ministered unto Him ; and many

[1] *Ut supra*, p. 124.   His account is referred to below.
[2] *Les Apôtres*, p. 6.   [3] *Vie de Jésus*, p. 431.

other women which came up with Him to Jerusalem "; [1] and how, at the burial, " Mary Magdalene and Mary the mother of Joses beheld where
He was laid." [2] These two, with Salome, are then
described as buying spices and coming to the tomb
on the Resurrection morning.[3] St. Matthew gives
the like story of " many women beholding from
afar, which had followed Jesus from Galilee,"
" among whom was Mary Magdalene, and Mary
the mother of James and Joses, and the mother of
the sons of Zebedee (Salome)," [4] and tells, as before,
of Mary Magdalene and the other Mary " sitting
over against the sepulchre." [5] It is extravagant
to suppose that because St. Matthew, following
up this statement, speaks of " Mary Magdalene
and the other Mary " [6] coming to the sepulchre
on the first day of the week, and omits the mention of Salome, he designs to contradict St. Mark,
who includes her. [7] St. Luke, likewise, knows of
" the women that followed with Him from Galilee," [8] and who (therefore not the two Marys only)
beheld where He was laid,[9] and came with their

---

[1] Mark xv. 40.   [2] Ver. 47.
[3] Mark xvi. 1.   [4] Matt. xxvii. 55, 56.
[5] Ver. 61.   [6] Matthew xxviii. 10.
[7] It would be as reasonable to accuse St. Mark of contradiction because in one verse he speaks of " Mary the
mother of James the less and of Joses," and in another
of " Mary the mother of Joses " only.
[8] Luke xxiii. 49.   [9] Ver. 55.

spices on the first-day morning.[1] St. Luke gives
the list afterwards as " Mary Magdalene, and Joanna,
and Mary the mother of James, and the other
women with them." (Salome is omitted and
Joanna the wife of Chuza, Herod's steward, appears.[2]) St. John corroborates the others in
speaking of Christ's " mother and His mother's
sister [probably Salome, so Meyer, Alford, etc.],
Mary the wife of Clopas and Mary Magdalene," [3]
at the Cross ; but at the Resurrection he speaks
only of Mary Magdalene,[4] of whom he has a special
story to tell. The " we," however, in St. John xx. 2,
implies the presence of others.

Is there really any difficulty of moment in these
various narratives ? They are incomplete, but
surely they are not contradictory. The same group
of women is in the background in each ; Mary
Magdalene and " the other Mary," are the prominent figures in all : the mention of other names
is determined by the preference or special object
of the Evangelist. It is most natural that the
mourning women should repair at the earliest
moment on the morning after the Sabbath to the
tomb of their crucified Master, to " see " it, as St.
Matthew says,[5] and, if access could be obtained,
to complete the rites of burial. There is no need
for supposing that they came together ; it is much

[1] Luke xxiv. 1.   [2] Ver. 10.   [3] John xix. 25.
[4] John xx. i.   [5] Matthew xxviii. 1.

more probable that they came in different groups
or companies—perhaps Mary Magdalene and the
other Mary, or these with Salome, first, to be
joined after by Joanna and other members of the
Galilean band.[1]   Nothing, as was before noted,
can be inferred from St. Matthew omitting to
mention the design of anointing. His story of
the guard, as rendering the anointing impossible,
may have influenced him : only that the women
knew nothing of the guard. It is not that the
Evangelist was ignorant of the custom of anointing ; [2] but, following up the picture he had drawn
of the two Marys " sitting over against " the sepulchre at the burial,[3] he gives prominence to the
yearning of love these women felt to see again where
the Lord slept.[4]

There remains (ii) the *time* of this visit of the
women, as to which, again, discrepancy is frequently alleged. Certain of the notes of time in
the Evangelists raise interesting exegetical questions (e.g., St. Matthew's " late on the Sabbath

---

[1] After enumerating the women Renan says : " They
came, probably each on her own account, for it is difficult
to call in question the tradition of the three Synoptical
Gospels, according to which several women came to the
tomb : on the other hand, it is certain that in the two
most authentic narratives [?] which we possess of the
Resurrection, Mary Magdalene alone played a part."
(*Les Apôtres*, p. 6.)

[2] Cf. Matthew xxvi. 12.   [3] Matthew xxvii. 61.
[4] Matthew xxviii. 1.

day " ; [1] St. Mark's " when the sun was risen " [2]) ; but real contradiction it is hard to discover. What can be readily observed is that no one of the Evangelists employs the precise expression of another —a strong proof of independence ; [3] and further, that all the expressions imply that the visits took place at, or about, early dawn, or daybreak, when darkness was passing into day. St. Matthew gives the description, " late on the Sabbath day " (ὀψὲ δὲ σαββάτων), as it began to dawn (τῇ ἐπιφωσ-κούσῃ) towards the first day of the week." [4] St. Mark says : " Very early (λίάν πρωΐ) on the first day of the week . . . when the sun was risen " (ἀνατεί-λαντος τοῦ ἡλίου). [5] St. Luke has the expression : " At early dawn " (ὄρθρου βαθέος). [6] St. John has : " Early (πρωΐ), while it was yet dark." [7] The discrepancies between these expressions are formal only. If contradiction there is, it lies chiefly in St. Mark's own apparently inconsistent clauses, " very early," and " when the sun was risen." [8]

---

[1] Matthew xxviii. 1.   [2] Mark xvi. 2.

[3] Alford wrote : " The independence and distinctness of the four narratives in this part have never been questioned " (on Matt. xxviii. 1). This, too, needs qualifying.

[4] Matthew xxviii. 1. Meyer observes : " Consequently the point of time mentioned here is substantially identical with that given in Luke xxiv. 1, and in John xx. i " (*in loc.*).

[5] Mark xvi. 2.   [6] Luke xxiv. 1.   [7] John xx. 1.

[8] Scholars are well agreed that the aorist participle here can only bear the sense : " After the sun was risen."

As the Evangelist cannot be supposed to intend verbally to contradict himself within the compass of one verse, his language must reasonably be construed to mean : " At early dawn, when the sun was just above the horizon." Similarly, St. Matthew's " late on the Sabbath day " cannot reasonably be put into contradiction with his own explanatory clause : " As it began to dawn towards the first day of the week." It is not, as the context shows,[1] Saturday night that is meant, but the period of darkness ending at dawn of the following morning (thus Meyer, Alford, etc.). The view advocated by some that St. Matthew, borrowing from St. Mark, here combines inconsistent clauses by dropping out St. Mark's mention of the purchase of spices between,[2] is, as Meyer remarks, untenable. It is not St. Mark's language that is used, and St. Matthew may be credited with

---

[1] Some, as McClellan, *The New Testament*, pp. 512–31, insist that St. Matthew's " late on the Sabbath " can only mean Saturday evening, and explain the subsequent clause by the help of Luke xxiii. 54, "And the Sabbath drew on " (ἐπέφωσκε). But the events that follow in St. Matthew plainly belong to the morning of the first day. McClellan acknowledges that " nearly every modern writer of importance [a long list] interprets St. Matthew's phrases as of Sunday morning."

[2] Thus Lake, p. 57 ; W. C. Allen, *St. Matthew*, pp. 300–1, etc. : so, too, Caspari (*Chron. Introd.*, E. T., p. 240). Allen says : " Matthew, by omitting Mark's reference to the purchase of perfumes, has combined two entirely inconsistent notes of time." But see Meyer, *in loc.*

sufficient knowledge of Greek to keep him from
perpetrating so obvious a blunder. St. John's
" while it was yet dark " presents no difficulty
when the situation is recalled. The women began
to arrive just as day was breaking, and it was daylight before they left the place. Mary Magdalene
had light enough to see that the stone was taken
away.[1]

3. The third crucial fact in the history—one
which, in connexion with succeeding incidents,
establishes the reality of the Resurrection, is that,
when the women reached the tomb of Jesus on that
Easter morning, after much dubiety as to how
they were to obtain entrance, they found *the stone
rolled away and the tomb empty.* Here, again, there
is entire unanimity among the witnesses.[2] St.
Matthew alone tells of *how* the stone was removed
—of " a great earthquake," and the descent of an
angel of the Lord, who rolled away the stone, and
sat upon it, before whose dazzling aspect the keepers
became as dead men.[3] But all the Evangelists
agree that the stone, the rolling away of which had
caused the women much concern (" who shall roll
us away the stone from the door of the tomb ? ")[4]

---

[1] John xx. 1 : " Twilight in that latitude does not last
for more than a quarter of an hour " (Latham, *The Risen
Master*, p. 225).

[2] Matthew xxviii. 2–7 ;   Mark xvi. 3–6 ;   Luke xxiv.
2–6 ; John xx. 1, 11, 12.

[3] Matthew xxviii. 2–4.   [4] Mark xvi. 3.

was found rolled away, and that the tomb was empty, when the women arrived. In St. Mark's words : " And looking up, they see that the stone is rolled back ; for it was exceeding great." [1] Or in St. Luke's : " And they found the stone rolled away from the tomb. And they entered in, and found not the body of the Lord Jesus." [2] According to St. John, the emptiness of the tomb was subsequently verified by St. Peter and St. John himself.[3] Moreover, while St. Matthew alone gives the story of the rolling away of the stone by the angel, the implication in all the other narratives is that the stone was removed by supernatural power. No human hand had effected this wonder. St. Matthew, therefore, only narrates in objective fashion—a reflection, possibly, of the terrified imagination of some of the guards—what the other Evangelists postulate. What really had happened the women were soon to learn from angelic announcements to themselves. Jesus had risen, as He said.[4]

Here, then, are two facts in the history of the Resurrection—*the stone rolled away*, and *the empty tomb*—attested about as well as facts can be, with the belief of the whole primitive Church behind them. There is not a hint anywhere that the fact

[1] Verse 4.   [2] Luke xxiv. 2, 3.
[3] John xx. 3–9 ; cf. Luke xxiv. 12.
[4] Matthew xxviii. 6.

of the empty tomb was ever questioned by either friend or foe. If would have been easy to question or disprove it when the Apostles were boldly proclaiming the Resurrection in Jerusalem a few weeks later.[1] But no one appears to have done so. The other fact of the rolling away of the stone with which the tomb had been closed is involved in the tomb being found empty. Taken as they stand —much more when taken in connexion with what succeeds—the two facts support belief in the Resurrection. What is to be said of them?

There are here only two courses if the Resurrection is disputed. Either (1) the facts may be denied, and the evidence set aside, as when it is argued that the empty tomb is itself an inference from belief in the Resurrection.[2] Or (2) the facts may be admitted, and a " natural " explanation be sought for them. The extremer view has already been alluded to, and need not longer detain us. It is interesting only for its implied admission that the belief of the Apostolic Church was belief in a bodily Rising. Undoubtedly every believer in the Resurrection of Christ, St. Paul included, held as part of that belief that the tomb of Jesus was left empty. But the emptiness of the tomb was not a deduction from prior belief in the Re-

---

[1] Acts ii. 24, 31 ; iii. 15 ; iv. 10, etc.
[2] Thus Strauss, Weizsäcker, Keim, etc.

surrection—the Apostles were guilty of no such *hysteron proteron*—but was a fact by itself, adequately attested, and one of the grounds of belief in that divine occurrence. In recent times, accordingly, the other alternative is that more commonly adopted. It is becoming usual to accept the fact of the empty tomb, and to seek for it, since the Resurrection is not admitted, some natural explanation. The study of these explanations is extremely instructive. Dr. Rashdall is quoted by Professor Lake as saying that " were the testimony fifty times stronger than it is, any hypothesis would be more possible than that " of a physical resuscitation.[1] Only in the light of these " more possible " explanations is the strength of the evidence for the Resurrection of Jesus fully disclosed.

If the tomb was empty on the morning of that third day, and Jesus did not rise, some other hands must secretly have removed the body. Who did it ? The old theory of fraud on the part of the disciples [2] has now no respectable advocates, and may be put out of account. Who, then, effected the removal ? Pilate ? The Sanhedrim—the enemies of Jesus ? This has been actually defended,[3]

---

[1] Lake, *ut supra*, p. 269.

[2] Reimarus and some of the Deists. The calumny noted in Matthew xxviii 12–15, is an additional proof that the tomb was found empty.

[3] E.g., by A. Réville, Schwartzkopff, etc.: cf. A. Meyer, *ut supra*, pp. 17–18.

but may also be passed over.[1]   But glance at more recent solutions.

O. Holtzmann gives the following account.   The honourable councillor, Joseph of Arimathæa, having first, as the Gospels relate, permitted the burial of Jesus in his rock-tomb, felt on reflection that it would not do to have the body of a man who had been crucified lying among the dead in his respectable family vault.   He, therefore, when the Sabbath was past, had the body of Jesus secretly removed, and buried elsewhere.   Such, this author thinks, is " the simplest explanation of the mysterious occurrence."[2]   It is implied, of course, that the secret was carefully kept from the disciples, who were allowed to believe that their Master had risen.   This interesting little deception of Joseph, so likely in a good man, and first brought to light in these last years, successfully took in the whole Christian Church, and, combined with imaginary appearances, created its faith in the Resurrection !

So transparent a piece of trickery does not appeal to Professor Lake, who gives a solution on different lines.   The facts, he thinks, were probably these.

[1] Renan admits the empty tomb, but judiciously refrains from explanations.   Cf. Latham, *The Risen Master*, pp. 6–9.

[2] *Leben Jesu*, pp. 392–3.   The germ of the theory is found in H. J. Holtzmann, *Die Synoptiker*, p. 105.   Cf. the criticism in A. Meyer, pp. 118–19.

The women came in the dusk of morning to an empty tomb, which they mistakenly took to be that of Jesus. The neighbourhood of Jerusalem was full of rock-tombs, and it was easy to go wrong. A young man, standing near, tried to convince them of their error, and pointed them to where the Lord really lay. [This is the young man, as previously seen, whom legend, according to Professor Lake, transforms into an angel, and also into the Risen Lord.] But the women fled. Professor Lake's own words deserve to be quoted : " The women came in the early morning to a tomb which they thought was the one in which they had seen the Lord buried. They expected to find a closed tomb, but they found an open one ; and a young man, who was in the entrance, guessing their errand, tried to tell them that they had made a mistake in the place. ' He is not here,' said he ; ' see the place where they laid Him,' and probably pointed to the next tomb. But the women were frightened at the detection of their error, and fled, only imperfectly or not at all understanding what they heard. If was only later on, when they knew that the Lord had risen [from visions of the disciples in Galilee], and—on their view—that His tomb must be empty, that they came to believe that the young man was something more than they had seen ; that he was not telling them of their mistake, but announcing the Resurrection,

and that his intention was to give them a message
for the disciples." [1]

As a " natural" explanation, this fairly rivals
Paulus. But will any one believe that such a
mistake of a few women is really the foundation
on which the Christian Church has built its Easter
hope, or affords an adequate explanation of the
revolutionary effects in the faith and hope of the
disciples which, according to all the narratives,
were wrought by the experiences of that Easter
morning ? If so, he has a strange idea of the relation of causes and effects. The theory, it need
hardly be pointed out, is itself an invention, without historical support or probability—a travesty
of the narratives as we have them. There is no
evidence of a mistake of the women, who knew
too well where the Lord was laid ; [2] or of the presence of the obliging young man, weeks after identified with an angel *within* the tomb ; or of a mistake of the import of the message. Were the
women the only persons who visited the spot ? Did
no one think of verifying their tale ? Did they
never themselves go back and discover their error ?
Whence this consentient and mistaken conviction
that the tomb was found empty on the third day, and
that a message came from it that the Lord had
risen ? As a " more possible " hypothesis Professor Lake's theory may safely be set aside.

[1] *Ut supra*, pp. 251–2.
[2] Mark xv. 47 ; Luke xxiii. 55.

A last example is taken from A. Meyer, who, in his book *Die Auferstehung Christi*, after criticizing and rejecting previous theories, gives what he conjectures may be the true version of events. The passage is an excellent example of the process of manufacturing history out of moonshine. He says : " If one seeks for an historical kernel behind the narrative of Mark, it is not difficult to picture to oneself how, perhaps, after some time [indefinite], in the early morning, veiled women, disciples of Jesus, crept forth, sad and despairing, to seek the tomb and the body ; how they, perchance, had inquired about the place, how they stood some time helpless before a huge stone, and said, ' Oh, if only some one would roll away that stone for us ' ; then again in doubt before an empty cave, not knowing whether the Lord might have lain there, and some one have taken Him away ; how they may have often repeated such search, until at last the news and summons came from Galilee, ' Why seek ye the living among the dead ? He is not there, give up your seeking : He is long ago risen and has appeared to Simon and the others ; come and hear it for yourselves.' " [1] It has only to be said of this flight of fancy that, when compared with the narrative of the Gospels, it has no substance or feature of reality in it. It contradicts the tradition at every point. There is no " historical

[1] P. 124.

kernel," for the ground of history is abandoned for imagination. The visit of the women is cut away from the third day : is unhistorically represented as repeated and resultless ; the message which came from the tomb is brought weeks later from Galilee, etc. Opposed to the Gospels, it is opposed equally to the theories already adduced. Unbelief here also lacks unity in its hypotheses. It shatters itself against the moveless rock of the facts.

4. And now the Easter history reaches its climax. The facts already reviewed—the third day, the visit of the women, the stone supernaturally removed, the empty tomb—lead up to, and find their natural culmination in, *the angelic vision and message that the Lord had risen.*[1] Here once more it is permissible to speak of at least essential agreement in the narratives. Particulars and phraseology in the accounts vary, as before, in a manner incompatible with dependence. St. Luke, e.g., speaks of two angels where St. Matthew and St. Mark mention only one ; and in the part of the angel's message relating to Galilee St. Luke gives the words a quite different turn from what they have in the other Gospels.[2] St. John's account stands again by itself. Yet all the Synoptical

[1] Matthew xxviii. 5–8 ; Mark xvi. 6–8 ; Luke xxiv. 4–11 ; John xx. 1, 11–12.
[2] Luke xxiv. 6, 7 ; cf. Matthew xxviii. 7 ; Mark xvi. 7.

narratives agree that, while the women stood, perplexed and affrighted at or within the tomb, they received a vision of angels ; that the announcement was made to them that the Lord had risen ; that they were invited to see the place where He had lain ; that they had given them a message to take to the disciples. In the central part of the message : " He is not here ; He is risen," there is *verbal* agreement : only St. Matthew and St. Luke reverse the order of the clauses. St. Mark breaks off with the women fleeing from the tomb in " trembling and astonishment " ; [1] but there can be no reasonable doubt that his Gospel also, not less than the others, contemplated a report of the angelic message to the disciples, and a narrative of certain of the appearances.[2] According to St. Matthew and St. Luke, the report was made on the same day.[3] The Apostles were, therefore, still in Jerusalem, and the fiction of their having already dispersed to Galilee is proved to be baseless.

The Lord had risen ! There were no witnesses of that august event ; but the fact was made certain to the faith of the disciples by the empty grave, by the angelic vision, and by the subsequent appearances of Jesus Himself. The time of the Resurrection is not told, but it is implied that it syn-

[1] Mark xvi. 8.
[2] Cf. the remarks in Menzies, *The Earliest Gospel*, p. 120.
[3] Matthew xxviii. 3 ; Luke xxiv. 9-11, 22, 23.

chronized with the convulsion of nature which
St. Matthew describes, and with the rolling away
of the stone by the angel which terrified and pros-
trated the guards. It therefore preceded by
some time the visit of the women. There is no
need to suppose that the guards were still there
when the women arrived. It may rather be presumed that, on recovery from their terror, they
betook themselves away as speedily as they could.
Neither need the angel of St. Matthew be understood to be still sitting on the stone as at the first.
His language to the women—" Come, see the place
where the Lord lay "—rather implies that, as in
other Gospels, he addresses them from *within* the
tomb.

It is not to be gainsaid that we have here a story
of supernatural events. The narratives are steeped
in the supernatural. The supernatural element
may be resisted, but it must at least be conceded
that the account goes together on its own assumption that a tremendous miracle—the Resurrection
of the Lord—really took place. It was before
remarked that in all the Gospels there is the implication of supernatural power in the removal
of the stone. A physical convulsion was the natural
accompaniment of so great a marvel.[1] The ap-

[1] Cf. the darkness, earthquake, and rending of the
Temple veil at the Crucifixion. Matthew xxvii. 15, 51 ;
Mark xv. 33, 37 ; Luke xxiii. 44, 45.

pearance of the angel is in keeping with what is told of the later appearances of the angels to the women. The reality of the angelic appearances, again, is vouched for by the message which, according to all the witnesses, the women received, and which they subsequently conveyed to the disciples. That message is the kernel of the whole story. It is the " Easter message " which has changed the face of the world. If anything stands fast in the Resurrection history, it is that this message did not spring from their own sad, despairing hearts, but was given them by celestial visitants at the tomb.

So closely, in truth, is this message which the women received bound up with the " vision of angels," [1] that it is difficult to see how the one is to be believed, if the other is rejected.[2] The difference in the accounts of the vision, though Strauss and later sceptics have made much of them, are not of a nature to occasion serious difficulty. There may really have been two angels, as in the experience of Mary Magdalene,[3] though only one is mentioned by St. Matthew and St. Mark : or St. Luke, in his summary narrative, may be combining the

[1] Luke xxiv. 23.

[2] There seems to the present writer no incredibility in the supposition of a higher spiritual world capable of manifesting itself, but much to favour the idea. Whatever the theory of Christ's knowledge, this is precisely one of the things on which His intuition might be trusted.

[3] John xx. 12.

experience of Mary Magdalene with that of the other women. But there is a further consideration suggested by the nature of vision itself. Whether or not it is right to speak of " ecstasy " in such an experience, it is certain that the state of " vision " (ὀπτασία) is not simply an extension of ordinary perception. It is not a state of pure objectivity. It is not on the outer but on the inner senses that an impression is made in the apprehension of the supersensible. There is, in Old Testament phrase, an " opening of the eyes," [1] a raising of consciousness to a higher plane. What is seen is real, but there is a subjective element in the seeing. It follows that in a vision like that of the women at the tomb the experience of one is not necessarily the measure of the experience of another. When notes were compared, all would not be found to have had exactly the same perceptions. Especially would this be the case if there were different companies, or if the experiences registered were not those of the same moment. Yet in the main the perceptions *did* agree. Forms of men ("a young man," Mark; " two men," Luke) ; [2] " appearance like lightning, and raiment

---

[1] Cf. Numbers xxiv. 3, 16 ; 2 Kings vi. 17, etc.

[2] Mr. Latham's idea that the " visitants to the tomb " (and at the Ascension) may have been persons (Essenes ?) from Jerusalem (*Risen Master*, pp. 412-19), is a strange aberration. The rationalistic theory that the women may have been deceived by the glint of the grave clothes is left unnoticed.

white as snow " (Matthew) ; " arrayed in white robe " (Mark) ; " in dazzling apparel " (Luke) ; " in white " (John). Above all do the narratives agree in the words of comfort : " Fear not ye : for I know that ye seek Jesus, which hath been crucified. He is not here ; for He is risen, even as He said. Come, see the place where the Lord lay " (Matthew). " Be not amazed ; ye seek Jesus the Nazarene, which hath been crucified : He is risen ; He is not here ; behold the place where they laid Him ! " (Mark). " Why seek ye the living among the dead ? He is not here, but is risen " (Luke).

From St. Mark and St. Luke [1] we learn that the women had " entered " and inspected the tomb before this wonderful experience befell them. It is not strange that, when it came, they were " amazed " (Mark) and " affrighted " (Luke), and needed the reassurance given them. The message they received for the disciples, that Jesus was going before them into Galilee, where they would see Him, with its important variation in St. Luke, will better be considered in connexion with the appearances. The events at the tomb ended with the hasty departure of the women—" with fear and great joy," says St. Matthew ; [2] " with trembling and astonishment," because of their fear, declares St. Mark,[3] saying nothing to any one, as they

[1] Mark xvi. 5 ; Luke xxiv. 5.
[2] Matthew xxviii. 8.   [3] Mark xvi. 8.

hasted to fulfil their commission to the disciples. St. Mark's Gospel, at this point, on the usual view, breaks off : not, however, before it has told us the things it is most essential for us to know.[1]

[1] The gospel, ending at chap. xvi. 8, is manifestly incomplete. Dean Burgon unquestionably makes out a strong case for suspense of judgment with regard to the remaining verses (9–20). (Cf. his *Last Twelve Verses of St. Mark*). But it is safer to regard the verses as an early Appendix. The problems which this raises must here stand over.

CREDIBILITY *continued*—THE POST-RE-
SURRECTION APPEARANCES

VI

CREDIBILITY *continued*—THE POST-RESURRECTION APPEARANCES

It is the testimony of all the New Testament witnesses—of the Gospels, of the Book of Acts, of St. Paul—that Jesus did appear to His disciples after His Resurrection. It was not simply the voices of angels proclaiming to the women that He had risen—not even the eloquent fact of the empty tomb—which produced in the disciples the immovable conviction that their Master had indeed burst the bands of death, and lived to die no more.[1] They believed, and unitedly testified, that they had seen Him, conversed with Him, eaten and drunk with Him ; [2] could give place, and date, and names, to His appearances to them. Often in the primitive circles, while the Apostles were still in their midst at Jerusalem, must the story of the time, occasion and manner of the chief of these manifestations, and of the incidents connected with them, have been recited.

[1] The reports of the women and of others were at first received with incredulity (Mark xvi. 11, 13, 14 ; Luke xxiv. 11).   [2] Acts x. 41.

144 THE CREDIBILITY OF THE WITNESS

There is a point here, it should be noted in passing, in which the weakness of the assault on the testimony for the Resurrection is specially apparent. The assumption, practically, of the hostile critics of that testimony is that the Church had no history ; that it knew nothing, really, of its own past ; that myths and legends grew up in rank abundance, and were everywhere eagerly received ; that the writers of the Gospels had no scrupulous conscience for truth, but imagined, manipulated, and altered their materials at pleasure.[1] Any Church of our own day could give a good account of its origin, and of the events in its history, say, for the past fifty years. But the Churches founded by the Apostles —even the Mother-Church at Jerusalem—are believed to have had no such capability. The early believers had a different opinion of their knowledge and responsibility,[2] and of their ability to discern between true and false. They were not so ready as the objectors imagine to be imposed on by " cunningly devised fables." [3] The Church to which they belonged had a continuous history ; they *thought* they knew how it originated, on what facts it was based, who were its early witnesses, and to what they testified ; and they told their story without doubt or hesitation.

---

[1] This is really the assumption, e.g., underlying the Abbé Loisy's newly published *Les Évangiles Synoptiques.*
[2] Cf. St. Paul, 1 Cor. xv. 15.   [3] 2 Peter i. 16.

This witness which the Apostles bore had nothing vague or intangible about it. It was in large part full, detailed, circumstantial. It was not "appearances" simply, but prolonged interviews, that were alleged. The testimony must be treated in view of the actual circumstances and relations between persons in the Apostolic community—another point often overlooked. When, e.g., it is argued, as by Weizsäcker [1] that, when the author of the Acts makes St. Peter say, " We ate and drank with Him after He rose from the dead," [2] he employs a mode of representing the Risen Christ impossible to St. Paul, it has to be asked whether St. Luke, who accompanied St. Paul for so many years, would have ventured to put into the mouths of St. Peter and of St. Paul himself [3] such speeches as are found in Acts, if they had been wholly alien to the Apostles' belief and testimony.[4] We are brought here, in short, to the alternative : either narratives of the kind must be dismissed as wilful fiction, for unconscious legend is impossible in face of the knowledge which the Church possessed of its own beginnings ; or if they are allowed to rest on original authentic tradition, they can leave no doubt upon the mind that Jesus was believed to

[1] *Apost. Age*, i. p. 10. Thus also Loisy, ii. p. 772.
[2] Acts x. 41. [3] E.g., Acts xiii. 31.
[4] Weizsäcker does not, of course, admit St. Luke's authorship of the Acts. His argument breaks down for every one who does.

have risen and to have appeared in bodily reality to His disciples.

The fact, however, as before, remains, and has now to be dealt with, that the narratives of the Resurrection appearances *are* challenged, and, line by line, point by point, the story which they tell is sought to be discredited. The grounds on which this is done are various. It is objected that the Gospels give different versions of these appearances, and that none gives *all* the appearances; that the evidence, even if allowed, is not of a kind to satisfy the demands of science—Renan, e.g., asks that the miraclé of resurrection be performed before " a commission composed of physiologists, physicists, chemists, persons accustomed to historical criticism," and be repeated as often as desired; [1] that Jesus appeared to none but His own disciples; that legends of resurrection are not uncommon, and are explicable from natural tendencies of the mind.[2] To all which it is sufficient at present to reply that

[1] *Vie de Jésus*, Introd. pp. i., ii.

[2] " Heroes," Renan declares, " do not die." " At the moment when Mohammed expired Omar issued from the tent sabre in hand, and declared he would strike off the head of any one who would dare to say that the Prophet was no more " (*Les Apôtres*, p. 3). But heroes *do* die, and the parallel is without relevance. Mohammed's followers never seriously claimed that the Prophet did not die, or had risen from the dead. There is no instance in history, apart from Christianity, of a religion established on belief in the Resurrection of its Founder. This is discussed later. Cf. chap. viii.

the evidence was not designed to satisfy scientific experts,[1] but to produce faith in those "chosen before of God,"[2] that they might be "witnesses" to others ; and that, as observed earlier, it is not here proposed to set up *a priori* demands for evidence, but to examine carefully what evidence we have, and to ask whether, with what else is known of Jesus, it is not sufficient to sustain the faith that He is risen from the dead, nay, to shut us up to that faith as the only reasonable explanation of the facts.

It is desirable to begin in this inquiry by collecting the evidence for the appearances, and considering generally the value to be attached to the same. The several appearances can then be discussed in order.

There *were*, as already said, appearances of the Risen Jesus, or what were taken to be such, to His followers. St. Paul's list in 1 Corinthians xv. 3–8 is allowed even by the most sceptical to afford unassailable testimony on this head.[3] It is further implied in the accounts, and is generally conceded, that these appearances extended over a considerable time—at least some days or weeks.

---

[1] Cf. Luke xvi. 30, 31. A mere intellectual conviction, even if produced, would have been of no avail for the end proposed. [2] Acts x. 40–1.
[3] Strauss, *New Life of Jesus*, i. p. 400. Renan, *Les Apôtres*, p. ix. Weizsäcker, *Apost. Age*, ch. i. Keim, *Jesus of Nazara*, vi. p. 279 and generally.

St. Luke states the period at " forty days." [1] " In Matthew," Strauss says, " the appearance of Jesus upon the mountain in Galilee must be supposed to have taken place long enough after the Resurrection to give time for the disciples to return back from Jerusalem to Galilee," [2] St. Paul [3] and St. John likewise assume a considerable period during which Jesus was manifested to His disciples. The chronological datum of St. Luke in Acts i. 3 must be allowed to rule the interpretation of the obviously condensed (" foreshortened ") account of the closing chapter of his Gospel. Events, as will be seen later, were there compressed which were afterwards to be narrated more in detail.

Furthermore, the witnesses to the appearances of Jesus are *many*, and all, it can be claimed, are entitled to be heard with a presumption of their honesty and credibility. Only leading points need be recalled. It was before stated that St. John is here unhesitatingly accepted as an eye-witness. St. Mark was the companion of St. Peter, St. Luke was the companion of St. Paul, and a zealous investigator on his own account. [4] St. Paul had direct communication with St. Peter, St. James, St. John, and other members of the original Apostolic company. [5]

---

[1] Acts i. 3.　　　　　　[2] *Ut supra*, ii. p. 420.
[3] Renan finds in 1 Cor. xv. 3–8 evidence of " the long duration of the appearances." Cf. Acts xiii. 31.
[4] Luke i. 1–4.
[5] Gal. i. 18, 19 ; ii. 1, 9 ; Acts ix. 26–7.

St. Matthew is believed to be connected with at least the original of his Gospel—to stand in a real way behind it. The Appendix to St. Mark is yet an unsolved problem. The fact that it appears in nearly all extant MSS. and versions [1] points to a very early date, and perhaps to a close relation with St. Mark himself. It does not seem warranted to regard it as simply a summary of incidents based on St. Luke and St. John.[2] It does not show linguistic dependence on the other Gospels ; furnishes original (Mark-like) details ; bears generally a stamp of a distinct and authentic tradition.[3]

The *amplitude* and *weight* of the evidence will best

[1] The section (chap. xvi. 9–20) is absent, as is well known, from Cod. Sin. and Cod. Vat., from Syr. Sin., from :om Armenian and Ethiopic MSS., etc. ; on the other hand. "it is supported by the vast majority of uncials," "by the cursives in a body," by all lectionaries and most versions. (Cf. art. "Mark" in Hastings' *Dict. of Bible*, iii. p. 252.) On the adverse patristic testimony, see Burgon, chap. v.

[2] Keim describes it unjustly as "a violent attempt at adjustment between Mark and Luke-John, between Galilee and Jerusalem " (vi. p. 318). The incidents in the Appendix must all have been well known in the early circles to which St. Mark (son of the Mary in whose home the Church met for worship, Acts xii. 12) belonged.

[3] Mr. Latham (*Risen Master*, pp. 202–3) is a little hard on the Appendix in fastening on its emphasis of "unbelief " (vers. 11, 16). It is precisely in St. Mark and St. Matthew that the emphasis is laid on ἀπιστία (Mark vi 6 ; ix. 24 ; Matt. xiii. 58 ; xvii. 20), St. Luke uses the verb in chap. xxiv. 11, 41. On upbraiding, cf. Luke xxiv. 25.

be seen by a survey of its particulars as furnished by these various witnesses :—

1. St. Mark breaks off at chapter xvi. 8, but in verse 7 forecasts a meeting of Jesus with the disciples in Galilee, as Jesus had foretold.[1] This is evidently the collective meeting which St. Matthew narrates.

2. St. Matthew narrates the meeting in Galilee (on " the mountain where Jesus had appointed them "),[2] but tells also of an appearance to the women on the morning of the Resurrection. The Galilean meeting, with its great Commission, " Go ye, therefore, and make disciples of all the nations," etc., is the objective of St. Matthew's Gospel, and to it he hastens without pausing on intermediate events. Yet the fact that he relates the appearance of the women (in which that to Mary Magdalene may be merged),[3] shows that the appointed meeting was not held to exclude earlier appearances.

3. St. Luke has a rich store of original tradition, confined, however, to Jerusalem and its neighbourhood. While St. Matthew concentrates on the meeting in Galilee, St. Luke is chiefly interested in the appearances on the Resurrection day and

[1] Cf. Mark xiv. 28 ; Matt. xxvi. 32. "After I am raised up I will go before you into Galilee."

[2] Matt. xxviii. 16–20. Regarding this "appointment" the Gospels are silent. Only the promise is given : "There shall ye see Him [Me]" (Matt. xxviii. 7–10 ; Mark xvi. 7).

[3] Matt. xxviii. 9, 10. Cf. John xx. 14–17.

in Jerusalem, as leading up to the promise of the Spirit, and the Ascension at Bethany. His accounts include an appearance to St. Peter,[1] the appearance to the two disciples on the way to Emmaus,[2] an appearance to the eleven in the evening [3]—these all on Easter Day—finally, a meeting, more fully reported in Acts, on the day of Ascension.[4] Nothing is said of appearances in Galilee, though ample room is left for these, if indeed they are not implied in the " forty days " of Acts i. 3.[5]

4. St. John, writing, it is to be remembered, with knowledge of the other Gospels, gives additional valuable information concerning the events of the Resurrection morning, and records, besides the appearance to Mary Magdalene in the garden, [6] an appearance to the assembled disciples that same evening,[7] another appearance to the eleven eight days after,[8] and an appearance to seven disciples some time later, at the Lake of Galilee.[9] St. John's narratives abound in minute touches which only personal knowledge could impart.

5. St. Paul's list in 1 Corinthians xi. 3–8—the earliest written testimony, and of undoubted genuineness—covers a wide area. It leaves un-

---

[1] Luke xxiv. 34. Cf. 1 Cor. xv. 5.
[2] Luke xxv. 13, 32.   [3] Vers. 33–43.
[4] Vers. 50, 51 ; cf. Acts i. 4–12.
[5] " Appearing to them by the space of forty days " (Acts i. 3).
[6] John xx. 14–17.   [7] John xx. 19–25.
[8] Vers. 26–28.   [9] John xxi. 1–14.

noticed the appearances to the women, but enumerates an appearance to St. Peter, one to the " twelve " (more strictly " the eleven ") [1] one to over five hundred brethren at once, the majority of them still living, one to St. James, and yet another to all the Apostles. To this series St. Paul adds, as of equal validity with the rest, the appearance to himself.

One point about this list is of interest in connexion with the question of " silence " in the Gospels. St. Luke was St. Paul's companion. Apart from what he must often have heard from St. Paul's own lips, he was undoubtedly familiar with this Epistle to the Corinthians, with its enumeration of appearances. Yet in his Gospel and in Acts he omits all mention of the great appearance to the five hundred brethren at once (probably to be identified with St Matthew's Galilean meeting), and of the appearance to St. James.[2] This bears also on the point of the Evangelist's supposed ignorance in his Gospel of any longer interval than a single day between the Resurrection and the Ascension.[3] How, it may be asked, was

---

[1] Professor Lake says : " ' The twelve ' is the title of a body of men who were originally twelve in number, but it had become a conventional name, and bore no necessary relation to the actual number " (p. 37).

[2] Cf. the remarks of Godet on this point in his *Com. on St. Luke*, E. T., ii. p. 363.

[3] Thus Strauss, Weizsäcker, Keim, etc., but also Meyer, Alford and others. Surely, however, it is evident of itself that St. Luke could not suppose that the journey to Beth-

this possible, in view of the explicit testimony of St. Paul, known to St. Luke, to Christ's numerous appearances ? Acts i. makes it plain that St. Luke did know.

6. Lastly, the Appendix to St. Mark contains brief notices of *three* of the above appearances— the appearance to Mary Magdalene, that to the two disciples, and an appearance to the eleven.[1] It is probable that, as in St. Luke, this one appearance to the eleven is made to stand for all, and that some of the injunctions attached to it really belong to other meetings.

In estimating the *value* of this range of testimony, the following points are of significance. It will be seen—(1) that, while certain of the appearances depend on one witness, most are doubly or even triply attested ; (2) that, while of one or two we have only brief notices, of most there are detailed accounts ; (3) that, if the narratives are at all to be trusted, they leave no room for doubt as to the Resurrection of the Lord in the body. Special weight in this connexion must be attached to the testimony of St. John and St. Paul—one a personal witness, the other basing on first-hand communications. It is of interest, accordingly, to note how large a part of the entire case is covered by the

any and the Ascension (chap. xxiv. 50, 51) took place late at night after a crowded day, and the prolonged evening meeting detailed in vers. 39–49. See next chapter.

[1] Mark xvi. 9–20.

testimony of these two. Thus St. John attests :
(1) the appearance to Mary Magdalene, whose summons brought him to the tomb ;[1] (2) *two* appearances to the eleven, at both of which he was present ;[2]
and (3) the meeting at the Lake of Galilee, at which
again he was present [3]—*four* instances out of a total
of ten. St. Paul again attests : (1) the appearance
to St. Peter ; (2) *two* appearances to the Apostles,
one coinciding with one of St. John's ; (3) the
appearance to the five hundred ; and (4) the appearance to St. James—*four* additional to St. John's,
or, between the two, *eight* appearances. A further
noteworthy result is that, with the exception of
the appearance to the women in St. Matthew,
the *singly* attested appearances are among the *best*
attested, for they are included in the above list ;
likewise the *greater* appearances, if, as is usually
assumed, the appearance to the five hundred is to
be identified with the meeting in Galilee, are, with
one exception (the appearance to the disciples on
the way to Emmaus), all included here. It will be
shown after that the Emmaus narrative, corroborated by the Appendix to St. Mark, is one of the
most credible of the series.

On the basis of this analysis, the attempt may
now be made to place the recorded appearances
in their *order*, and to exhibit the degree of attestation
that pertains to each. It is only to be borne in mind

[1] John xx. 3.   [2] Vers. 19–29.   [3] John xxi. 2.

what formerly was said, that in no case is it the design of the Evangelists to furnish *proofs* for the Resurrection.[1] Their object is simply to supply information, each in accordance with his particular aim, regarding a fact already universally believed. Each gives his own selection of incidents, and no single narrative makes any pretence to be complete.[2]

The appearances to the disciples may be arranged as follows :—

1. The appearance to Mary Magdalene (John, Appendix to Mark). According to the Marcan Appendix this appearance was the " first."

2. The appearance to the women on their way to the disciples (Matt.). The relation to (1) is considered below.

3. The appearance to St. Peter (Luke, Paul). St. Paul doubtless had the fact from St. Peter himself. St. Luke probably had it from St. Paul But it was known from the beginning.[3]

4. The appearance to the two disciples on the road to Emmaus (Luke, Appendix to Mark). St. Luke gives the detailed account.

---

[1] This should be partially qualified in the case of St. John, who does exhibit an evidential purpose (chap. xx. 31 ; xxi. 24).

[2] Each Evangelist would have been ready to endorse the concluding words in St. John: " There are also many other things which Jesus did," etc. (xxi. 5 ; cf. xx. 31).

[3] Luke xxiv. 34. St. Mark may have had this appearance in view in the words : " Go, tell His disciples and Peter " (xvi. 7).

5. The appearance to the assembled disciples in the evening (Luke, John, Paul, Appendix to Mark). The details are given in St. Luke and St. John.

These five appearances all occurred on the day of Resurrection.

6. The second appearance to the eleven, " eight days after " (John). St. John had told how, on the previous occasion, Thomas was not present. The doubt of Thomas was now removed.

7. An appearance to seven disciples at the Lake of Galilee (John).

8. The great appearance to over five hundred brethren at once (Paul). This, as above said, is probably identical with the " appointed " meeting in Galilee, when the " eleven " received their Lord's great Commission (Matt).

9. An appearance to St. James (Paul).

10. The final appearance to the eleven (Paul), identical with the meeting of Jesus with His disciples prior to His Ascension (Luke in Gospel and Acts ; Appendix to Mark).

It will be perceived from this enumeration that there were in all no fewer than *five* appearances of Jesus—half of the total number—to the Apostles, when all, or a majority, were present ; in one instance at a large gathering of over five hundred. Of the remaining instances, three were private (to Mary, St. Peter, St James) : one was to two

disciples on a journey; one was to the group of
women. St. Matthew probably introduces the last
because of the message then repeated to meet the
Lord in Galilee. St. Luke, as shown, confines himself
to the meetings in and about Jerusalem. St. Paul
dwells naturally for his purpose on the appearances
to the Apostles, including that to James, and the
meeting with the five hundred. St. John fills up
from his reminiscences what the others had left
untold—the tender scene with the Magdalene, the
second appearance to the Apostles, the appearance
to the seven in Galilee. It all seems very natural.
The pieces of the puzzle are perhaps not so hard
to put together after all.

The circumstances of the several appearances
must now be more carefully investigated, with a
view to the further elucidation of their *nature* and
reality. But, first, there are certain threads of the
Synoptical narratives which require to be gathered
up, and related to what follows.

1. Two of the Evangelists, St. Matthew and St.
Mark, agree that the women at the tomb *received
a message* to give to the disciples.[1] St. Luke does
not mention this message, yet relates: " They
returned from the tomb, and told all these things
to the eleven, and to all the rest " [2] (the implication of a wider company should be noted). In the
report of the words spoken by the angels to the

---

[1] Matt. xxviii. 7; Mark xvi. 7.   [2] Luke xxiv. 9.

women, however, there is an important variation in St. Luke, which needs consideration. In the two other Synoptics, the women are directed to tell the disciples that Jesus goes before them into Galilee, and that there they will see Him. Instead of this message, St. Luke reads : " Remember how He spake unto you when He was yet in Galilee, saying that the Son of Man must be delivered up unto the hands of sinful men and be crucified, and the third day rise again. And they remembered His words." [1] In St. Matthew, further, the words which in St. Mark appear in connexion with the direction about Galilee (" as He said unto you ")[2] are transferred to the announcement of the Resurrection (" as He said "),[3] and the angel's message closes with the statement, " Lo, I have told you." The difficulty of deriving either of these forms from the other is obvious (the word " Galilee " occurring in both should not mislead). The simple explanation seems to be that it is not the design of St. Luke to relate the appearances in Galilee (cf., however, Acts i. 3 ; " appearing to them by the space of forty days ") ; he therefore omits the part of the message bearing on this point. For the rest, Jesus did do both things there stated : (1) announce when in Galilee His approaching death and Resurrection [4] (so in Matt.), and St. Luke

[1] Luke xxiv. 6–8.   [2] Mark xvi. 7.   [3] Matt. xxviii. 6.
[4] Cf. Matt. xvi. 21 ; xvii. 9–13, etc.

simply repeats His words ; and (2) announce that He would meet His disciples in Galilee [1] (" as He said unto you," Mark). This second part St. Luke passes over.

2. In the close of his narrative of the Resurrection, St. Matthew gives *the sequel to his story of the guard* at the tomb [2] previously alluded to. Certain of the guard, hastening to the city, told the chief priests what had happened. These, after counsel with the elders, bribed the soldiers to spread the report that the disciples had stolen the body of Jesus while they (the guard) slept, promising to use their interest with Pilate to secure them from harm. This episode, as was before seen, is rejected by the critics as fabulous. Yet it is difficult to believe that a narrative so circumstantial could be simple invention,[3] or have no foundation in fact. Nor are the grounds alleged adequate to sustain this view of it. The central point in the story— the charge of stealing the body—is evidently historical. It is given as a current report when the Gospel was written,[4] and is independently attested.[5]

---

[1] Matt. xxvi. 32 ; Mark xiv. 28.

[2] Matt. xxvii. 11–15. Cf. chap. xxvii. 62–66.

[3] Professor Lake thinks that the episode has " neither intrinsic nor traditional probability." It is, in his view, " nothing more than a fragment of controversy " between Jews and Gentiles, " in which each imputed unworthy motives to the other, and stated suggestions as established fact " (p. 180).   [4] Matt. xxviii. 15.

[5] Justin Martyr, *Dialogue with Trypho*, 108 ; Tertullian, *On Spectacles*, 30.

As giving the Jewish version of the Resurrection, it has value as a left-hand testimony to the fact of the grave being found empty. When it is asked, Is it likely that the soldiers should accept a bribe to plead guilty to a military offence—sleeping on duty— which was punishable by death ? [1] it is overlooked that the breach of discipline had already been committed in their flight from the tomb, and admission that the tomb was open and the body gone. The theft by the disciples was only a pretext to cover an event which both soldiers and priests were aware had really a more marvellous character. The case would be presented in a truer light to Pilate, and the soldiers screened. It was probably from some of the guards themselves—led, like the centurion, to say, "Truly this man was the Son of God," [2]—that the facts were ascertained.[3]

This leads to the consideration of the distinct appearances.

1. Little use has up to this point been made of the testimony of St. John. It is now necessary to consider that testimony in its relation to the Synoptics, as embodying the narrative of the first of our Lord's recorded appearances—that to *Mary Mag-*

[1] Lake, p. 178.   [2] Mark xv. 39.

[3] Dr. Forrest, in his *Christ of History and Experience*, says : This "incident related by Matthew . . . though it is not corroborated in any of the other Gospels, has, I think, every mark of probability " (p. 145). Cf. Alford on Matt. xxvii. 62–66.

dalene.[1]   St. John has the supreme qualification as a witness that he himself was *magna pars* in the transactions he records.   His narrative has an autoptic character.   Part of its design apparently is to give greater precision to certain events which the other Gospels had more or less generalized.   It is a piece of testimony of the first importance.

In the story of the appearance to Mary Magdalene, St. John so far goes with the Synoptics that he tells how Mary Magdalene came in the early morning to the tomb of Jesus, and found the stone taken away.[2]   Mention is not made of companions, but probably at least one other is implied in Mary's words : " They have taken away the Lord out of the tomb, and *we* know not where they have laid Him." [3]   The same words may suggest that, either by her own inspection or that of others, Mary had ascertained that the tomb was empty—not simply open.

But here St. John diverges.   We learn from him how, concluding that the body had been removed, Mary at once ran to carry the news to St. Peter and St. John.   It was still very early, and the disciples had to be sought for in their private—perhaps separate—lodgings (ver. 10).   Aroused by her tale, they lost not a moment in hastening to the

---

[1] John xx. 11–18.
[2] Ver. 1.   [3] Ver. 2.

spot.[1] St. John—for he only can be meant by
" the other disciple "[2]—outran St. Peter, and coming first to the tomb, stooped and looked in, and
saw (βλέπει) the linen cloths (ὀθόνια) lying, but
did not go farther. St. Peter followed, but, with
characteristic energy, at once entered, and beheld
(θεωρεῖ, implying careful note), not simply the
disposition of the cloths, but the peculiarity of the
napkin for the head lying rolled up in a place by
itself.[3] St. John then found courage to enter, and
" having seen, believed."[4] It is a weakening of
this expression to suppose it to mean simply, " believed that the tomb was empty." Both disciples
believed this. But with a flash of true discernment
St. John grasped the significance of what he saw,
viz., that Jesus had risen—a truth to which the
Scriptures had not yet led him.[5] St. Peter, it is
implied, though wondering,[6] had still not attained
to this confidence. The two disciples then returned
home.[7]

Meanwhile Mary Magdalene had come back, and
was " standing without at the tomb weeping."[8]
Afterwards she too stooped and looked into the

---

[1] Ver. 3–10. [2] Vers. 2, 3, 8.
[3] Ver. 7. Mr. Latham's ingenious reasoning from the
disposition of the grave-cloths to the manner of the Resurrection should be studied in his *Risen Master*, chaps. i–iii.
[4] Ver. 8. [5] Ver. 9.
[6] Cf. Luke xxii. 12, below.
[7] Ver. 10. [8] Ver. 11.

tomb, and had, like the other women, a " vision of angels "—in her case " two angels in white raiment," one at the head, the other at the foot, of the ledge or slab where the body of Jesus had lain.[1] Then came the meeting with the Lord described in the succeeding verses. At first Mary took the person who addressed her for the gardener, and besought him, if it was he who had borne away her Lord from the tomb, to tell her where he had laid Him.[2] Little trace here of the *hallucinée*, whose passion, according to Renan, " gave to the world a resuscitated god."[3] Christ's tender word " Mary " illuminated her at once as to who He was, and with the exclamation " Rabboni," she would have clasped Him, had He permitted her.

The words with which the Risen Lord in this interview gently checked the movement of Mary at once to worship and to detain Him—to hold Him, now restored to her, as if never more to let Him go—have been the subject of sufficiently diverse interpretations. " Touch me not " ($\mu\acute{\eta} \mu o\upsilon \ \acute{a}\pi\tau o\upsilon$; R.V. marg., " Take not hold on Me "), Jesus said, " for I am not yet ascended unto My Father ; but go unto My brethren, and say to them, I ascend unto My Father and your Father, and My God and your God." [4] The meaning that lies on the surface is : " Do not hold me now, for I am not yet ascended

---

[1] Vers. 11–13, see the plates of the tomb in Latham,
[2] Ver. 15.   [3] *Vie de Jésus*, p. 434.   [4] Ver. 17.

unto My Father, but go at once unto My brethren,"
etc. But the terms of the message to the brethren
(" Say unto them, I ascend," etc.) show that a
deeper reason lay behind. " Tell them," its purport is, " that I am risen ; the same, yet entered on
a higher (the Ascension) life, in which old relations
cannot be renewed, but better ones begin." [1]

If this striking narrative of St. John stood alone,
it would be sufficiently attested, but it is corroborated by two notices which probably are independent of it. The Appendix to St. Mark tells of the
early morning appearance to Mary Magdalene ; [2]
St. Luke records the visit of St. Peter to the tomb,
in language closely resembling St. John's, with an
indication later that he was not alone. St. Luke
xxiv. 12, reads : " But Peter arose and ran into
the tomb ; and stooping and looking in, he seeth
(βλέπει) the linen cloths (ὀθόνια) by themselves,
and he departed to his home, wondering at
that which was come to pass." In verse 24, the
disciples journeying to Emmaus say : " And certain of them that were with us went to the tomb,
and found it even as the women had said : but

---

[1] The chief interpretations of the passage can be seen
in Godet, *Com. on St. John*, iii. pp. 311–13, and in Latham,
ut supra, pp. 419–20. Godet takes it to mean : " I have
not reached the state in which I shall be able to live with
you in the communion I promised you " (p. 311).

[2] On the supposed dependence on St. John, cf. remark
above.

Him they saw not." [1]   On the ground of its absence
from certain Western texts, the former passage (ver.
12) is regarded by textual critics with suspicion.[2]
This doubt does not attach to verse 24, which plainly
has in view the visit described by St. John.   Its
genuineness, in turn, supports that of verse 12,
where St. Peter only is mentioned.   It may reasonably be supposed that St. John, in his fuller narrative,
has the aim of rectifying a certain inexactitude in
St. Luke's summary account.   St. Luke, e.g.,
speaks of St. Peter, at the tomb, as " stooping and
looking in."   St. John, the disciple who accompanied
St. Peter, explains that, while this was true of himself (cf. chap. xx. 5), St. Peter did more, actually
entering the tomb and inspecting the contents.
In his consecutive account, he makes clear also the
precise time of this visit.

2. At this point a question of some nicety arises
as to the relation of this appearance to Mary Magdalene, and *the appearance to the women recorded*
in St. Matthew xxviii. 9, 10, which stands next upon
our list.   Are these appearances different ?   Or

---

[1] Meyer remarks : " Of the ' other disciple ' of John
xx. 3, Luke says nothing, but, according to ver. 24, does
not exclude him " (*Com. in loc.*).

[2] The preponderance of early MSS. authority sustains
the passage.   Godet, who, in his *Com. on St. Luke* (ii. p. 352)
upholds the genuineness, treats it in his *Com. on St. John*
(iii. p. 308) as " a gloss borrowed from St. John."   Had
it been so, it would surely have avoided the appearance
of contradiction !

is the second (that in Matthew) merely a generalized form of the first (that in John)? The latter
is the view taken by many scholars.[1] In favour
of it is the fact that only two women, Mary Magdalene and the other Mary, are mentioned in St.
Matthew's narrative.[2] We know, however, that
there were other women present, and there is a
marked contrast in the circumstances in the two
narratives. The women in St. Matthew are already
on their way to tell the disciples; they hold
Jesus by the feet, and are apparently unrebuked
(the act was *only* one of worship); the message, too, is different. The appearance to Mary
may well be grouped (probably is) with that of
the other women; it is not so easy to identify the
latter with Mary's solitary experience. If, on the
other hand, the appearances are taken to be distinct, a difficulty arises as to the order of time.
The appearance to the women coming from the
tomb would now seem to claim precedence over
that to Mary, who had in the interval gone to
Jerusalem and had returned. There is nothing
absolutely to preclude this, if the note of order
in the Appendix to St. Mark ("appeared first to
Mary Magdalene") be surrendered. Some, accordingly, do place the appearance to the other women
first.[3]

---

[1] E.g., Ebrard, Godet, Alford, Swete.   [2] Ver. 1.
[3] E.g., Milligan, *The Resur. of our Lord*, pp. 259–60.

But even on the ordinarily received view that the appearance to Mary Magdalene was the prior, the problem, when the circumstances are fairly considered, does not seem insoluble. Both appearances took place in early morning, with at most an hour or two between them. The disciples, mostly lodging apart—in Jerusalem,[1] in Bethany, elsewhere [2]—could not be convened till later. The women, after their first hurried flight (cf. Mark xvi. 8) must have paused to regain their self-possession, to confer with one another on what they had seen and heard, to consider how they should proceed in conveying their tidings to the still scattered disciples. In such a pause, their hearts aflame with love and holy desire, Jesus, who a little earlier had made Himself known to Mary in the garden, appeared to them. Even before He approached a single Apostle, He disclosed Himself to this company of faithful hearts. His " All hail ! " and the renewed commission to the disciples sealed the message at the tomb.

It is not unlikely that, before long, on her way back to the city, Mary Magdalene joined her sisters, and that, after interchange of experiences, the errand to the disciples was undertaken by the women together. Keen indeed must have been the chill to their enthusiasm at the reception their message

[1] As St. Peter and St. John above.
[2] Two were from Emmaus.

met with when they did deliver it. Their words received no credence : were treated as " idle talk." [1] That the tomb was found empty, the Apostles did not dispute ; but stories of visions of angels and appearances of Jesus they refused to accept. There was astonishment, but not belief. Yet it is this sceptical circle, antipathetic to visionary experiences, in which belief in the Resurrection is supposed spontaneously to have arisen through visions of their own.

3. It must have been still early on this eventful day, probably soon after the Apostle's visit to the tomb, and while he was still brooding on what had happened, that the third appearance of Jesus took place—*the appearance to St. Peter*, attested by both St. Paul [2] and St. Luke. [3] The critics, as will be found, transfer this appearance from Jerusalem to Galilee, but without a shadow of a valid reason. It was in harmony with the tender, considerate spirit displayed by Jesus in all these manifestations that such an appearance should be granted, so soon after the Resurrection, to the disciple who had denied, yet who so devotedly loved Him—whom He Himself had named the " Rock." [4] Like the appearance to St. James at a later period, the meeting was entirely private. It can only be

---

[1] Luke xxiv. 10, 11, 22, 23. Cf. Mark xvi. 9–11.
[2] 1 Cor. xv. 5.   [3] Luke xxiv. 34.
[4] Matt. xvi. 18 ; John i. 42.

conjectured how, with another look, reproachful perhaps, but gracious and forgiving, the memory was banished of that look turned upon St. Peter in the High Priest's palace, which had overwhelmed him with such sorrow.[1] The great stone was now rolled away from his heart, as before the stone had been rolled from the tomb. The transformation which this appearance of Christ wrought in the Apostle is reflected in the excitement which the report of it created in the circle of the disciples. " The Lord hath risen indeed and hath appeared to Simon." [2] The disciples might disbelieve the women ; they could not doubt the reality of the experience of St. Peter. The " conversion " which Jesus had predicted was realized, and thereafter the Apostle was to " strengthen " his brethren.[3]

4. As it is with the appearance to St. Peter, so it is with the other appearance which may be associated with this, as of the same private order—the *appearance to St. James.*[4]

It is among the latest of the appearances, as that to Peter is among the earliest. With regard to both,

---

[1] Luke xxii. 61.

[2] Luke xxiv. 34. Prof. Lake thinks it " uncertain " whether Simon Peter or another is intended in this passage —a characteristic excess of scepticism. He cannot believe that St. Luke has in view the appearance to Cephas referred to by St. Paul. He prefers, " with the courage of despair," as he calls it, to " think that St. Luke himself did not write " the passage (pp. 101–3).

[3] Luke xxii. 32.   [4] 1 Cor. xv. 7.

while the facts are well-attested, no particulars are given. It is not doubted that the person intended in St. Paul's notice is the well-known James, the " brother of the Lord." [1] This of itself explains much. James, so far as is known, was not a believer in Jesus up to the time of the Crucifixion.[2] Yet immediately after the Ascension, he, and the other brethren of Jesus, are found in the company of the disciples.[3] Thereafter he became a " pillar " [4]—finally the chief personage—in the Church at Jerusalem.[5] He ranked with the Apostles.[6] What could explain such a change, save that, like the other Apostles, he had " seen the Lord ? " [7] Christ's appearance to St. James was not simply His revelation to His own family—His kinsfolk according to the flesh—but was the qualification for lifelong Apostolic service. St. James exercised an authority at Jerusalem hardly second to that of St. Paul among the Churches of the Gentiles.

The remaining appearances will introduce us to the problems connected with the nature of the Resurrection body of the Lord.[8]

[1] Gal. i. 19. Cf. Matt. xiii. 35 ; Mark vi. 3.
[2] Cf. John vii. 5.   [3] Acts i. 14.   [4] Gal. iii. 9.
[5] Acts xii. 17 ; xv. 13 ; xxi. 18.
[6] Gal. i. 19 ; ii. 9 ; 1 Cor. ix. 5.   [7] Cf. 1 Cor. ix. 1.
[8] Cf. Hegisippus in Eusebius, *Ecc. Hist.*, ii. 23. There is a legend about St. James in the *Gospel according to the Hebrews* (cf. Westcott, *Introd. to Gospels*, p. 463 ; Lightfoot, *Galatians*, p. 274), to which, however, little, if any, weight can be attached. Apocryphal ideas will be considered later.

THE SIGNIFICANCE OF THE APPEAR-
ANCES—THE RISEN BODY

VII

THE SIGNIFICANCE OF THE APPEARANCES —THE RISEN BODY

THE appearances of Jesus already considered—those, viz., to Mary Magdalene, to the women, to St. Peter, on the day of Resurrection, and that to St. James later—were all of a private or semi-private nature. Isolated, under varying conditions, designed for personal comfort and confirmation, taking place well-nigh simultaneously, the manifestations to one and another on the Resurrection day afforded no room for self-deception, or for collusion, or the contagious action of sympathy. It would seem as if, on this first day, by manifestations to individuals chosen for their peculiar receptiveness or representative character, Jesus desired to lay a broad basis for certainty in His Rising, before He appeared to His disciples as a body.

Another example of this semi-private form of manifestation to which attention must now be directed was the appearance of Jesus to *the two disciples on their way to Emmaus*, the full account

of which is furnished by St. Luke.[1] The name
of only one of these favoured disciples is given—
Cleopas :[2] otherwise both are unknown. Chosen
for this honour as representatives of the wider circle
of disciples, doubtless also for the susceptibility
discerned in them for the reception of Christ's
communications, they form a link with the general
Apostolic company. From it they had just come,
after hearing the reports of certain of the women
and of others who had visited the tomb,[3] and to
it they returned after their own meeting with
Jesus, to find the company in excitement at the
news of the Lord's appearance to St. Peter, and to
witness another appearance of the Master.[4] Theirs
was the singular privilege, shared, so far as is
known, by St. Peter only, of beholding the Risen
Lord twice on one day !

The story of St. Luke is simple and direct, with
every internal mark of truthfulness. The disciples were on their way to Emmaus, a village
about two hours' walk from Jerusalem,[5] when
Jesus overtook them, and questioned them as to
the nature of their communings. Their inability
to recognize Him is explained by the statement :
" Their eyes were holden that they should not
know Him."[6] Their simple recital of the events of

---

[1] Luke xxiv. 12–35.   [2] Ver. 18.   [3] Vers. 22–24.
[4] Vers. 34–36.
[5] Ver. 13 ; cf. Josephus, *Jewish War*, vii. 6, 6.   [6] Ver. 16.

the past few days and expression of their disappointed hopes—" We hoped that it was He who should redeem Israel "[1]—with their mention of the women's tale of the " vision of angels, who said that He was alive," [2] gave Jesus the opportunity of reproving their unbelief, and of expounding to them in His own way the meaning of the Scriptures regarding Himself.[3] As the day was closing, they constrained Jesus to abide with them ; then, at the evening meal, as Jesus blessed and brake the bread, and gave it to them, " their eyes were opened and they knew Him ; and He vanished out of their sight." [4] Recalling how their hearts had burned within them as He opened to them the Scriptures, they hastily rose, and returned at once to Jerusalem.[5] According to the Appendix to St. Mark, their testimony, like that of the women earlier, was not at first believed [6]—a fact very credible when the strangeness of their story, and the difficulty of harmonizing the appearance at Emmaus with

---

[1] Ver. 21.   [2] Ver. 23.

[3] Vers. 25–27. The Lord's exposition of the Scriptures here and later (vers. 44–46) may have turned on the sufferings and fate of righteous men and prophets in all ages, and on the predictions of the future triumph and glory of the Sufferer in Ps. xxii. (vers. 22–31), and Is. liii. Psalms like the 16th and prophecies like Zech. xiii. would also have place (cf. Hengstenberg, *Christologie*, iv. App. iv.).

[4] Vers. 30–31.   [5] Vers. 32–33.

[6] Mark xvi. 12, 13.

that to St. Peter at Jerusalem, are considered.[1] It is apparent from many parts of his Gospel that St. Luke had access to a Jerusalem tradition of primitive origin and high value, and this narrative, which probably took shape at the time from the report of the disciples,[2] is, in its clear, straightforward character, evidently one of the best preserved parts of that tradition. Critics, accordingly, while of course rejecting its testimony to the bodily appearance of Jesus, commonly treat the Emmaus narrative with considerable respect. As examples, Renan, after his manner, takes the picturesque story simply as it stands, transforming the stranger into "a pious man well versed in the Scriptures," whose gesture in the breaking of bread at the evening repast vividly recalled Jesus, and plunged the disciples into tender thoughts. When they awoke from their reverie, the stranger was gone.[3] A. Meyer sees in the appearance to Simon and the naming of Cleopas and Emmaus evidence that St. Luke's source contained "valuable old material." His

[1] It is told in Luke xxiv. 41 that, even when the Lord Himself appeared among them, the Apostles and disciples "disbelieved for joy."

[2] Cf. Latham, *The Risen Master*, pp. 135–7.

[3] *Les Apôtres*, pp. 18–21. Renan's descrption is characteristic. "How often had they not seen their beloved Master, in that hour, forget the burden of the day, and, in the abandon of gay conversation, and enlivened by several sips of excellent wine, speak to them of the fruit of the vine," etc. (p. 11).

chief objection is that St. Paul does not mention an incident which, if true, must have been " of price-less significance as a proof of the Resurrection." [1] Professor Lake allows that the story " reads as though it were based on fact," and thinks it " is probably a genuine remnant of the original tradition of the Church at Jerusalem, which has suffered a little in the process of transmission." [2] It is supposed to preserve a recollection of appearances in the neighbourhood of Jerusalem, afterwards woven into connexion with the Apostles (thus also A. Meyer). The reference to the appearance to Simon, assumed to be Galilean, is excised. [3] Against these arbitrary conjectures, the simplicity and direct-ness of the narrative—its " air of reality "—suffi-ciently speak. [4]

The real points of difficulty in the narrative are those which touch on the mystery of the Lord's Re-surrection body. Such are (1) His non-recognition by the disciples through " their eyes " being " holden " (or, as in the Appendix to St. Mark, His appearance to them " in another form " [5]) ; (2) His vanishing from their sight at the table ; (3) His appearing on the same evening at Jerusalem. These points are

---

[1] *Die Auferstehung Christi*, pp. 132–3.
[2] *Res. of Jesus Christ*, pp. 218–19.
[3] Ibid. pp. 103, 219.
[4] On general objections to the narrative cf. Loof's *Die Auferstehungsberichte und ihr Wert*, pp. 27–8.
[5] Mark xvi. 12.

better held over till all the facts of a similar nature are in view.

The time had now arrived when these private appearances of Jesus were to give place to His more public manifestations of Himself to His disciples. Accordingly, still on the Resurrection-evening, and in connexion with the visit of the Emmaus disciples just described, we come to the *first* in order of the important series of *the appearances of the Lord to His assembled Apostles.* This, as in a marked degree typical, will repay careful study.

1. The witnesses to this *first appearance to the Apostles* are St. Luke [1] and St. John,[2] supported by St. Paul.[3] The story, in St. Luke, is the continuation of the Emmaus narrative ; in St. John it is a distinct episode, and furnishes in its commencement the important detail that, when Jesus appeared, " the doors were shut where the disciples were, for fear of the Jews." [4] This makes more emphatic the marvel of Christ's sudden appearance in the midst of the disciples, which yet is implied in both narratives. " Jesus," St. Luke says, " Himself stood ($\mathring{\epsilon}\sigma\tau\eta$) in the midst of them." [5] St. John speaks similarly : " Jesus came and stood in the midst." [6] This practical identity of lan-

---

[1] Luke xxiv. 36–43.   [2] John xx. 19–23.
[3] I Cor. xv. 5.   [4] John xx. 19.
[5] Luke xxiv. 36.   [6] John xx. 19.

guage in an undoubted part of the text should predispose us to consider favourably the two succeeding clauses in St. Luke, likewise identical with, or closely akin to St. John's, on which doubt is cast by their absence from some Western texts. They are these : (1) Ver. 36 reads, as in St. John [1] : " And saith unto them, Peace be unto you." (2) Ver. 40 reads : " And when He had said this, He showed them His hands and His feet," where St. John has : " And when He had said this He showed unto them His hands and His side." [2] The passages are here accepted as genuine ; [3] but whether expressed or not, the showing of the hands and the feet in the latter is implied in St. Luke's preceding words : " See My hands and My feet," etc.[4]

Up to a certain point, therefore, the two narratives agree almost verbally. That of St. John an immediate witness, confirms that of St. Luke and with it supports the authenticity of St. Luke's narrative generally. The astonishment and doubt which the Lord's sudden appearance occasioned

[1] John xx. 19.　　[2] John xx. 20.
[3] Alford's notes may be quoted. On ver. 36 : "Possibly from John ; but as the whole is nearly related to that narrative, and the authority for the omission weak, Tischendorf is certainly not justified in expunging it." On ver. 40 : "Had this been interpolated from St. John, we certainly should have found ' feet ' altered by some to ' side,' either here only, or in ver. 39 also." The R.V. retains both clauses in the text.
[4] Luke xxiv. 39.

is reflected in both. St. Luke's language is the more vivid. " They were terrified and affrighted, and supposed that they beheld a spirit." [1] Even after the Lord's reassurances, and His invitation, " Handle Me, and see : for a spirit hath not flesh and bones, as ye behold Me having," it is declared, " They still disbelieved for joy, and wondered." [2] The removal of doubt is implied in St. John in Christ's showing of His hands and His side, and the " joy " is corroborated in the words : " The disciples therefore were glad when they saw the Lord." [3] The whole account is psychologically most natural, and sheds vivid light by contrast on the theories which see the origin of belief in the Resurrection in an eager credulity and proneness to mistake hallucinations for reality on the part of the Apostles.

At this point St. Luke and St. John part company, each giving an incident not related by the other. St. Luke tells how, at His own request, the disciples gave Jesus a piece of a broiled fish [the words "and of a honey-comb " are doubtful] and He " ate before them " [4] (a like " eating " seems implied in the later scene in St. John at the Lake of Galilee).[5] St. John, on the other hand, tells of a renewed commission to the Apostles, and of how Jesus " breathed on them, and said unto them,

[1] Ver. 37.   [2] Ver. 41.   [3] John xx. 20.
[4] Luke xxiv. 43.   [5] John xxi. 4–13.

Receive ye [the] Holy Spirit. Whosesoever sins
ye forgive, they are forgiven unto them ; whosesoever sins ye retain, they are retained." [1] Into
the controversies connected with these solemn
words, this is not the place to enter. It may be
that here, as elsewhere, Jesus is contemplating the
existence of a spiritual Society, and is investing
His Apostles with disciplinary authority to deal
with sins which affect the standing of members
in that Society.[2] Or the deeper thought may be
that the remission or retention of sins is bound up
ipso facto with the reception or rejection of the
message which He commits to the Apostles to bear.
Whatever the nature of the authority, the text
makes plain that its exercise is conditioned by
the possession of the Holy Spirit. It is not necessary to assume that the actual imparting of the
Spirit was delayed till Pentecost. The act of
breathing and the words used by Jesus imply that
the Spirit was *then* given in a measure, if not in the
fulness of the later affusion.[3] St. John, too, knew
that the Spirit was not given till Christ was glorified.[4]

In this incident, as in the earlier appearances,
while proof is given of the reality of Christ's risen

[1] John xx. 21–3.
[2] Cf. Matt. xviii. 17, 18. See also Latham, *ut supra*,
pp. 168–74.
[3] " Arrha Pentecostes " (Bengel). " That preparatory
communication, that anticipatory Pentecost " (Godet).
[4] John vii. 39.

body, and of its identity with the body that was
crucified and buried, not less plain evidence is
afforded of the changed conditions under which
that body now existed. The fact is meanwhile,
again, only noted. When, however, the critics
import into these narratives a contradiction with
St. Paul's conception of Christ's Resurrection
body,[1] and, to heighten the variance, arbitrarily
transfer the appearance to "the twelve" mentioned by St. Paul in 1 Cor. xv. 5, to Galilee,
it must be pointed out that they not only break
with a sound Jerusalem tradition, of which the
Apostle must have been perfectly aware, but assert
what, on the face of it, is an incredibility. What
motive or occasion can be suggested for a convening
of "the twelve" (or eleven) in Galilee to receive
an appearance?[2] And how difficult to conceive
of the simultaneous experience of such a vision
by a band of men so brought together! Better
with A. Meyer, to cast doubt on the appearance
altogether.[3]

[1] Thus Henson (*Hibbert Journal*, 1903–4, pp. 476–93,
Weizsäcker, A. Meyer, Loisy (*Les Evangiles*, ii. p. 772),
etc. On the other hand, cf. Loofs, *ut supra*, pp. 27–9, 33.

[2] According to Loisy, it was St. Peter, who had one
day seen Jesus when fishing on the Lake of Tiberias (see
below), who "no doubt [!] gathered the eleven, and kindled
with his ardour their wavering faith" (ii. p. 224).

[3] *Ut supra*, p. 139. After disposing of all details, Meyer
concludes that there is a "kernel" of truth in the story
The vision theory is discussed in next chapter.

2. Eight days after this first appearance—St. John here again being witness—*a second appearance of Jesus to the Apostles* took place in the same chamber, and under the like conditions ("the doors being shut").[1] The peculiar feature of this second meeting was the removal of the doubt of St. Thomas, who, it is related, had not been present on the earlier occasion.[2] St. Thomas, in a spirit which the "modern" mind should appreciate, refused to believe in so extraordinary a fact as the Resurrection of the Lord in the body on the mere report of others, and demanded indubitable sensible evidence of the miracle for himself. "Except I shall see in His hands the print of the nails, and put my finger into the print of the nails, and put my hand into His side, I will not believe."[3] Graciously, at this second appearance, Jesus gave the doubting Apostle the evidence he asked—"Reach hither thy hand,"[4] etc.—though, as the event proved, the sign was not needed. The faith of the disciple was greater than he thought, and the sight and words of Jesus sufficed, without actual examination, to bring him to his Lord's feet in adoring acknowledgment. The love and reverence that lay beneath his doubts came in a surge of instantaneous devotion to the surface: "My Lord and my God."[5] Yet, as Jesus reminded him, there is a higher faith still

[1] John xix. 24–9   [2] John xx. 24.   [3] Ver. 25.
[4] Ver. 27.   [5] Ver. 28.

—that which does not need even seeing, but apprehends intuitively that in the nature of the case nothing else could be true of One in whom the Eternal Life was revealed. " Because thou hast seen Me, thou hast believed ; blessed are they that have not seen, and yet have believed." [1]

The confidence instinctively awakened by this striking narrative of the Lord's treatment of a doubting spirit is not disturbed by the inability that may be felt to explain why the Apostles should still be at Jerusalem a whole week after they had received the direction to meet the Lord in Galilee. Various reasons might be suggested for the delay. It appears from St. Matthew that place and time of the Galilean meeting were definitely " appointed." [2] There was therefore no need for departure till the time drew near. It was, besides, the week of the Passover feast, and there was urgent cause why the Apostles, in the new circumstances that had arisen, should remain at Jerusalem to bear their own testimony, allay doubts, meet inquirers, check false rumours and calumnies. [3] When they did journey northwards it would probably still be in company. The departure may well have taken place in the course of the week succeeding that renewed appearance of Jesus on the eighth day. Very significant must

[1] Ver. 29.   [2] Matt. xxviii. 18.
[3] Godet suggests as a reason " the obstinacy of Thomas " (St. John, iii. pp. 319, 339).

that second meeting on " the first day of the week "—
the anniversary of the Rising—have been felt by
the disciples to be! It consecrated it for them
anew as " the Lord's Day " ! [1]

3. In harmony with this view of the succession
of events, the scene of manifestation is now transferred to Galilee, and *the third appearance* of the Lord
to His disciples takes place, as recorded in St. John
xxi, on the shore of the Lake of Galilee (" Sea of
Tiberias ").[2] The chapter (xxi.) is a supplement
to the rest of the Gospel, but is so evidently
Johannine in character that, with the exception
of the endorsement in verses 24-5, it may safely
be accepted as from the pen of the beloved disciple.[3]
Seven disciples were present on this occasion, of
whom five are named (" Simon Peter, Thomas,
Nathanael, the Sons of Zebedee "). [4] All five are
Apostles, if, as is probable, Nathanael is to be
identified with Bartholomew. This creates the likelihood that " the two other of His disciples " were
Apostles also—unnamed, perhaps, as Luthardt
suggests,[5] because not elsewhere mentioned in the

[1] Rev. i. 10.   [2] John xxi. 1.
[3] " Some (e.g. Zahn) prefer to take the chapter as the
work of a disciple, or disciples, of St. John. But style,
allusions, marks of eye-witness speak to its being from
the same hand as the rest of the Gospel (thus Lightfoot,
Meyer, Godet, Alford, etc.). The attestation (ver. 24),
covers this chapter equally with the others. The Gospel
never circulated without it.
[4] Ver. 2.   [5] *Com. on St. John*, iii. p. 358.

186 SIGNIFICANCE OF APPEARANCES

Gospel. At every point the life-like touches in the story attest the writer as an eye-witness. The disciples had spent a night of fruitless toil in fishing. At break of day, Jesus appeared to them on the shore, and, as yet unrecognized, bade them cast their net on the right side of the boat.[1] The unprecedented draught of fishes which rewarded their effort revealed at once to St. John the presence of the Lord. " It is the Lord," he said.[2] St. Peter, on hearing the words, girt his fisher's coat about him (" for he was naked "), and cast himself into the sea, while the others dragged the net to shore.[3] Arrived there, they found a fire of coals, with fish laid on it, and bread ; after other fish had been brought, Jesus invited them to eat, and with His own hand distributed the bread and the fish.[4] It is remarked that, whilst the disciples now knew it was the Lord, none durst inquire of Him, " Who art Thou ? "[5] It seems implied, though it is not directly stated, that Jesus Himself shared in the meal. The scene that followed of St. Peter's reinstatement (the three-fold question, answering to the three-fold denial, with its subtle play on the word " lovest,"[6] St. Peter's replies, Christ's " Feed My lambs," " Feed My sheep ") is familiar to every reader of Scripture.[7]

It need hardly be said, that, with all its delicate

[1] Ver. 4.   [2] Ver. 7.   [3] Vers. 7, 8.
[4] Vers. 9–13.   [5] Ver. 12.
[6] ἀγαπᾷς (vers. 15, 16) ; φιλεῖς (ver. 17). St. Peter uses φιλῶ.   [7] Vers. 15–19.

marks of truth, this narrative of the Fourth Gospel meets with short shrift at the hands of the critics. Its symbolical character is thought to rob it of all claim to historicity. The theories propounded regarding it are as various as the minds that conceive them. One curious speculation, adopted by Harnack,[1] is that St. John xxi. represents the lost ending of St. Mark. Professor Lake thinks that " there is certainly not a little to be said for this hypothesis."[2] In reality it has *nothing* in its favour, beyond the probability that the lost section of St. Mark contained the account of some appear-ance in Galilee.[3] Most take the first part of the chapter to be a version, with adaptations, of St. Luke's story of the miraculous draught of fishes. Strauss sees in it a combination of this "legend " in St. Luke with that of St. Peter walking on the sea.[4] Only in this case St. Peter does *not* walk on the sea. The newest tendency is to find in it a reminiscence of the appearance of Jesus to St. Peter, transferred to the Lake of Galilee.[5] The second

---

[1] *Chronologie*, i. pp. 696 ff.   Harnack follows Rohrbach. Others see the lost conclusion of St. Mark behind Matt. xxviii. 16–20.

[2] *Ut supra*, p. 143.

[3] As already said, style, names (Nathanael, Cana in Galilee, Didymus, etc.), and whole cast of the narrative speak for Johannine authorship and rebut this Marcan theory.   [4] *New Life of Jesus*, ii. pp. 131–2.

[5] Thus, e.g. Loisy : " He [St. Peter] had seen Jesus one day in the dawn when fishing on the Lake of Tiberias," etc. (*ut supra*, p. 224).

part of the story Renan accounts for by " dreams."
(" One day Peter, dreaming, believed that he heard
Jesus ask him, ' Lovest thou Me ? ' " [1]) : most
regard it as a free invention. [2] In these hypotheses
it is the imagination of the critics, not that of the
Evangelist, that is active. It is enough here to
oppose to them, conflicting and mutually destructive
in themselves, the direct and satisfying testimony
of the disciple who was *there*. It is, no doubt, a
miracle that is recorded—one of the " providential "
order—but the resemblance with that in St. Luke
begins and ends with the fact that it is a draught
of fishes. Circumstances and connexion are totally
different. In a symbolical respect it may well have
been designed as a reminder and renewal of the call
originally given, and a confirmation, suitable to
this period of new commissions, of the pledge which
accompanied that call : " From henceforth thou
shalt catch men."[3]

Noteworthy in this narrative, as in the preceding,
is the combination in Christ's Resurrection body
of seemingly opposite characters ; on the one hand,
mysterious (supernatural) traits, veiling recognition, and exciting awe in the beholders ; on the
other, attributes and functions which attest its full

[1] *Les Apôtres*, pp. 33–34.
[2] Keim takes this view of the whole chapter (*Jesus of
Nazara*, vi. pp. 314–18).
[3] Luke v. 10.

physical reality, and identity with the body that was crucified.

4. Chief among the appearances of Jesus after His Resurrection is unquestionably to be ranked the great meeting *on the mountain in Galilee*, of which St. Matthew alone preserves the record. [1] St. Matthew's testimony, however, is not wholly without corroboration. It is commonly assumed that St. Mark also had intended to give some account of this meeting, [2] which is usually, and no doubt correctly, identified with the appearance which St. Paul mentions " to above five hundred brethren at once, of whom the greater part remain until now." [3] St. Matthew, indeed, speaks only of " the eleven disciples " in connexion with the meeting. He does so because it is with the Commission to the Apostles he is specially concerned. But the wider scope of the gathering is already evident in his own intimations regarding it. The meeting had been in view from the day of Resurrection. The summons to it was addressed to the " disciples," [4] who are by no means to be confined to the Apostles. The place and, we must suppose, the time also, had been definitely " appointed." [5]   It was to be in " a mountain " in Galilee—a place suitable for a

[1] Matt. xxviii. 16–20.
[2] Cf. Mark xvi. 7.   [3] 1 Cor. xv. 6.
[4] Matt. xxviii. 7, 9.   In ver. 10, " brethren."
[5] Ver. 16. On whole incident, cf. Latham, *ut supra*, pp. 280–94.

general gathering. The intention, in short, was a collective meeting of disciples.

To this place, accordingly, at the appointed time, the Apostles and other disciples repaired and there, faithful to His promise, Jesus appeared to them. The expression " when they saw Him " [1] suggests some sudden appearance, while the clause " came unto them," [2] in the succeeding verse, points to approach from some little distance. In so large a company susceptibility would vary, and it is not surprising that it is on record that, when Jesus was first seen, " they worshipped Him, *but some doubted.*" [3] The statement is a testimony to the genuineness of the narrative ; it is also an indirect indication of the presence of others. [4] In the small body of the eleven there is hardly room for a " some." Whatever doubt there was would vanish when the Lord drew near and spoke.

With such a view of the Galilean meeting, objections to the genuineness of the great Commission, " Go ye, therefore, and make disciples of all the nations," etc., lose most of their force. Based as it is on the august declaration, " All authority hath been given unto Me in heaven and on earth," and culminating in the promise, " Lo, I am with you always, even unto the end of the world," [5] the

[1] Ver. 17.   [2] Ver. 18.   [3] Ibid.
[4] Cf. Latham, pp. 291–3 ; Allen, *St. Matthew*, pp. 303, 305.
[5] Cf. Latham, pp. 282–6 ; Allen, pp. 306–7.

Commission will be felt by most to hold its proper place. If Jesus really rose, these, or words like these, are precisely what He might be expected to use on such an occasion. Doubt of the words, as a rule goes along with doubt of the Resurrection itself.[1]

[The appearance to St. James [2] was dealt with in last chapter.]

5. Shortly after the great meeting in Galilee, the Apostles returned again to Jerusalem—from this time on, as every one admits, the continuous scene of their residence and labours. The fact that they did return is confirmatory evidence that some decisive experience had awaited them in the north. A link, however, is still wanting to connect previous events with the waiting for Pentecost, and the bold action immediately thereafter taken in the founding of the Church. That link is found in *the last appearance of the Lord to the Apostles*—the appearance alluded to by St. Paul in the words, " then, to all the Apostles" [3] and more circumstantially narrated by St. Luke, who brings it into direct

---

[1] The critical questions in this section are chiefly two : (1) Whether St. Matthew here follows the lost ending of St. Mark (some, as Allen, favour ; others doubt or deny) ; and (2) whether the words, " Baptizing them into the name," etc., should be omitted (after Eusebius). Prof. Lake says : " The balance of argument is in favour of the Eusebian text " (p. 88). Against this another sentence of his own may be quoted : " The text is found in all MSS. and versions " (p. 87).

[2] 1 Cor. xv. 7.   [3] Ibid.

relation with the Ascension.[1] A difficulty is found here in the fact that in his Gospel (chap. xxiv.) St. Luke proceeds without break from Christ's first appearance to " the eleven " to His last words about " the promise of the Father " and the Ascension at Bethany ; whereas in Acts i. he interposes " forty days " between the Resurrection and Ascension, and assumes appearances of Christ spread over the whole period. Not only Strauss, Keim, Weizsäcker, etc., but also Meyer, and many other critics, emphasize this " contradiction." It may reasonably be suspected, however, that " contradiction " occurring in books by the same writer, addressed to the same person, one of which is formally a continuation of the other, has its origin, less in fault of the author, than in the failure of the critics to do justice to his method. St. Luke, in his second work, betrays no consciousness of " contradiction " with his first, and his acquaintance with St. Paul, and knowledge of the list of appearances in 1 Corinthians,[2] make it, as formerly urged, unthinkable that he should have supposed all the events between the Resurrection and Ascension to be crowded into a single day. Neither, as a more careful inspection of his narrative in the Gospel shows, does he suppose this. The sequence of events in chap, xxiv. makes

---

[1] Luke xxiv. 44–53 ; Acts i. 5–12.

[2] Weizsäcker thinks that St. Luke's mention of the appearance of St. Peter " depended on the writer's acquaintance with the passage in Paul " (*Apost. Age*, ii. p. 11).

it clear that it was already late in the evening
when Jesus appeared to "the eleven."[1]   A meal
followed.   After this, if all happened on the same
evening, there took place a lengthened exposition
of the prophetic Scriptures.   The disciples were
then led out of Bethany, a mile and a half from the
city. There they witnessed the Ascension. Afterwards they returned to Jerusalem "with great
joy," and were continually in the Temple. Is it not
self-evident that there is compressed into these
closing verses of the Gospel far more than the events
of one day ?[2] Conscious of his purpose to write a
fuller account of the circumstances of the Lord's
parting with His disciples, the Evangelist foreshortens
and summarizes his narrative of the instructions and
promises which had their beginning at that first
meeting, and were continued later.[3] Similarly, the
citation of Christ's words in the closing verses of
the Appendix to St. Mark must be regarded as a
summary.

The last meeting of Christ with His Apostles took

[1] The disciples had returned from Emmaus after an
evening meal there.

[2] Latham justly says : " I will not listen to the supposition that the events of Luke xxiv. 36–53 all happened
in the one evening—this would make the Ascension take
place in the dead of night " (p. 155).

[3] Cf. Godet, *St. Luke*, ii. p. 358 ; Plummer, *St. Luke*,
pp. 561, 564. Luthardt says : "Luke draws into one
the entire time from the day of the Resurrection to the
Ascension " (*St. John*, iii. p. 356).

place, as we definitely learn from Acts i. 4, when He was " assembled together with them " at Jerusalem. It was then His final instructions were given. Even here the scene changes insensibly to Olivet, where the Ascension is located. Jesus might have simply " vanished " from the sight of His disciples, as on previous occasions, but it was His will to leave them in a way which would visibly mark the final close of His temporal association with them. He was " taken up," and " a cloud received Him out of their sight." [1] As they stood, still gazing at the spot where He had disappeared, angels, described as " two men in white apparel " (if ever angels were in place, it surely was at the Resurrection and Ascension), admonished them that, as they had seen Him depart, so in like manner He would come again. The visible Ascension has its counterpart in the visible Return.

It is the same picture of the Ascension, essentially, which is given in the close of St. Luke's Gospel : " He parted from them, and was carried up into heaven." [2] It matters little for the sense whether the last clause is retained, as probably it should be, or, with some authorities, is rejected, for the context plainly shows the kind of " parting " that is intended (cf. " received up," $\dot{\alpha}\nu\alpha\lambda\dot{\eta}\mu\psi\epsilon\omega\varsigma$, in chap. ix. 51). The Appendix to St. Mark, likewise, correctly gives the meaning : " He was received up

[1] Acts i. 10, 11.   [2] Luke xxiv. 51.

($\dot{a}\nu\epsilon\lambda\dot{\eta}\mu\phi\theta\eta$) into heaven, and sat down at the right hand of God." [1] Not in these passages only, but thro ghout the whole of the New Testament, it is implic d that Jesus after His Resurrection " passed into the heavens," was exalted and glorified. [2]

The facts are now before us. It remains, as far as it can be reverently done, to sum up the *results* as to the nature of the body of the Lord during this transitional period between Resurrection and Ascension, and to consider briefly the problems which these raise. This, with the full recognition that, in the present state of knowledge, these problems are, in large part, necessarily insoluble.

[1] Mark xvi. 19.
[2] John vi. 62, xx. 17 ; Eph. iv. 8–10 ; 1 Tim. iii. 16 ; Heb. iv. 14 , 1 Pet. iii. 21, 22, etc. On the Ascension, cf. Godet, *St. Luke*, iii. pp. 367–71 ; Latham, chap. xii. Only a word need be said on the objection urged from Strauss down that the Ascension is confuted by its connexion with a now exploded cosmogony. A recent writer, Prof. A. O. Lovejoy, states the objection thus in *The Hibbert Journal*, April 1908, p. 503 : "This story [of the Resurrection] is inextricably involved with, and is unintelligible apart from, the complementary story of the Ascension, with its crude scene of levitation ; and this, in turn, is meaningless without the scheme of cosmic topography that places a heaven somewhere in space in a direction perpendicular to the earth's surface at the latitude and longitude of Bethany." The objection really rests on a crudely realistic view of the world of space and time, as if this was not itself the index and symbol of another and (to us) invisible world, to which a higher reality belongs (in illustration, cf. Stewart and Tait's *The Unseen Universe*). Reception into this world is not by way of spatial transition.

"I am not yet ascended " . . . " I ascend." [1] In these two parts of the one saying of Jesus the mystery of the Resurrection body is comprised

On *earth*, as the history shows, Jesus had a body in all natural respects, corruptibility excepted, like our own. He hungered, He thirsted, He was weary, He suffered, He died of exhaustion and wounds. In *heaven*, that body has undergone transformation ; has become " the body of His glory." [2] In comparison with the natural, it has become a spiritual— " a pneumatic "—body, assimilated to, and entirely under the control of, the spiritual nature and forces that reside in it and work through it. In the interval between the Resurrection and the Ascension its condition must be thought of as *intermediate* between these two states—no longer merely natural (the act of Resurrection itself proclaimed this), yet not fully entered into the state of glorification. It presents characters, requisite for the proof of its identity, which show that the earthly condition is still not wholly parted with. It discovers qualities and powers which reveal that the supra-terrestrial condition is already begun. The apparently inconsistent aspects, therefore, under which Christ's body appears in the narratives do not constitute a bar to the acceptance of the truthfulness of the accounts ; they may rather, in their congruity with what is to be

[1] John xx. 17.   [2] Phil. iii. 21.

looked for in the Risen One,who has shown His power over death, but has not yet entered into His glory, be held to furnish a mark of credibility. How unlikely that the myth-forming spirit—not to say the crudeness of invention—should be able to seize so exactly the two-fold aspect which the manifestation of the Redeemer in His triumph over the grave must necessarily present !

Let these peculiarities of the Lord's Risen body be a little more closely considered.

1. On the one side, the greatest pains are taken to prove that the body in which Jesus appeared was a *true body*—not a spirit or phantasm, but the veritable body which had suffered on the Cross, and been laid in the tomb. It could be seen, touched, handled. It bore on it the marks of the Passion. To leave no room for doubt of its reality, it is told that on at least two, probably on three, occasions, Jesus *ate* with His disciples. With this accords the fact that the grave in which the body of Jesus had been buried on the Friday evening was found empty on the Easter Sunday morning. It was seen before that it was undeniably the belief of St. Paul and of the whole Apostolic Church that Jesus rose on the third day in the very body which had been buried.[1]

[1] Ménégoz says : " The mention of the third day would have no sense if Paul had not accepted the belief of the community of Jerusalem that on the third day Jesus went

2. On the other hand, it is equally evident that
the Resurrection body of Jesus was *not simply
natural*. It had attributes proclaiming its connexion with that supra-terrestrial sphere to which
it now more properly belonged. These attributes,
moreover, however difficult to reconcile with the
more tangible properties, can still not be regarded
as mere legendary embellishments, for they appear
in some degree in all the presentations.

The peculiarities chiefly calling for notice in this
respect are the following :—

(1) There is the mysterious power which Jesus
seems to have possessed of withdrawing Himself in
greater or less degree from the *recognition* of those
around Him.   In more than one of the narratives,
as has been seen, it is implied that there was something strange—something unfamiliar or mysterious
—in His aspect, which prevented His immediate
recognition even by those intimate with Him ;
which held them in awe ; while again, when some
gesture, word, or look, revealed to them suddenly
who He was, they were surprised, as the truth
flashed upon them, that they had not recognized
Him sooner.

The instances which come under this head, indeed,
differ in character.   It is possible that the failure
of Mary Magdalene to recognize Jesus at the begin-

forth alive from the tomb " (*La Péché et la Redemption
d'apres S. Paul,* p. 261 ; quoted by Bruce).

ning [1] may have been due to her absorption in her grief ; but it was probably in part occasioned also by some alteration in His appearance. It is said of the Emmaus disciples that " their eyes were holden that they should not know Him," [2] elsewhere that He appeared to them " in another form." [3] The former expression need not, perhaps, be pressed to imply a supernatural action on their senses. It may mean simply that they did not know Him ; that there was that about Him which prevented recognition. Yet when He was revealed to them in the breaking of bread, they appear to have marvelled at their blindness in not discerning Him sooner. In the incident at the Sea of Tiberias, the disciples may have been hindered from recognizing Jesus by the distance or the dimness of the dawn. The narrative, nevertheless, implies something in Christ's aspect which awed and restrained them, so that, even when they knew Him, they did not ask, " Who art Thou ? " [4]

(2) It is an extension of the same supernatural quality when the power is attributed to Jesus of withdrawing Himself from *sensible perception* altogether. At Emmaus, we are told, " He vanished out of their sight." [5] On other occasions He appeared and disappeared.[6] Here, apparently, is an emerging from, and withdrawing into, complete invisibility.

[1] John xx. 14.   [2] Luke xxiv. 16.   [3] Mark xvi. 12.
[4] John xxi. 12.   [5] Luke xxiv. 31.
[6] Luke xxiv. 36 ; John xx. 19, 26.

(3) The climax in supernatural quality is reached when Jesus is represented as withdrawing Himself wholly from conditions of space and time, and as *transcending physical limitations*—in appearing, e.g., to His disciples within closed doors,[1] or being found in different places at short intervals, or, finally, in ascending from earth to heaven in visible form.[2] A body in which powers like these are manifested is on the point of escaping from earthly conditions altogether—as, in truth, the body of Jesus was.

Little help can be gained from natural analogies in throwing light on properties so mysterious as those now described, or in removing the feeling of incredulity with which they must always be regarded by minds that persist in applying to them only the standards of ordinary experience. Daily, indeed, are men being forced to recognize that the world holds more mysteries than they formerly imagined it to do. Probably physicists are not so sure of the absolute impenetrability of matter,[3] or even of the conservation of energy, as they once were ; and newer speculations on the etheric basis of matter, and on the relation of the seen to an unseen universe (or universes), with forces and laws largely un-

---

[1] Luke xxiv. 36 ; John xx. 19, 26.
[2] Luke xxiv. 51 ; Acts i. 9. On the Ascension, see note above, p. 195.
[3] Cf. Stallo's *Concepts of Modern Physics* (Inter. Scien. Lib.), pp. 91-2, 178-82.

known,[1] open up vistas of possibility which may hold in them the key to phenomena even as extraordinary as those in question. In another direction, Mr. R. J. Campbell finds himself able to accept the physical Resurrection, and " the mysterious appearances and disappearances of the body of Jesus," on the ground of a theory of a " three-dimensional " and " four-dimensional " world,[2] which probably will be incomprehensible to most. Then the Society for Psychical Research has its experiments to prove a direct control of matter by spirit in extraordinary, if not preternatural, ways.[3] Such considerations may aid in removing prejudices, but they do little really to explain the remarkable phenomena of the bodily manifestations of Jesus to His disciples. These must still rest on their connexion with His unique Person.

Specially suggestive in this last relation are the indications in the Gospels themselves that, even during His earthly ministry, Christ's body possessed powers and obeyed laws higher than those to which ordinary humanity is subject. Two of the best attested incidents in the cycle of Gospel tradition —His Walking on the Sea,[4] and the Transfigura-

[1] Cf. *The Unseen Universe* (Stewart and Tait), pp. 166, 189–90.

[2] *The New Theology*, pp. 220–24.

[3] Cf. Myers, *Human Personality*, ii. pp. 204 ff. ; Sir Oliver Lodge, *Hibbert Journal*, April, 1908, pp. 574 ff.

[4] Matt. xiv. 22–33 ; Mark vi. 45–52 ; John vi. 15–21. In St. Matthew's narrative St. Peter also shared this power till his faith failed.

tion [1]—will occur as examples. Mighty powers worked in Him which already suggested to Herod One risen from the dead ; [2] powers which might be expected to manifest themselves in a higher degree when He actually did rise.

---

[1] Matt. xvii. 1–8 ; Mark ix. 2–8 ; Luke ix. 28–36. Well-hausen (*Das Evang. Marci*, pp. 75–6) actually supposes that the Transfiguration was originally an appearance of the Risen Christ to St. Peter. Loisy follows him in the conjecture (ii. p. 39).

[2] Matt. xiv. 2.

THE APOSTOLIC CHURCH—VISIONAL
AND APPARITIONAL THEORIES

VIII

THE APOSTOLIC CHURCH—VISIONAL AND APPARITIONAL THEORIES

It has been seen that the facts of the historical witness for the Resurrection form a chain of evidence extending from the empty grave on the morning of the third day and the message of the women, through the successive appearances of Jesus in Jerusalem and Galilee, till the day that He was finally " taken up " [1] into heaven in the view of His disciples. On these facts was based, in the immediate witnesses, the firm conviction, which nothing could shake, that their Lord, who had been crucified, had risen from the dead, and had been exalted to heavenly dominion. Their testimony, held fast to under the severest trial of privation, suffering, and death, was public, and no attempt was ever made, so far as is known, to refute their assertion. The effects of the faith in the first disciples, and in the hearts and lives of their converts, were of a nature to establish that they were the

[1] Acts i. 2.

victims of no illusion ; that they built on rock, not sand.

For this is the point next to be observed : the historical evidence for the Resurrection of Jesus is not all the evidence. As the Resurrection had its antecedents in the history and claims of Jesus, so it had its *results*. Pentecost is such a result. The Apostolic Church is such a result. The conversion of St. Paul, the Epistles of the New Testament, the Spirit-filled lives of a multitude of believers are such results. The Church founded on the Apostolic witness has endured for nineteen centuries. Christian experience throughout all these ages is a fact which only a Living Christ can explain or sustain. The Apostle speaks of the " power " of Christ's Resurrection.[1] That which continuously exerts " power " is a demonstrable reality.

There is space only for a glance at one or two of these results in the Apostolic Age.

1. The *Day of Pentecost*, in the Book of Acts, is the *sequel* to the Resurrection and Ascension. " Being, therefore," said St. Peter, " by the right hand of God exalted, and having received of the Father the promise of the Holy Spirit, He hath poured forth this, which ye do see and hear." [2] The cavils which have been raised against the general historicity of the first chapters of the Acts,

---

[1] Phil. iii. 10.   [2] Acts ii. 33.

which narrate the outpouring of the Spirit, and
the origin of the Church at Jerusalem,[1] are met,
apart from the note of clear remembrance and full
information in the narrative itself, by one single
consideration. It is as incredible that the Mother
of all the Churches—the undoubted seat of Apostolic residence and activity for many years—should
have been unaware of, or have forgotten, the circumstances of its own origin, as that, say, Germany
should forget its Reformation by Luther, or America
its Declaration of Independence.

2. The crucial fact of *St. Paul's conversion* took
place at most five or six years after the Resurrection.[2] It happened, therefore, when the original
witnesses were still alive and located at Jerusalem,
and when remembrance had as yet no time to grow
obscure, or tradition to become corrupted or per-
verted. Three years later St. Paul lodged for a
fortnight with St. Peter [3]—chief of the Apostles
—at Jerusalem, and there also met James, the
Lord's brother. Then, if not before, he must have
made himself familiar with the chief details of the
Jerusalem tradition regarding Christ's death and
Resurrection. Earlier, while yet a persecutor, he

[1] Even Harnack, who partly shares in the objection,
admits that " the instances of alleged incredibility have
been much exaggerated by critics " (*Lukas der Arzt*, p. 88).

[2] The dates range from 31–2 A.D. (Harnack), 33 (Ram-
say), 35–6 (Conybeare and Howson, Turner).

[3] Gal. i. 18.

had shared in the martyrdom of that precursor of
his own, St. Stephen, who, in dying, had the vision
of Jesus in heaven waiting to receive his departing
spirit.[1]

No fewer than three times in the Book of Acts
the circumstances of St. Paul's vision of Jesus on
the way to Damascus are narrated,[2] and it can
scarcely be doubted by any one who accepts St.
Luke's authorship of the Book that the information which these accounts contain was derived
originally from St. Paul's own lips.[3] This, again,
alone should suffice to set aside the contradiction
which some have imagined between the Apostle's
own conception of his conversion and the narratives
in Acts, as well as the charge of vital contradictions
in the narratives themselves.[4] As penned by the
same writer, in the compass of the same work,
the accounts must, in all reason, be supposed to be
in harmony with each other to the author's own
thought, whatever critics may now choose to make
of them.

[1] Acts vii. 51–60.

[2] Acts. ix. 1–22 ; xxii. 1–16 ; xxvi. 1–18.

[3] The first is St. Luke's narrative ; the second is in St.
Paul's defence before Lysias, when St. Luke was probably
present (a " we " section) ; the third is in St. Paul's defence before Agrippa, when St. Luke again was probably
present.

[4] Particulars given in one narrative and not in another
are not contradictions. The writer being the same, the
particulars must in each case have been known to him,
though not expressed.

It is not necessary to discuss at length the reality and objectivity of this appearance of the glorified Jesus to Saul the persecutor, when his mad rage against the saints was in full career. The sudden and revolutionary change then wrought, with its lasting moral and spiritual effects, is one which no " kicking against the goads " [1] in Saul's conscience, or " explosion " of forces of the subliminal consciousness which had been silently gathering to a head, can satisfactorily explain. Objective elements are implied in the great light, " above the brightness of the sun," that suddenly shone around the whole company, causing all, as the longer narrative shows, to fall to the ground, and in the voice which all heard, though Saul alone apprehended its articulate purport. [2] It is not so clear whether Saul not simply heard the Lord speak, [3] but beheld His form in the heavenly glory. That the latter, really, was the case, is suggested by the contrast in the words used of his companions, " hearing the voice, but beholding no man," [4] and by the words of St. Paul himself, " Have I not seen Jesus our Lord ? " [5] Most certain it is that St. Paul himself was absolutely convinced, both at the time of the vision and ever after, of the reality of

[1] Acts. xxvi. 14.
[2] Cf. Acts ix. 3, 7 ; xxvi. 13, 14.
[3] Weizsäcker and Loisy urge that St. Paul only saw a light and heard words.
[4] Acts ix. 7.   [5] 1 Cor. ix. 1.

Christ's appearance to him, and of the call he then received to be the Apostle of the Gentiles. Accordingly, he confidently ranks the appearance to himself with those to the other Apostles.[1] With the outward vision went an inward revelation of God's Son to his soul [2]—outward and inward com_ bining to effect an entire transformation in his conceptions of God, man, Christ, the world : everything.[3] This was the turning-point in St. Paul's history ; a turning-point, also, in the history of Christianity. Before, Christ's enemy, he was now Christ's devoted " slave " (δοῦλος) and Apostle. The Spirit that thenceforward wrought in him with mightiest results was the surest attestation of the genuineness of his experience.

3. In the prominence naturally given to the testimony of St. Paul, it should not be overlooked how pervasive is the witness of the *entire New Testament* to this same great primary fact of the Lord's Resurrection. It was seen that St. Peter was one of the first to whom Jesus appeared. But St. Peter has left an Epistle (the question of the second Epistle may here be waived), which rings throughout with the joyful hope and confidence begotten by the Resurrection of Jesus from the dead.[4] Jesus appeared to St. James ; and St.

[1] I Cor. xv. 8.   [2] Gal. i. 15, 16.   [3] Cf. 2 Cor. v. 16.
[4] I Pet. i. 3, 21 ; iii. 21, 22.

James has likewise an Epistle which extols Jesus as "the Lord of glory," and looks for His coming as nigh at hand.[1] St. John also, in Gospel, Epistle, and Apocalypse, presupposes or declares the Resurrection. The hope he holds out to believers is that, when He—Jesus—shall be "manifested," they shall be like Him, for they shall see Him even as He is.[2]

The historical attestation of the Resurrection in the New Testament has now been examined, and, so far as the inquiry has gone, the Resurrection of Jesus, as the foundation of the faith, hope, and life of the Church, stands fast. But the question will still be pressed—Is there no alternative conclusion ? Is it not possible that the facts which appear to render support to the belief in the Resurrection in the Apostolic Age may be explained in another way ? It has already been seen that this is the contention of a large class of writers in our own day. It has also been made apparent that there is as yet little approach to agreement among them in the rival theories they advance to supplant the Apostolic belief. The study of these "modern" theories may, indeed, well be ranked as a supplementary chapter in the exhibition of the positive evidence for the Resurrection. It is in this corroborative light it is proposed here principally to regard them.

[1] Jas. ii. 1 ; v. 7–9.   [2] I John iii. 2.

The two main pillars of belief in the Resurrection were found to be the empty tomb on the morning of the third day, and the actual appearances of the Risen Lord to His disciples.

1. Some light has already been cast on the various expedients by which it is attempted in the newer theories to get rid of the fact of *the empty tomb*. Either, as by not a few, the story is treated as unhistorical,[1] and roundabout attempts are made to explain its origin by inference from the (visionary) appearances to the disciples in Galilee ; or, granting a basis of fact in the narratives, it is conjectured that the body of Jesus had been secretly removed from the tomb, and disposed of elsewhere ; or, as by Professor Lake, it is supposed that the women made a mistake in the tomb which they visited. These curiosities of theory need not be further dwelt upon. Christian people to whom they are offered may be excused for echoing the lament of Mary Magdalene : " They have taken away my Lord, and I know not where they have laid Him."[2] For the critics do not even profess to know where the body of Jesus was put. The disciples, indeed, are now usually exonerated from participation in a deliberate fraud, and speculation varies between Pilate, the Sanhedrim, and Joseph of Arimathæa

---

[1] " An empty grave was never seen by any disciple of Jesus " (A. Meyer, p. 213).

[2] John xx. 11.

as persons who may have removed the body. Others, more wisely, leave the matter in the vagueness of ignorance.[1] There remains the fact which cannot be got over—a fact fatal to all this arbitrary theorising—that within a few weeks at most of the Crucifixion, at Pentecost and in the days immediately thereaftert, he disciples, raised from despair to a joyful confidence which nothing could destroy, were, as already told, boldly and publicly proclaiming in the streets of the very city where Jesus had been crucified that He was risen from the dead ; were maintaining the same testimony before the tribunals ; were stirring the city, and making thousands of converts. Yet not the least attempt was made, either by the rulers, or by any one else interested, to stay the movement, and silence the preachers, as might easily have been done, had their testimony been false, by pointing to where the body of Jesus still lay, or by showing how it had come to be removed from the tomb in which it had, after the Crucifixion, to the knowledge of all, been deposited. *Did not* in this case spells *could not*, and the empty tomb remains an unim-

---

[1] Thus Renan ; now also Loisy. The latter says : " It appears useless to discuss here the different hypotheses regarding the removal of the body [assumed by the critic to be a fact], whether by Joseph of Arimathæa, or by the proprietor of the tomb, or by the orders of the Sanhedrim, or by Mary of Bethany, or by the Apostles there " (*Les Évangiles Synoptiques*, ii. p. 720).

peachable witness to the truth of the message that the Lord had risen.

2. If the empty tomb cannot be got rid of, may it not at least be possible to show that *the appearances of Jesus* can be explained on another hypothesis than that of a physical Resurrection—either by subjective hallucinations, which is the older form of the visional theory, or, if that be thought inadequate, by real apparitions of the (spiritually) risen Christ, which is the form of theory now preferred by many ? The aim in both of these classes of theories, is to relieve the mind from the difficulty of believing in an actual rising of the body from the grave ; in other words, to do away with the physical miracle. Only, while the purely visional theory takes away all ground for belief in the Resurrection, the other, or apparitional, by substituting a spiritual rising for the corporeal, and allowing real manifestations of the Risen Jesus, proposes in a certain way to conserve that belief. Is this admissible ? It is hoped that a brief examination will make clear how far either theory is from furnishing a tenable explanation of the facts it has to deal with.

(1) Attention has to be called, first, to an interesting fact which has already been repeatedly alluded to in the course of these discussions. It is to be observed with regard to most of these modern visional and apparitional theories that, in complete break

with tradition, they feel the necessity of *transferring the appearances of Jesus from Jerusalem*, where the earlier of them are related to have happened *to the more remote region of Galilee*, and so of dissociating them wholly from the message of the women at the tomb.[1] A slight qualification of this is that some are disposed to see in St. Luke's narrative of the appearance at Emmaus a reminiscence of appearances in the *neighbourhood* of Jerusalem.[2] But the greater appearances—all those included in the list of St. Paul in 1 Corinthians xv. 3–8—are transported without further ado to Galilee.

The advantage of this change of *locale* for the theory is obvious. It separates the visions from the events of the Easter morning, gives time for visions to develop, transfers them to scenes where memory and imagination may be supposed to be more prepared to work, frees them from the control of the hard realities of the situation. As Strauss puts it : "If the transference of the appearances to Galilee disengages us from the third day as the period of the commencement of them, the longer time thus gained makes the reaction in the minds of the disciples more conceivable."[3]

The real course of events after the Crucifixion

[1] Thus Strauss, Keim, Weizsäcker, Pfleiderer, Harnack, O. Holtzmann, Lake, Loisy, etc.

[2] Thus A. Meyer (pp. 134, 136) ; Lake (pp. 218–19).

[3] *New Life of Jesus*, i. p. 437.

is alleged to be unmistakably indicated by the statement of the Evangelists : "They [the disciples] all left Him and fled " (whither should they flee but to their old home ?), supported as this is by the words of Jesus : "It is written, I will smite the shepherd," etc., which He expressly connects with His going before them into Galilee ; [1] and again by the fact that St. Mark and St. Matthew point to Galilee as the place of Christ's meeting with His disciples.[2] It is true that St. Luke and St. John—in part also St. Matthew—locate the first appearances in Jerusalem ; but this representation, declared to be irreconcilable with the other, is promptly set aside as unhistorical.[3] Internal probability is likewise claimed in favour of Galilee.[4] To Galilee, therefore, without hesitation, all the leading appearances of Jesus—the appearance to St. Peter, the appearances to the Apostles, to the five hundred, to St. James, etc.—are carried.[5]

---

[1] Matt. xxvi. 31, 32, 56 ; Mark xiv. 27, 28, 50 ; John xvi. 32.

[2] Matt. xxviii. 7 ; Mark xvi. 7.

[3] " This last conception is irreconcilable with the first " (Strauss, i. p. 435). " Now these two representations are irreconcilable " (Weizsäcker, i. p. 2). " This is evidently not genuine but coloured history " (Keim, vi. p. 284).

[4] Strauss, i. pp. 436–7.

[5] Keim is emphatic : " These appearances of Jesus took place, according to the plainest evidence, in Galilee, not in Jerusalem " (p. 281). " Nothing can be plainer than that all the appearances are to be located in the mother country of Christianity " (p. 283).

It is not difficult to show that this hypothesis, directly opposed as it is to nine-tenths of the tradition we possess, has no real foothold even in the facts alleged in its support.[1] To give it any colour, it is necessary to get behind the tradition even in St. Mark, the supposed original, and in St. Matthew, and to reinterpret the *data* in a way fatal to the good sense and veracity of the narratives. There is nothing in St. Matthew, St. Mark, or St. John to countenance the idea that the " scattering " and " fleeing " of the disciples had reference to a flight into Galilee. On the very night of the " fleeing "[2] St. Peter is found in the High Priest's palace. The threefold denial into which he was there betrayed does not look like a purpose to go at once into Galilee. St. Matthew and St. Mark, again, who announce that Jesus will go before the disciples into Galilee, as plainly imply that the disciples to whom the message is sent are still in Jerusalem.[3] St. Matthew himself records an appearance in Jerusalem in which the same direction to go into Galilee is embodied.[4] St. John predicts the " scattering," [5] yet gives detailed accounts of the meetings

---

[1] For a criticism of the theory, cf. Loofs, *Die Auferstehungsberichte*, pp. 18–25. Loofs, however, is himself arbitrary in transferring *all* the appearances to Jerusalem.

[2] Matt. xxvi. 58 ; Mark xiv. 54.

[3] This is supposed to be an expedient to cover the earlier disgrace of the flight. Cf. Loofs in criticism (p. 20).

[4] Matt. xxviii. 9, 10.   [5] John xvi. 32.

in Jerusalem. It is not easy to see, therefore, how Keim can suppose that St. John's words " preserve the reminiscence that they [the disciples] fled towards their home, that is, towards Galilee." [1] St. Luke knew something of St. Paul's beliefs. He must have known something also of St. Paul's understanding of the locality of the appearances in 1 Corinthians xv. Yet he places the appearance to St. Peter in Jerusalem on the very day of the Resurrection.[2] And where is there the least evidence that St. Paul, who knew Jerusalem, but never mentions Galilee, intended all the appearances he enumerates to be located in that region ?

There *were* Galilean appearances. St. Matthew tells of one, St. Mark probably intended to tell of one, St. John tells of one. But how extremely unlikely, assuming the departure into Galilee to have been simply a chance scattering, that the eleven Apostles should be found on different occasions convened to receive visions ? Or that above five hundred brethren should be brought together in that region, without previous appointment, for a similar purpose ? Or that immediately afterwards Apostles and disciples should be found again at Jerusalem, a united body, animated by a common purpose and hope, and ready to testify at all hazards that Jesus had been raised *from the tomb* ?

[1] *Jesus of Nazara*, vi. p. 283.
[2] Luke xxiv. 34.

The theory of the transference of the earlier appearances to Galilee being discarded as one which a sound treatment of the sources cannot justify, the way is cleared for a judgment on the *visional* and *apparitional* theories which are put forward to explain the appearances themselves.

(2) The theory of *subjective visions*, or *mental hallucinations*, though its glaring weaknesses have often been exposed, by none more effectively than by Keim himself—is still the favourite with many.[1] Visions, under excitement, or in persons of a high-strung, nervous temperament, especially among ascetics, are an often-recurring phenomenon in religious history.[2] Visions, too, in an emotional atmosphere, are contagious. Here then, it may be thought, is a principle which can be invoked to furnish an easy and natural explanation of the abnormal experiences of the disciples

[1] It was the theory of Strauss and Renan, and is favoured by Weizsäcker, Harnack, A. Meyer, O. Holtzmann, Loisy, etc.

[2] See the long chapter of instances in A. Meyer, *Die Auferstehung Christi*, pp. 217–70. Cf. Keim, iv. pp. 346–8 : " Thus, not to speak of the Old and New Testaments with their long lists of examples, Maximilla and the Montanists saw Christ, the Maid of Orleans received the Archangel Michael and S.S. Catherine and Margaret, Francis of Assisi saw the Lord as a seraph, and Savonarola looked upon both obscure and clear pictures of the future through the ordinary ministry of angels. In the same way, the eccentric Mohammed, the pious Swedenborg, the illuminated bookseller Nicolai, have had visions," etc. (p. 346)

after the Resurrection. From St. Paul's " vision "
of Jesus on the way to Damascus, it is argued that
the earlier appearances which he enumerates must
have been visionary also.

The forms which the vision-theory assumes are
legion. Renan's is the most naïve, idyllic, and
fanciful. Renan has no difficulty with the
appearances at Jerusalem. According to him, the
minds of the disciples swam in a delicious intoxi-
cation almost from the hour of the Crucifixion.
" Heroes do not die." ¹ Their Master must rise
again. It was Mary Magdalene who set the train
of visions in motion.² In the garden she believed
that she saw and heard Jesus.³ Divine hallucination ! Her enthusiasm gave to the world a resuscitated god ! ⁴ Others at once caught the infec-
tion.⁵ The most trifling incidents—" a current of
air, a creaking window, a casual murmur " ⁶—
sufficed to start a vision. St. Peter's vision (which
St. Paul misunderstood) was really his glimpse of
the white grave-clothes in the tomb.⁷ The dis-

---

¹ *Les Apôtres*, p. 3. See above, p. 146.

² " Mary alone loved enough to dispense with nature,
and to have revived the phantom of the perfect Master . . .
The glory, then, of the Resurrection belongs to Mary Magdalene " (pp. 12, 13).

³ " The vision gently receded, and said to her : ' Touch
Me not ! ' Gradually the shadow disappeared " (p. 11).

⁴ *Vie de Jésus*, p. 434 ; *Les Apôtres*, p. 13.

⁵ Ibid., pp. 16, 17.   ⁶ P. 22.

⁷ P. 12.

ciples at Emmaus, in their rapture, mistook the
" pious Jew " who had expounded to them the Scriptures for Jesus. Suddenly he had vanished ![1]
A breath of wind made the disciples in the closed
room think they recognized Jesus. " It was impossible to doubt ; Jesus was present ; He was
there, in the assembly."[2] Visions multiplied on
every hand.[3] Sometimes, " during meal time,
Jesus was seen to appear, taking the bread, blessing it, breaking it, and offering it."[4] When the
enthusiasm chilled, the disciples revived it by going
in a joyous company to Galilee.[5] There they had
new experiences.[6] It was all too lovely to last, so
by and by the excitement died away, and the visions
ceased ![7]

The falsetto note in these descriptions is all too
obvious, and sober-minded advocates of the vision
hypothesis usually now take another, if hardly
more successful, line. Jerusalem, as has been seen,

[1] Pp. 20–1.   [2] P. 22.
[3] " Visions were multiplied without number " (p. 25).
There is not a word in the narratives to countenance this.
[4] P. 26.
[5] " In a melancholy mood, they thought of the lake
and of the beautiful mountains where they had received
a foretaste of the Kingdom of God. . . . The majority
of the disciples then departed, full of joy and hope, perhaps
in the company of the caravan, which took back the pil-
grims from the Feast of the Passover " (pp. 28, 29).
[6] " The visions, at first, on the lake appear to have
been pretty frequent " (p. 32). Again quite unhistorical.
[7] Pp. 45 ff.

is abandoned as too near the scene of events ; the third day also is set aside as affording too little time for the recovery of the disciples from despair. But Galilee, whither the disciples are carried, with its memories and tender associations, revives hope, and brings back the image of the Master. One day, perhaps by the Lake of Galilee (a reminiscence is discerned in St. John xxi.[1]), St. Peter sees a bright light, or something of the kind, and fancies it is Jesus.[2] By a mysterious telepathy, his experience affects the remaining Apostles, who happen to be gathered together, and they also have visions The contagion spreads, and on another occasion 500 brethren at once have visions. By and by the visions cease as suddenly as they began. Returning to Jerusalem, the Apostles are met by the women, and for the first time (thus Professor Lake, etc.) hear of the empty tomb. Their faith is confirmed, and the women are established by the visions in their conviction that Jesus is risen.

It will be seen, to begin with, that to gain for this visional theory any semblance of plausibility, every fact in the Gospel history has to be changed— time, place, nature of the events, mood of the disciples, etc.—while scenes, conditions, and experiences are invented of which the Gospels know nothing. It is not the facts on record that are

---

[1] Thus Harnack, Loisy, etc.
[2] Cf. Weizsäcker, A. Meyer, etc.

explained, but a different (imaginary) set of facts
altogether. According to the history, the first
appearances took place in Jerusalem on the very
day of the Resurrection. They took place independently. There was no preparedness to see
visions, but, on the contrary, deep depression and
rooted incredulity, not removed till Jesus, by sensible tokens, put his corporeal reality beyond doubt.
The appearances were not momentary glimpses,
but, at least in several of the cases, prolonged
interviews. They were not excited by every trifling
circumstance, nor ceaselessly multiplied. They
numbered only ten altogether, five of them on the
first day. The subjects of them were not nervous,
hysterical persons, but men of stolid, practical
judgment, fishermen, a tax-gatherer like St. Matthew, a matter-of-fact, unideal man like St. Philip,
a sceptic like St. Thomas. In no case is there the
slightest trace of preparatory excitement. If, when
Jesus appeared, the disciples were " affrighted,"
it was at the thought that a spirit appeared to them,[1]
and this idea (a chance for the vision hypothesis) had
to be dispelled before they would believe that it
was Jesus. Ordinarily they were calm and collected. It is obvious that for the explanation of
such appearances a vision theory is useless.

Even on its own ground, however, it must be
held that the vision theory breaks down in the

----

[1] Luke xxiv. 37–8.

most essential points. It is not, for instance, the case that there is any general predisposition to believe in the resurrection of " heroes," or to affirm that heroes have actually risen. No single example can be produced of belief in the resurrection of an historical personage such as Jesus was : none at least on which anything was ever founded. What *is* found is an unwillingness to believe, or to admit, in certain cases,[1] for a time, that the hero is really dead. The Christian Resurrection is thus a fact without historical analogy. There was, moreover, nothing in the nature of visions, assuming that the disciples had them, to give rise to the idea of a *bodily* Resurrection. " Visions " are phantasmal, and would be construed as " apparitions " of the dead, not as proofs of resurrection.[2] This is precisely what the Apostles at first did think about the appearances of Jesus. Lastly, as checking a purely visional theory, there is the immovable fact of the empty tomb. It would, indeed, be an extraordinary coincidence if, in the environs of Jerusalem, the tomb of Jesus was found empty, while, without previous knowledge of a Resurrection, the disciples began in Galilee to have visions of a Risen Lord !

[1] The cases are not numerous ; that of Mohammed, which Renan cites, is not really one. Mohammed's death was never really doubted.

[2] Cf. B. Weiss, *Life of Christ*, iii. p. 390 (E. T.).

Psychologically, no good cause has ever been shown why the disciples should have this marvellous outburst of visionary experience ; should have it so early as the third day, should have it simultaneously, should have it within a strictly limited period, after which the visions as suddenly ceased, should never afterwards waver or doubt about it, should be inspired by it for the noblest work ever done on earth.[1] If anything is certain historically, it is that the death of their Master plunged the disciples into deepest despondency, that their hearts, always " slow to believe," were sad, and their hopes broken, and that, so far from expecting a Resurrection, they could hardly be persuaded of the fact even after it occurred. Even the words which Jesus had spoken on the subject had not been apprehended in a sense which helped them to believe. The women who visited the tomb had assuredly no expectation of finding the Lord risen. Even had their faith been stronger than it was, that would not have caused the appearances.

Equally unaccountable on a purely visional theory is the *outcome* of belief in the Resurrection. It was this consideration which weighed most of all with Keim, whose view is thus summed up by Godet : " It would be difficult to understand how,

[1] Keim forcibly urges against the vision-theory the orderly, regular character and early cessation of the appearances (vi. pp. 356–7). Cf. also Beyschlag, *Leben Jesu*, i. pp. 430–50.

from a society held together by over-excitement, issuing in visions, could have proceeded the Christian Church, with its lucidity of thought and earnestness of moral activity." [1] The visions not only cease, but as Keim points out, make way for a diametrically opposite mental current. From enthusiastic excitement, the impetus of which would have gone on working, as in Montanism, for a long period, there is a sudden transition to self-possession and clear-mindedness. "If therefore," Keim argues, "there was actually an early, an immediate transition from the visions to a calm self-possession, and to a self-possessed energy, then the visions did not proceed from self-generated visionary over-excitement and fanatical agitation among the multitude." [2]

(3) Impressed by these difficulties, it is not surprising to find a tendency exhibiting itself among recent writers to concede the inadequacy of a purely subjective account of the appearances to the disciples, and to fall back on a theory of spiritual yet *real* manifestations of the Risen Christ—on what is called above an *apparitional* theory. Keim is not the earliest, but he is one of the best known representatives of this theory,[3] which is now thought by certain "moderns" to receive support from the

---

[1] Godet, *Defence of the Christian Faith*, p. 88.
[2] Keim, vi. pp. 357–8. Cf. Weiss, *ut supra*, iii. p. 387.
[3] *Ut supra*, vi. pp. 361–5.

evidence collected by the Society for Psychical
Research on apparitions of the dead, or phantasms
of persons at the time of death.[1] The view is one
which commends itself to prominent Ritschlians,
e.g. to Johannes Weiss.[2] It is put forward as
probable by Professor Lake.[3] Keim thinks that
in this way he saves the truth of the Resurrection
("thus, though much has fallen away, the secure
faith-fortress of the Resurrection remains.") [4]

Keim's theory, in brief, is that, while the body
of the Crucified Jesus slept on in the tomb in which
it had received "honourable burial," [5] His spirit
manifested itself by supernatural impressions on the
minds of the disciples—what he calls "telegrams
from heaven" [6]—giving them the assurance that
He still lived, and grounding a firm hope of immortality. Keim will not even refuse to those who
may require it the belief that the vision took the
form of "corporeal appearances." [7] The newer
theories rely more on the evidence of apparitions
to bring the appearances of Jesus within the scope
of natural law—the idea of "law" being widened to
take in psychical manifestations from the unseen
world.[8] So far from belief in immortality being

---

[1] Cf. Lake, *Resur. of Jesus Christ*, pp. 271-6 ; Myers,
Human Personality, i. p. 288.
[2] *Das Nachfolge Christi*, pp. 99, 151.
[3] *Ut supra.*   [4] P. 365.   [5] P. 271.   [6] Pp. 364-5.
[7] P. 362.
[8] Cf. Prof. Lake, in agreement with Dr. Rashdall : " A

based on the Resurrection, Professor Lake, in a passage earlier quoted, would seem to say that this belief (including the survival of Christ's personality) must remain an hypothesis till experts have sifted the evidence for the alleged psychical manifestations.[1]

It is not necessary here to investigate the degree of truth which belongs to the class of phenomena with which psychical research deals, or to discuss the alternative explanations which may be given of such phenomena. There is no call to deny the reality of telepathic communication between living minds, or the possibility of impressions being conveyed from one mind to another in the hour of death. The whole region is obscure, and needs further exploration. What it is necessary to insist upon is that nothing of the kind answers to the proper Scriptural idea of Resurrection, and that it is a mistake, involving a real yielding up of the Christian basis, to rest the proof of Christ's rising from the dead in any degree on *data* so elusive,

---

real though supernormal psychological event, but which involved nothing which can properly be spoken of as a suspension of natural law " (p. 269 ; cf. p. 277).

[1] " It remains merely an hypothesis until it can be shown that personal life does endure beyond death, is neither extinguished nor suspended, and is capable of manifesting its existence to us . . . but we must wait until the experts have sufficiently sifted the arguments for alternative explanations of the phenomena " (p. 245).

precarious, and in this connexion so misleading, as those to which attention is here directed. The survival of the soul is not resurrection.[1] An apparitional theory is not a theory of the Resurrection of Jesus as Apostolic Christianity understood it, but a substitute, which is in principle a negation, of the Apostolic affirmation.

It is speedily apparent, further, that apparitional theories of the Resurrection, quite as much as the visional, break on the character of the facts the theories are intended to explain. The empty tomb, once more, stands as an insuperable barrier in the way of all such theories. The testimony of the Apostles again stands on record, and cannot be spirited away. The witness of the Apostles was that they had actually seen and conversed with Jesus—not with an apparition or ghost of Jesus, but with the living Christ Himself. It is an acute criticism which the late Professor A. B. Bruce makes on Keim's " telegram " theory when he says : " It is open to the charge that it makes the faith of the disciples rest on a hallucination. Christ sends a series of telegrams from heaven to let His disciples know that all is well. But what does the telegram say in every case. Not merely, My spirit lives with God and cares for you ; but, My

---

[1] Prof. Lake says : . " What we mean by resurrection is not resuscitation of the material body, but the unbroken survival of personal life " (p. 265 ; cf. p. 275).

body is risen from the grave. . . . If the Resurrection be an unreality, if the body that was nailed to the tree never came forth from the tomb, why send messages that were certain to produce an opposite impression ? " [1]

After all, on such a theory supernaturalism is not escaped, and most will feel that Keim's spiritualistic hypothesis is a poor exchange for the Apostolic affirmation that Jesus actually burst the bands of death, and came forth living from the tomb, on the morning of the third day. Dr. Bruce says of it : " Truly this is a poor foundation to build Christendom upon, a bastard supernaturalism, as objectionable to unbelievers as the true supernaturalism of the Catholic creed, and having the additional drawback that it offers to faith asking for bread a stone." [2] It does not help much to plead that, if apparitions can be proved in the present day, the whole subject is brought within the domain of natural law. The reality of appartions is never likely to be proved to the general satisfaction of mankind ; but, if it were, they would certainly be regarded as facts belonging to a supernatural world, and not as mere phenomena of nature. The root of the whole difficulty, as Professor Lake frankly admits, is the naturalistic assumption that the reanimation of a dead body—

[1] *Apologetics*, p. 393.   [2] Ibid.

even of the body of the Son of God—could not take place.[1] Anything, he says, rather than that.[2], Hence the need of resorting to the fantastic theories just described, which yet, as seen, have an element of the supernatural inhering in them.

Visional and apparitional theories once parted with, there is only one remaining explanation, viz., *that the Resurrection really took place.* As Beyschlag truly says : " The *faith* of the disciples in the Resurrection of Jesus, which no one denies, cannot have originated, and cannot be explained otherwise than through the *fact* of the Resurrection, through the fact in its full, objective, supernatural sense, as hitherto understood."[3] So long as this is contested, the Resurrection remains a problem which rival attempts at explanation only leave in deeper darkness.

[1] *Ut supra,* pp. 264–5, 268–9.
[2] " Such a phenomena is in itself so improbable that any alternative is preferable to its assertion " (p. 267).
[3] *Leben Jesu,* i. p. 440.

NEO-BABYLONIAN THEORIES—JEWISH
AND APOCRYPHAL IDEAS

IX

NEO-BABYLONIAN THEORIES—JEWISH AND APOCRYPHAL IDEAS

THE inadequacy of previous attempts to explain the Resurrection of Jesus out of natural grounds is convincingly shown by the rise of a new mythological school, which, discarding, or at least dispensing with, theories of vision and apparition, proposes to account for the " Resurrection-legend " —indeed for the whole New Testament Christology [1]—by the help of conceptions imported into Judaism from Babylonia and other parts of the Orient (Egyptian, Arabian, Persian, etc.). The rise of this school is connected particularly with the brilliant results of exploration in the East during the last half century, and with the consequent vast enlargement in our knowledge of peoples and religions of remote antiquity. The mythologies of these ancient religions—the study of comparative mythology generally—puts, it is thought, into the hands of scholars a golden key to open locks in Old

---

[1] Cf. Gunkel, *Zum religionsgeschichtlichen Verständniss des Neuen Testaments*, pp. 61, 89–95.

and New Testament religion which have hitherto remained closed to the most painstaking efforts of the learned.[1] The prestige which this new Babylonian school has already gained through its novelty and boldness of speculation entitles it to a consideration which, perhaps, if only its own merits were regarded, would hardly be accorded to it.

It is well to apprehend at the outset the position taken up by this revolutionary Babylonian school. It is the fact that myths of resurrection, though in vague, fluctuating form, to which the character of historical reality cannot for a moment be attached, are not infrequent in Oriental religions.[2] They are traceable in later even more than in earlier times, and specially are found in connection with the Mysteries. The analogies pressed into the service of their theories by scholars are often sufficiently shadowy,[3] but it is admitted that the myths used in the Mysteries and related festivals, whether Egyptian, Persian, Phrygian, Syrian, or Greek,

[1] Gunkel, p. 78 : "Already in the Old Testament there are mysterious portions [he instances the "servant of Jehovah" in Isaiah] which hitherto have defied all attempts at interpretation," etc.

[2] For examples, see Cheyne, *Bible Problems*, pp. 119–22 ; Farnell, *The Evolution of Religion*, pp. 60–62 ; Frazer, *Golden Bough*, ii. pp. 115–168 ; Zimmern in Schrader's *Keilinschriften*, pp. 387 ff., 643.

[3] As when Zimmern connects this idea with the Babylonian god Marduk ; or Cheyne (*ut supra*, p. 119) instances the myth of Osiris, "who after a violent death lived on in the person of his son Horus ! "

had all a certain family likeness. They all turn, as Boissier remarks in his *La Religion Romaine*, on the death and resurrection of a god, and, in order still more to inflame the religious sensibility, in all the tales the god is loved by a goddess, who loses and refinds him, who mourns over his death, and ends by receiving him back to life. " In Egypt, it is Isis, who seeks Osiris, slain by a jealous brother ; in Phoenicia, it is Astarte or Venus who weeps for Adonis ; on the banks of the Euxine, it is Cybele, the great mother of the gods, who sees the beautiful Attis die in her arms." [1] Older than any of these, and, on the new theory, the parent of most of them, is the often-told Babylonian myth of Ishtar and Tammuz.[2] All, in truth, are nature-myths, telling the same story of the death of nature in winter, and its revival in spring, or of the conquest of light by darkness, and the return of brightness with the new sunrise.[3] But in the Mysteries an allegorical significance was read into these myths, and they became the instruments of a moral symbolism, in which faint resemblances to Christian ideas can be discerned.

All this is old and tolerably familiar. But the

[1] Boissier, i. p. 408.

[2] See the story in full in Sayce's Hibbert Lectures, *The Religion of the Ancient Babylonians*, Lect. IV., " Tammuz and Ishtar."

[3] Cf. Gunkel, *ut supra*, p. 77 ; A. Jeremias, *Babylonisches im N.T.*, pp. 8 ff., 11, 19, etc.

Babylonian school goes much further. It is no longer parallels merely which are sought between the Gospel narratives and pagan myths, but an actual derivation is proclaimed. Ancient Babylonia had developed a comprehensive world-theory of which its mythology is the imaginative expression. These myths spread into all countries, receiving in each local modification ; Israel, which came into contact with, and in Canaan deeply imbibed, this culture, could not escape being affected by it. Winckler, and in a more extreme form Jensen, find in Babylonian mythology the key not only to the so-called legends of the patriarchs, of Moses and Aaron, and of the Judges, but to the histories of Samuel, of Saul and David, of Elijah and Elisha. Now, by Gunkel, Cheyne, Jensen, and others, the theory is extended to the New Testament. Filtering down through Egypt, Canaan, Arabia, Phoenicia, Persia, there came, it is alleged, myths of virgin-births, of descents into Hades, of resurrections and ascensions ; these, penetrating into Judaism, became attached to the figure of the expected Messiah—itself of old-world derivation—and gave rise to the idea that such and such traits would be realized in Him. Dr. Cheyne supposes that there was a written " pre-Christian sketch " of the Messiah, which embodied these features.[1] One form of the Jewish concep-

[1] *Ut supra*, p. 128.

tion is seen in the picture of the woman clothed with the sun in Revelation xii. More definitely, the form which the conception assumed in Christian circles is seen in the legends of Christ's birth and infancy, in the incidents and miracles of His ministry, in the three days and nights of His burial in the tomb, and in the stories of His Resurrection and Ascension. It is the mythical theory of Strauss over again, with the substitution of Babylonian mythology for Old Testament prophecy as the foundation of an imaginary history of Jesus.

The shapes which this theory assumes in the hands of the writers who advocate it are naturally various. A few instances may be given.

Dr. Cheyne goes far enough in assuring us that " there are parts of the New Testament—in the Gospels, in the Epistles, and in the Apocalypse— which can only be accounted for by the newly-discovered fact of an Oriental syncretism which began early and continued late. And the leading factor in this is Babylonian." Among the beliefs the " mythic origin " of which is thus accounted for, is " the form of the belief in the Resurrection of Christ." [1] His " pre-Christian sketch " theory is alluded to below.

Gunkel's position is not dissimilar, and is wrought out in more detail. Judaism and Christianity, he

---

[1] *Bible Problems*, pp. 19, 117.

holds, are both examples of syncretism in religion.[1]
Both are deeply penetrated by ideas diffused
through the Orient, and derived chiefly from Babylonia. He states his thesis thus : " That in its
origin and shaping (*Ausbildung*) the New Testament
religion stood, in weighty, indeed essential points,
under the decisive influence of foreign religions,
and that this influence was transmitted to the
men of the New Testament through Judaism." [2]
He traces the penetrative influence of Oriental
conceptions in Judaism, with special respect to the
doctrine of the Resurrection ; [3] finds in it the origin
of the Messianic idea, and of the Christology of St.
Paul and St. John ; [4] and derives from it the Gospel
narratives of the Infancy,[5] the Transfiguration,[6]
the Resurrection from the dead on the third day,[7]
the appearance to the disciples on the way to
Emmaus,[8] the Ascension,[9] the origin of Sunday
as a Christian festival,[10] etc.

A. Jeremias, from a believing standpoint, cri-
ticizes this position of Gunkel's, and the denial of

[1] *Ut supra*, pp. 34, 117. Judaism must be named
" Eine synkretistische Religion." So, " Das Christentum
ist eine synkretistische Religion."

[2] *Ut supra*, p. 1.   [3] Pp. 31–35.

[4] Pp. 24–5, 64, 89–95. " The form of the Messiah
belongs to this original mythological material " (p. 24).

[5] Pp. 65–70.

[6] P. 71 (likewise the Baptism and Temptation narratives,
pp. 70–1).   [7] Pp. 76–83.   [8] P. 71.

[9] Pp. 71–2.   [10] Pp. 73–76.

the absoluteness of Christianity connected with
it.[1] Sharing the same general view that " the
Israelitish-Judaic background " of the New Testament writings " is no other than the Babylonian,
or better, the old Oriental background,"[2] he sees
in the Babylonian mythology a pre-ordained providential preparation for the Gospel history and
the Christian religion, the essential truths of which
he accepts.[3] The resurrection of a god formed
part of the universally-spread mythus.[4]

Everything hitherto attempted, however, in the
application of this theory to the Biblical history
is hopelessly left behind in the latest book which
has appeared on the subject—Professor Jensen's
Das Gilgamesch-Epos in der Weltliteratur of which,
as yet, only the first volume has appeared. But
this extends to 1,030 pages. It treats of the origins of the legends of the Old Testament patriarchs, prophets, and deliverers, and of the New
Testament legend of Jesus, embracing all the incidents of His history—birth, life, miracles, death,

[1] *Bab. im N.T.*, p. 1. [2] P. 3.
[3] Pp. 6, 46, 48, etc. The heathen myths are " Schatten-
bilder " (prefigurations, foreshadowings) of the Christian
verities.
[4] Pp. 8–10. Jeremias has, however, little to say on
the application to the Resurrection of Christ. He makes
much more of the Virgin-birth (pp. 46 ff.). He says that
no one who understands the circle of conceptions of the
ancient Orient will doubt that Is. vii. 14, in the sense of
the author, really means a " virgin " (p. 47).

and Resurrection. All, as the title suggests, are treated as transformations and elaborations of the old Babylonian epic of Gilgamesh and Eabani. We have Abraham-*Gilgamesh*, Jacob-*Gilgamesh*, Moses-*Gilgamesh*, Joshua-*Gilgamesh*, Samson-*Gilgamesh*, Samuel-*Gilgamesh*, Saul-*Gilgamesh*, David-*Gilgamesh*, Solomon-*Gilgamesh*, Elijah-*Gilgamesh*, Elisha-*Gilgamesh*, etc. With endless iteration the changes are rung on a few mythical conceptions; personages are blended, and attributes and incidents are transferred at will from one to another; the most far-fetched and impossible analogies are treated as demonstrations. The basis being laid in the Old Testament, the stories of John the Baptist and Jesus are then affiliated to the Gilgamesh myths through their supposed Old Testament parallels. For instance, the Resurrection of " Jesus-*Gilgamesh* " is supposed to be suggested by such incidents as the revival of the dead man cast into the grave of Elisha, on touching the bones of the prophet,[1] and the removal of the bones of Saul [2] and Samson [3] from their respective tombs ! [4] " Incredible, such trifling," one is disposed to exclaim. Not incredible, but the newest and truest " scientific " treatment of history, on the most approved " religionsgeschichtliche "

---

[1] 2 Kings xiii. 21.   [2] 2 Sam. xxi. 12–14.
[3] Judges xvi. 31.
[4] *Gilgamesch-Epos*, p. 923 ; cf. pp. 471, 697.

methods, thinks Jensen himself. The result, at least, in this author's learned pages, is the removal of the last particle of historicity from the life of Jesus in the Gospels. Such a person as Jesus of Nazareth " never existed "—" never lived." [1] " The Jesus-legend is an Israelitish *Gilgamesh*-legend," [2] attached to some person of whom we know absolutely nothing—neither time nor country.[3] " This Jesus has never walked the earth, has never died on earth, because He is actually *nought* but an Israelitish *Gilgamesh—nought* but a counterpart (*Seitenstück*) to Abraham, to Moses, and to innumerable other forms of the legend." [4]

It is needless to confront a reasoner like Jensen, confident in his multiplied proofs (?) that the Gospel history is throughout simply a Gilgamesh-legend, with the testimony of St. Paul. Everything that St. Paul has to tell of Jesus in his four accepted Epistles (Romans, 1 and 2 Corinthians, Galatians) belongs with the highest probability to the Gilgamesh-legend.[5] True, St. Paul tells how he abode fifteen days with St. Peter at Jerusalem, and then saw, and doubtless spoke with St. James, the Lord's brother ; and again how fourteen years later he met this same brother at Jerusalem. That is, he met the brother of this perfectly legendary character.[6] Jensen's reply is simple. Since the

---

[1] P. 1026.   [2] P. 1024.   [3] P. 1026.
[4] P. 1029.   [5] P. 1027.   [6] P. 1028.

Jesus of the Gospels and of the Epistles never existed, St. Paul could not have done what he describes. If these notices actually come from him, " the man either tells a falsehood, or he has been mystified in a wonderful way in Jerusalem." [1] It is a suspicious circumstance that St. Paul has to confirm his statement about seeing St. James with an oath.[2] It adds to the doubt that in 1 Corinthians xi., in its present form, this same St. Paul is found declaring that he received the quite mythical account of the institution of the Lord's Supper as a revelation of the Lord ! [3] " The ground here sinks beneath our feet." [4]

Jensen is an extremist, and his book may be regarded as the *reductio ad absurdum* of a theory which, before him, had been getting cut more and more away from the ground of historical fact. It is to that ground the endeavour must be made to bring it back. The Resurrection of Jesus, it has already been shown, is a fact which rests on historical evidence. What has the theory just described to say to this evidence ? It is a theory, obviously, which may be applied in different ways. It may be applied, e.g., to explain special *traits* in the narratives without denying the general facts of a death, a burial, and subsequent appearances of Jesus. It may be combined with a vision

[1] P. 1028.   [2] Ibid.
[3] Ibid.   [4] P. 1029.

theory, and used, as indeed in part it is, by A. Meyer [1] and Professor Lake, [2] to explain how the stories of these appearances came to take on their present form. Or, treating the whole account of the Resurrection as mythical, it may give itself no concern with the facts, and simply seek to account for the origin of the legend.

It is probably doing the theory no injustice to say that, in the hands of its chief exponents, it is the latter point of view which rules. There is no necessity for discussing the empty tomb, or the reality of Christ's appearances. Enough to show that the history, as we have it, is a deposit of mythological conceptions. Gunkel, e.g., excuses himself from discussion of the origin of faith in the Resurrection, [3] and confines himself to elucidating the form of the legend. Jensen, as just seen, regards the whole as a purely mythological growth. Cheyne has nearly as little to say on the historical basis. If this view be adopted, it cuts belief in the Resurrection away from the ground of history altogether, and it might be enough to reply to it —the history is *there*, and it is utterly impossible, by any legerdemain of the kind proposed, to get rid of it. You do not get rid of facts by simply proposing to give an artificial mythological ex-

---

[1] *Die Auferstehung Christi*, 184–5, 353–4.
[2] *Resur. of Jesus Christ*, pp. 260–3.
[3] Pp. 76–7.

planation of them. The Gospels, the Acts, and
the Epistles still stand, as containing the well-
attested accounts which the Church of Apostolic
days had to give of its own origin. These accounts
had not the remotest relation to Gilgamesh epics,
nature-myths of Egyptian, Greek, or Persian
Mysteries, or pagan speculations of any kind, but
were narratives of plain facts, known to the whole
Church, and attested by Apostles and others who
were themselves eye-witnesses of most of the things
which they related. It was the fact that on the
Friday the Lord was publicly crucified, and died ;
that He was buried in the tomb of Joseph of Arimathæa, in presence of many spectators ; that on
the morning of the third day—" the first day of
the week "—the tomb was visited by holy women,
who found it empty, and received the message
that Jesus had risen, as He said ; that on the same
day He appeared to individual disciples (Mary, St.
Peter, the disciples going to Emmaus), and, in the
evening, to the body of the disciples (the eleven) ;
that afterwards there were other appearances
which the Evangelists and St. Paul recount ; that,
after forty days, He was taken from them up to
heaven. The attempts to break down this history
have been studied in previous chapters, and proof
has been given that these attempts have failed.

Now, in lieu of the history, and as a new discovery, there is offered us this marvellous mytho-

logical construction, by which *all* history, and most previous theories of explanation as well, are swept into space. In dealing with it as a rival theory, not of the origin of belief in the Resurrection, for that it can hardly be said to touch, but of the Gospel story of the Resurrection, it must in frankness be declared of it that it labours under nearly every possible defect which a theory of the kind can have. This judgment it is necessary, but not difficult, to substantiate.

1. One thing which must strike the mind about the theory at once is the *baselessness* of its chief assumptions. Nothing need be said here of the general astral Babylonian hypothesis with which it starts, or of the assumed universal diffusion of this astral theory throughout the East. That must stand or fall on its own merits.[1] Nor need the traces of the influence of Oriental symbolism in Old Testament prophecy, or in Jewish and Christian Apocalyptic, be denied, if such really can be established. But what is to be said of the

[1] Winckler's theory on this subject is still the subject of much dispute among scholars (cf. Lake, *Resur. of Jesus Christ*, pp. 260–2). Prof. Lake says on its application to Scripture : "The difficulty is to decide how far this theory is based on fact, and how far it is merely guess-work" (p. 262). For a popular statement of Winckler's theory, see his *Die Babylonische Kultur in ihren Beziehungen zur unsrigen* (1902), and in criticism of Winckler and Jeremias, E. König, "*Altorientalische Weltanschauung*" und *Altes Testament*.

allegation, on the correctness of which the application to the New Testament depends, of a wholesale absorption of Babylonian mythology by the Jewish nation, and the crystallisation of this mythology round the idea of the Messiah in Jewish popular thought in pre-Christian times? What proof worthy of the name can be given of such an assumption? Dr. Cheyne's form of the theory, already referred to, had best be stated in his own words. "The four forms of Christian belief," he says, "which we have been considering are the Virgin-birth of Jesus Christ, His descent into the nether world, His Resurrection, and His Ascension. On the ground of facts supplied by archæology, it is plausible to hold that all these arose out of a pre-Christian sketch of the life, death, and exaltation of the expected Messiah, itself ultimately derived from a widely current mythic tradition respecting a solar deity." [1] And earlier, "The Apostle Paul, when he says (1 Cor. xv. 3, 4) that Christ died and that He rose again 'according to the Scriptures,' in reality points to a pre-Christian sketch of the life of Christ, partly—as we have seen—derived from widely-spread non-Jewish myths, and embodied in Jewish writings." [2] With this drapery it is assumed that the figure of Jesus of Nazareth was

---

[1] *Ut supra*, p. 128; cf. note xi., p. 252.
[2] P. 113. Gunkel may be compared, *ut supra*, pp. 68–9, 78–9.

clothed. But where is the faintest trace of evidence
of such a pre-Christian Jewish sketch of the Messiah
embracing Virgin-birth, Resurrection, and Ascension ? It is nothing but an inferential conjecture
from the Gospel narratives themselves, eked out
by allusions to myths of deaths and resurrections
of gods in other religions. These, as said above,
are, in their origin, nature-myths. The Resurrection of Jesus was no nature-myth, but an event
which happened three days after His Crucifixion,
in an historical time, and in the case of an historical
Personage. Parallels to *such* an event utterly
fail.[1]

2. The baselessness of the foundation of the
theory is only equalled by the *arbitrariness* of the
methods by which a connexion with the Gospel,
story is sought to be bolstered up. Specimens of
Professor Jensen's reasonings have been given
above, and no more need be said of them. But
a like arbitrariness, if in less glaring form, infects

[1] Gunkel admits that " this belief in a dying and rising
Christ was not present in *official* Judaism in the time of
Jesus " ; but thinks it may have lurked " in certain private
circles " (*ut supra*, p. 79). Cheyne, in his own note, can
give no evidence at all of writings alluding to a resurrection (*ut supra*, p. 254).
Jesus and His Apostles found, indeed, a suffering and
rising Christ in the O.T., but their point of view (on this
see Hengstenberg, *Christology*, vol. iv., app. iv.) was not
that of contemporary Judaism. The disciples themselves
were " slow of heart " to believe the things that Jesus
spoke to them (Luke xxiv. 25-6, 44-6).

the whole theory. In the Protean shapes assumed by Oriental mythology it is never difficult to pick out isolated traits which, by ingenious, if far-fetched combinations, can be made to present some resemblance to some feature or other in the Gospel story. Thus, as parallels to " the death of the world's Redeemer," we are told by Dr. Cheyne: " That the death of the solar deity, Marduk, was spoken of, and his grave shown, in Babylonia, is an ascertained fact ; the death of Osiris and of other gods was an Egyptian belief, and, though a more distant parallel, one may here refer also to the empty grave of Zeus pointed out in Crete." [1] [Gunkel gives this last fact more correctly ; " In Crete is shown the grave of Zeus, naturally an *empty* grave." [2]] Where facts fail, imagination is invoked to fill the gaps, this specially in the parts which concern the Resurrection. Thus, in Jeremias : " The ' grave of Bel ' (Herod. i. 18), like the grave of Osiris, certainly stands in connexion (*zusammenhängt*) with the celebration of the death and resurrection of Marduk-Tammuz (Lehmann, i. p. 276), even *though we still possess no definite testimonies to a festival of the death and resurrection of Marduk-Tammuz* " [3] (italics ours). Gunkel thinks that the Jewish belief in the resurerection compels us to " postulate " that " in the

---

[1] Pp. 253-4.   [2] *Ut supra*, p. 77.
[3] *Ut supra*, p. 9.

Orient of that time belief in the resurrection must have ruled." [1] Jensen has to face the fact, that the Gilgamesh epic has nothing about a resurrection. But, he says, " that the Babyloniana Gilgamesh, who must die, in the oldest form of his legend (*Sage*) rose again from the dead, appears self-evident. For he is a Sun-god, and sun-gods, like gods of light and warmth, who die, must also, among the Babylonians, rise again." [2] The oldest form of the Elisha-*Gilgamesh* legend, he thinks probably included a translation to heaven, and, as an inference from this, a resurrection.[3] Simiarly, the Resurrection of Jesus is a " logical postulate " from the fact of His exaltation, in accordance with a long series of parallel myths.[4]

A special application of the theory to the Gospel history connects itself with the Resurrection " on the third day," and the origin of the Sunday festival. It is very difficult, indeed, to find suitable illustrations connecting resurrection with " the third day "—indeed, none are to be found. We are driven back on Jonah's three days in the fish, which Dr. Cheyne says is not sufficient to justify St. Paul's expression ; [5] on the Apocalyptic " time and times and half a time," and three days and a half ; on a Mandæan story of a " little boy of

[1] *Ut supra*, p. 33.   [2] *Ut supra*, p. 925.
[3] Pp. 923-4.   [4] P. 924.
[5] *Ut supra*, p. 254.

three years and one day"; on the Greek myth of
Apollo slaying the serpent Pytho on the fourth
day after his birth; on the festival of the resurrection of the Phrygian Actis on the fourth day
after the lamentations over his death.[1] This is
actually supposed to be evidence. Gunkel makes
a strong point of the festival of Sunday. How
came the Resurrection of Jesus to be fixed down
to a Sunday? How came this to be observed
as a weekly festival? "All these difficulties are
relieved, so soon as we treat the matter from
the 'historical-religious' point of view"[2] The
"Lord's Day" was the day of the Sun-god; in
Babylonian reckoning the first day of the week.
Easter Sunday was the day of the sun's emergence
from the night of winter.[3] Can it be held, then,
as accidental that this was the day on which Jesus
arose?[4] It is really an ancient Oriental festival
which is here being taken over by the primitive
Christian community, as later the Church took
over December 25 as Christmas Day.[5] It fails to
be observed in this ingenious construction—wholly
in the air, as if there was no such thing as history
in the matter—that there is not a single word in

---

[1] Pp. 110–13; cf. Gunkel, *ut supra*, pp. 79–82; Lake,
p. 263.

[2] Gunkel, p. 74.

[3] Pp. 74, 79. Thus also Loisy, *Les Évangiles Synoptiques*, ii. p. 721.

[4] P. 79.   [5] Pp. 74–5, 79.

the Gospels or in the New Testament connecting
" the first day of the week "—reckoned in purely
Jewish fashion by the " Sabbath "—with the day
of the sun, or any use or suggestion of the name
" Sunday." The " primitive community " had
other and far plainer reasons for remembrance
of the " Lord's Day " (Jesus alone was their " Lord,"
and no sun-god), viz., in the fact that on the Friday
of the Passover week He was crucified and en-
tombed, and on the dawn of the first day of the
week thereafter actually came forth, as He had
predicted, victorious over the power of death, and
appeared to His disciples.

This theory, in brief, destitute of adequate foundation, laden with incredibilities, and disdainful
of the world of realities, has no claim whatever
to supersede the plain, simply-told, historically
well-attested narratives of the four Gospels as to
the grounds of the Church's belief from the beginning in the Resurrection of the Lord from the
dead. As has frequently been said in these pages
—*the Church knew its own origin,* and could be
under no vital mistake as to the great facts on
which its belief in Christ as its Crucified and Risen
Lord rested. It is difficult to imagine what kind
of persons the Apostles and Evangelists in some
of these theories are taken for—children or fools ?
They were really neither, and the work they did,
and the literature they have left, prove it. Who

that has ever felt on his spirit the power of the
impression of the picture and teaching of Jesus
in the Gospels could dream of accounting for it
by a bundle of Babylonian myths? Who that
has ever experienced the power of His Resurrection
life could fancy the source of it an unreality?

It may be appropriate at this point to say a
few words on the state of *Jewish belief* on the
subject of resurrection. That the Jews in the
time of Jesus were familiar with the idea of a
resurrection of the dead (the Sadducees alone denying it [1]) is put beyond question by the Gospels,[2]
though there is no evidence, despite assertions to
the contrary,[3] that they connected death and
resurrection with the idea of the Messiah. The
particular ideas entertained by the Jews of the
resurrection-body,[4] while of interest in themselves,
have therefore only a slight bearing on the origin
of belief in the Resurrection of Jesus from His
tomb on the third day. That was an event *sui
generis*, outside the anticipations of the disciples,
notwithstanding the repeated intimations which
Jesus Himself had given them regarding it,[5] and

[1] Matt. xxii. 23, etc.; cf. Acts xxiii. 6–8.

[2] As above; cf. John v. 28, 29; xi. 24; Matt. xiv. 2;
and the instances of resurrection in the Gospels (Jairus's
daughter, son of widow of Nain, Lazarus).

[3] Gunkel and Cheyne give no proof, and none is to be
had.

[4] On these, cf. Lake, *ut supra*, pp. 23–7, with references.

[5] As already seen, these were persistently misunder-

only forced upon their faith by indubitable evidence of the actual occurrence of the marvel. There is no reason to suppose that the idea of the resurrection of the body was a form subsequently imposed on a belief in the Lord's continued life [1] originally gained in some other way. The Resurrection of Jesus never meant anything else in the primitive community than His Resurrection in the body.

Of greater importance is the question raised by Gunkel in his discussion as to *whence* the Jews derived their idea of the resurrection. It is to be granted that Gunkel has a much profounder view of what he calls " the immeasurable significance " of this doctrine of the resurrection for the New Testament [2] than most other writers who deal with the topic. He claims that " this doctrine of the resurrection from the dead is one of the greatest things found anywhere in the history of religion," [3] and devotes space to drawing out its weighty implications. Just, however, on account of " this incomparable significance " of the doctrine, he holds that it cannot be derived from within Judaism itself, but must take its origin from a ruling belief in the Orient of the later time.[4] The existence of such a belief is a " postulate " from its presence

stood by the disciples. The critics mostly deny that they were given.

[1] Thus Harnack and others.

[2] *Ut supra*, p. 31.   [3] P 32.   [4] P. 33.

in Judaism, and is thought to be supported by Oriental, especially by Egyptian and Persian, parallels.[1] He discounts the evidence of the belief in the Old Testament furnished by passages in the Psalms, the prophets, and in Job. The doctrine, in short, "is not, as was formerly commonly maintained, and sometimes still is maintained, a genuine product of Judaism, but has come into Judaism from without."[2] If this be so, it may be argued that it is really a pagan intrusion into Christianity, and ought not to be retained.

The "immeasurable significance" of the belief in resurrection among the Jews may be admitted, but Gunkel's inferences to the foreign origin of the belief can only be contested. For—

1. The *link fails* to connect this belief with any foreign religions. Gunkel seems hardly aware of the paradox of his theory of a world filled with belief in the resurrection, while yet the Jews, till a late period, are supposed to have had no knowledge of it. But the theory itself is without foundation. There is no evidence of any such *general* belief in a resurrection of the dead in ancient religions. No evidence of such general belief can be adduced from ancient Babylonia. Merodach may be hailed in a stray verse as "the merciful one, who raises the dead to life," and Ishtar may rescue Tammuz from Hades. But this falls far

[1] P. 33.   [2] P. 31.

short of the proof required. Belief in the reanimation of the body may underlie the Egyptian
practice of embalming, though this is disputed,
but the developed Osiris-myth is comparatively
late, and without provable influence on Judaism.[1]
The alleged Persian or Zoroastrian influence is
equally problematical. It is very questionable
how far this doctrine is found in the old Persian
religion at all.[2] The references to it are certainly
few and ambiguous,[3] and totally inadequate to
explain the remarkable prominence which the
doctrine assumed among the Jews.

2. The *adequate grounds* for the development
of this doctrine are found in the Old Testament
itself. It may be held, and has been argued for
by the present writer,[4] that, so far as a hope of
immortality (beyond the shadowy and cheerless
lot of Sheol) appears in the Old Testament, it is

[1] On Merodach, Osiris and Resurrection, cf. Sayce,
Religions of Ancient Egypt and Babylonia, pp. 24, 153 ff.,
165, 168, 288, 329, etc.

[2] Schultz remarks : " This point [of influence] will be
the more difficult to decide, the more uncertain it becomes
how far this doctrine, the principal witness to which is the
Bundehesh [a late work], was really Old Persian " (*O.T.
Theol.* ii. p. 392).

[3] This can be tested by consulting the translation to
the Zend-Avesta in *The Sacred Books of the East*. The
indexes to the three volumes give only one reference to
the subject, and that to an undated " Miscellaneous Fragment " at the end.

[4] In *The Christian View of God and the World :* Appendix
to Lect. V., " The Old Testament Doctrine of Immortality."

always in the form of deliverance from Sheol, and renewed life in the body. The state of death is neither a natural nor normal state for man, whose original destiny was immortality in the completeness of his personal life in a body ; and the same faith which enabled the believer to trust in God for deliverance from all ills of life, enabled him also, in its higher exercises, to trust Him for deliverance from death itself. This seems the true key to those passages in the Psalms and in Job which by nearly all but the new school of interpreters have been regarded as breathing the hope of immortality with God.[1] In the prophets, from Hosea down, the idea of a resurrection of the nation, including, may we not say, at least in such passages as Hosea vi. 2 ; xiii. 14, and Isaiah xxv. 6–8 ; xxvi. 19, the individuals in it, is a familiar one. A text like Daniel xii. 2 only draws out the individual implication of this doctrine with more distinctness. In later books, as 2 Maccabees, the Book of Enoch, Ezra iv., the doctrine is treated as established (sometimes resurrection of the godly, sometimes of righteous and wicked).

[1] E.g., Pss. xvi. 8–11 ; xvii. 15 ; xlix. 14, 15 ; lxxiii. 24 ; Job xiv. 13–15 (R.V.) ; xix. 25–27. In his *Origin of the Psalter* Dr. Cheyne accepts the resurrection reference of several of these passages, seeing in them a proof of Zoroastrian influence (pp. 382, 406, 407, 431, etc.). This, however, as he himself acknowledges, is where leading scholars fail to support him (pp. 425, 451). Cf. Pusey, Daniel, pp. 512–17.

Little has been said in these discussions of the New Testament *Apocryphal* books,[1] the statements of which it has become customary to draw into comparison with the accepted Gospels. Only a few remarks need be made on them now. They have been kept apart because, in origin, character, and authority, they stand on a completely different footing from the canonical Gospels, and because there is not the least reason to believe that they preserve a single authentic tradition beyond those which the four Gospels contain. This has long been acknowledged with regard to the stories of the Infancy, the puerilities of which put them outside the range of serious consideration by any intelligent mind. No more reason exists for paying heed to the fabulous embellishments of the narratives of the Resurrection. A romance like *The Gospel of Nicodemus* (fifth cent.), whether based on a second century *Acts of Pilate* or not, receives attention from no one. It is simply a travesty and tricking out with extravagances of the material furnished by St. Matthew and the other Evangelists. More respect is paid to the recently-discovered fragment of *The Gospel of Peter*,[2] which begins in the middle of Christ's trial, and breaks

---

[1] A collection of some of the chief of these, edited and annotated by the present writer, may be seen in *The New Testament Apocryphal Writings*, in the "Temple Bible" series (Dent).

[2] A Gnostic Gospel of the 2nd century.

off in the middle of a sentence, with Peter and Andrew returning to their fishermen's toils, after the feast of unleavened bread is ended. Here, it is thought, is a distinct tradition, preserving the memory of that flight into Galilee which the canonical Gospels ignore. Yet at every point this Gospel shows itself dependent on St. Matthew and the rest, while freely manipulating and embellishing the tradition which they contain. A single specimen is enough to show the degree of credit to be attached to it. From St. Matthew is borrowed the story of the watch at the tomb, with adornments, the centurion, e.g., being named Petronius. The day of the Resurrection is called " the Lord's Day." Then, we read, as that day dawned, " While the soldiers kept watch two and two at their post, a mighty voice sounded in the heaven ; and they saw the heavens opened, and two men descending from thence in great glory, and approaching the sepulchre. But that stone which had been placed at the door of the sepulchre rolled back of itself, and moved aside, and the tomb opened, and both the young men went in. When, therefore, those soldiers behold this, they awakened the centurion and the elders—for they also were there to watch—and while they were telling what they had seen, they behold coming forth from the tomb three men, and the two supporting the one, and a cross following them. And the heads of the two reached indeed unto heaven, but the head of the one who was led by them reached far above the heavens. And they heard a voice from heaven that said : Hast thou preached unto those that sleep ? And the answer was heard from the Cross : Yes. . . . And while they were yet pondering the matter, the heavens open again, and a man descends and goes into the sepulchre." [1] This may be placed alongside of the narrative in the Gospel without comment.

[1] If it is argued that this is a simple expansion of St. Matthew's story of the watch, as the latter is an addition to St. Mark's, it may be observed that St. Matthew's story is an expansion or embellishment of nothing, but a distinct, independent narrative ; while the story in *The Gospel of Peter* has evidently no basis but St. Matthew's account, which it decorates from pure fancy.

DOCTRINAL BEARINGS OF THE RESURRECTION

X

DOCTRINAL BEARINGS OF THE RESUR-RECTION

IT will probably be evident from the preceding discussion that a movement is at present in process which aims at nothing less than the dissolution of Christianity, as that has hitherto been understood. It is not simply the details of the recorded life of Jesus that are questioned, but the whole conception of Christ's supernatural Person and work, as set forth in the Gospels and Epistles, which is challenged. If the Virgin Birth is rejected at one end of the history, and the bodily Resurrection at the other, not less are the miracles and supernatural claims that lie between. With this goes naturally on the part of many a hesitancy in admitting even Christ's moral perfection.[1] A sinless Personality would be a miracle in time, and miracles are excluded by the first principles of the new philosophy.

---

[1] This tendency is seen in various recent pronouncements. E.g., Mr. G. L. Dickinson, in the *Hibbert Journal* for April, 1908, asks : " How many men are really aware of any such personal relation to Jesus as the Christian religion presupposes ? How many, if they told the honest truth, really hold Him to be even the ideal man ? " (p. 522).

Bolder spirits, taking, as they conceive, a wider outlook on the field of religion, and on the evolutionary advance of the race, would cut loose the progress of humanity from Christianity altogether.[1] It is an illusion to imagine that a tendency of this kind can be effectively met by any half-way, compromising attitude to the great supernatural facts on which Christianity rests. It is only to be met by the firm reassertion of the whole truth regarding the Christ of the New Testament Gospel—a Christ supernatural in origin, nature, works, claims, mission, and destiny ; the divine Son, incarnate for the salvation of the world, pure from sin, crucified and risen, ever-living to carry on to its consummation the work of the Kingdom He founded while on earth.   None need really fear that the ground is about to be swept from beneath his feet with respect to this divine foundation by any skill of sceptics or revolutionary discoveries in knowledge. One notices in how strange ways the wheel of criticism itself comes round often to the affirmation of things it once denied. To take only one point : how often has the contrast between the Jesus of the Synoptics and the Pauline and Johannine Christ been emphasized ? The contrast is, of course, still maintained, yet with the growing admission that the difference is at most one of *degree*, that the Jesus

[1] The same writer rejects Christianity, and advocates a return to " mythology " (p. 509).

of the Synoptics is as truly a supernatural being as the Jesus of St. John. Bousset, e.g., states this frankly : " Already," he says, " the oldest Gospel is written from the standpoint of faith ; already for Mark is Jesus not only the Messiah of the Jewish people, but the miraculous eternal Son of God, whose glory shone in this world. And it has been rightly emphasized, that in this respect, our first three Gospels are distinguished from the fourth only in degree. . . . For the faith of the community, which the oldest Evangelist already shares, Jesus is the miraculous Son of God, in whom men believe, whom men put wholly on the side of God." [1]

In the history of such a Christ as the Gospels depict the Resurrection from the dead has its natural and necessary place. To the first preachers of Christianity an indissoluble connexion subsisted between the Resurrection of Jesus and the Gospel they proclaimed. Remove that foundation, and in St. Paul's judgment, their message was gone. " If Christ hath not been raised," he says, " then is

---

[1] *Was wissen wir von Jesus ?* pp. 54, 57. To explain these traits some scholars feel it necessary to postulate a revision of St. Mark's Gospel from a Johannine standpoint. Thus J. Weiss, in the *Dict. of Christ and the Gospels*, ii. p. 324 : " For our own part we have been able to collect a mass of evidence in support of the theory that the text of Mark has been very thoroughly revised from the Johannine standpoint, that a host of Johannine characteristics were inserted into it at some period subsequent to its use by Matthew and Mark." There is no real proof of such revision.

our preaching vain, your faith also is vain. . . . If Christ hath not been raised, your faith is vain ; ye are yet in your sins." [1] To " modern " thought, on the other hand, the Resurrection of Jesus, in any other sense, at least, than that of spiritual survival, has no essential importance for Christianity. The belief in a bodily Resurrection is rather an excrescence on Christianity, that can be dropped without affecting it in any vital way.   Is this really so ?   It may aid faith if it can be shown that, so far from being a non-essential of Christianity, the Resurrection of Jesus is, as the Apostles believed, in the strictest sense, a *constitutive* part of the Christian Gospel.

1. In the older mode of treatment of the Resurrection, peculiar stress was laid upon its *evidential* value.   It was the culminating proof of Christ's claim to be " a Teacher come from God," [2] or, from a higher point of view, the crowning demonstration of His divine Sonship and Messiahship.   It was also the supreme attestation of the fact of immortality. The angle of vision is now considerably changed, and it has rightly become more customary to view the Resurrection in the light of Christ's claims and manifested glory as the Son of God, than to regard the latter as deriving credibility from the former.   But care must be taken that the element of truth in the older view is likewise conserved.

[1] I Cor. xv. 14.   [2] John iii. 2.

(1) With respect to the *divine Sonship*. It is doubtless the case that faith in the Resurrection is connected with, and in part depends on, the degree of faith in Jesus Himself. It is the belief that Jesus is such an One as the Gospels represent Him to be—"holy, guileless, undefiled, separated from sinners,"[1] divinely great in the prerogatives He claims as Son of God and Saviour of the world, yet in His submission to rejection and death at the hands of sinful men the perfect example of suffering obedience—which above all sustains the conviction that He, the Prince and Lord of life, cannot have succumbed to the power of death, and prepares the mind to receive the evidence that He actually *did* rise, as the Gospels declare.

This connexion of faith in the Resurrection with faith in Jesus, however, it must now be remarked, in no way deprives the Resurrection of Jesus of the apologetic or evidential value which justly belongs to it as a fact of the first moment, amply attested on its own account, in its bearings on the Lord's Person and claims. The attempt to set faith and historical evidence in opposition to each other, witnessed specially in the Ritschlian school, must to the general Christian intelligence, always fail. Since, as is above remarked, it is implied in Christ's whole claim that He, the Holy One, should not be holden of death,[2] not merely that He has a spiritual

[1] Heb. vii. 26.
[2] Acts ii. 24. This is further illustrated below.

life with God—faith would be involved in insoluble contradictions if it could be shown that Christ
has not risen, or, what comes to the same thing,
that there is no historical evidence that He has risen.
It may be, and is, involved in faith that He should
rise from the dead, but this faith would not of itself be
a sufficient ground for asserting that He had risen,
if all historical evidence for the statement were
wanting.   Faith cherishes the just expectation that,
if Christ has risen, there will be historical evidence
for the fact ; and were such evidence not forthcom-
ing, it would be driven back upon itself in questioning whether its confidence was not self-delusion.

In harmony with this view is the place which
the Resurrection of Jesus holds in Scripture, and
the stress there laid upon its historical attestation.
" Declared," the Apostle says, " to be the Son of
God with power, according to the Spirit of holiness,
by the Resurrection of the dead." [1]   It is undeniable
that, if historically real, the Resurrection of Jesus
is a confirmation of His entire claim.   No mind can
believe in that transcendent fact, and in the exaltation that followed it, and continue to apply to Christ
a mere humanitarian standard.   The older Socinians
attempted this, but the logic of the case proved too
strong for them.   Both assertions hold good :
Christ's Personality and claims demand a Resurrection, and, conversely, the Resurrection is a retro-

[1] Rom. i. 4.

spective attestation that Jesus was indeed the
exalted and divinely-sent Person He claimed to be.

(2) Not very dissimilar is the position to be taken
as to the evidential value of the Resurrection with
regard to *immortality*. The relation here is, indeed,
more vital than at first appears. The Christian
hope, it will immediately be seen, is not merely
that of an " immortality of the soul," nor is " eternal
life " simply the indefinite prolongation of existence
in a future state of being. Keeping, however, at
present to the general question of the possibility
and reality of a life beyond the grave, it is to be asked
what bearing the Resurrection of Jesus has as evidence on this. None whatever, a writer like Professor Lake will reply, for the physical Resurrection is
an incredibility, and can prove nothing. Apparitional
manifestations are possible, but even these can only
be admitted if, first of all, proof is given of the survival of the soul by the help of such phenomena as
the Society of Psychical Research furnishes.[1] Others
base on the natural grounds for belief in a future life
supplied by the constitution of the human soul, eked
out, in the case of recent able writers, by appeal to the
same class of psychical phenomena.[2] On a more

---

[1] *Res. of Jesus Christ*, pp. 245, 272–3.

[2] Cf. the interesting paper on Immortality by Sir Oliver
Lodge in the *Hibbert Journal* for April, 1908. The persistence of the soul (which damage or destruction of the
brain is held not to disprove) is argued from the " priority
in essence of the spiritual to the material " and from such

spiritual plane, Herrmann and Harnack would argue
that immortality is given as a " thought of faith "
in the direct contemplation of Christ's life in God.
A soul of such purity, elevation, and devotion to the
Father as was Christ's cannot be thought of as
extinguished in death.[1]

It seems evident that, if man is really a being
destined for life hereafter, indications of this vast
destiny cannot be absent from the make and constitution of his nature. Capacities will reveal themselves in him proportionate to the immortality that
awaits him. It is not denied, therefore—at least
here—that there are grounds in man's nature abundantly warranting a reasonable faith in a life beyond
death, and awakening the craving for more light
regarding that future state of being. History and
literature, however, are witnesses how little these
" natural intimations of immortality " can of themselves do to sustain an assured confidence in a future
conscious existence, or to give comfort and hope at
the thought of entrance into it. Browning may be
styled a poet of immortality, but a long distance is
traversed between the early optimism of a *Pauline*,[2]
and the soul-racking doubts of a *La Saisiaz*, when

facts as telepathy (pp. 570 ff.), præter-normal psychology
(pp. 572 ff.), automatism (pp. 574 ff.), subliminal faculty
(pp. 547 ff.), genius (pp. 580 ff.), mental pathology (pp.
582 ff.).

[1] Cf. Herrmann, *Communion with God* (E. T.), pp. 221-2.
[2] Cf. Browning, *Works*, i. pp. 27, 29.

the question has to be faced and answered in the light of reason, " Does the soul survive the body ? Is there God's self, no or yes ? "[1]

The spiritual faith that roots itself in Christ's unbroken communion with the Father has, indeed, an irrefragable basis. But is it adequate, if it does not advance to its own natural completion in belief in the Resurrection ? For Christ's earthly history does not end as an optimistic faith would expect. Rather, it closes in seeming defeat and disaster. The forces of evil—the powers of dissolution that devour on every side—seem to have prevailed over Him also. Is this the last word ? If so, how shall faith support itself ? " We hoped that it was He which should redeem Israel."[2] Is not the darkness deeper than before when even He seems to go down in the struggle ?

Will it be doubted that, as for the first disciples, so for myriads since, the Resurrection has dispelled these doubts, and given them an assurance which nothing can overthrow that death is conquered,[3] and that, because Jesus lives, they shall live also ?[4] Jesus, who came from God and went to God, has shed a flood of light into that unseen world which has vanquished its terrors, and made it the bright home of every spiritual and eternal hope. It is open to any one to reject this consolation, grounded

[1] *Works*, xiv. p. 168. [2] Luke xxiv. 21.
[3] 1 Cor. xv. 54–7. [4] John xiv. 19.

in sure historical fact, or to prefer to it the star-light—if even such it can be named—of dubious psychical phenomena. But will it be denied that for those who, on what they judge the best of grounds, *believe* the Resurrection, there is opened up a " sure and certain hope " of immortality which nothing else in time can give ?

2. The Resurrection is an evidential fact, and its importance in this relation is not to be minimized. But this, as a little consideration may show, after all, only touches the exterior of the subject. The core of the matter is not reached till it is perceived that the Resurrection of Jesus is not simply an external seal or evidential appendage to the Christian Gospel, but enters as a *constitutive element* into the very essence of that Gospel. Its denial or removal would be the mutilation of the Christian doctrine of Redemption, of which it is an integral part. An opposite view is that of Herrmann, who lays the whole stress on the impression produced by Christ's earthly life. Such a view has no means of incorporating the Resurrection into itself as a constitutive part of its Christianity. The Resurrection remains at most a deduction of faith without inner relation to salvation ? It is apt to be felt, therefore, to be a superfluous appendage. In a full Scriptural presentation it is not so. It might almost be said to be a test of the adequacy of the view of Christ and His work taken by any school, whether

it is able to take in the Resurrection of Christ as a constitutive part of it.

In New Testament Scripture, it will not be disputed that these two things are always taken together—the Death and the Resurrection of Christ —the one as essentially connected with, and completed in, the other. " It is Christ Jesus that died," says St. Paul, " yea, rather, that was raised from the dead." [1] " Who was delivered up for our trespasses, and was raised for our justification." [2] " Who through Him," says St. Peter, " are believers in God, which raised Him from the dead, and gave Him glory ; so that your faith and hope might be in God." [3] " The God of peace, who brought again from the dead the great shepherd of the sheep, with the blood of the everlasting covenant," [4] we read in Hebrews. " I am the Living One ; and I was dead, and behold, I am alive for evermore," [5] says the Lord in the Apocalypse.

What is the nature of this connexion ? The answer to this question turns on the manner in which the death of Christ itself is conceived, and on this point the teaching of the New Testament is again sufficiently explicit. The Cross is the decisive meeting-place between man's sin and God's grace. It is the point of reconciliation between man and

[1] Rom. viii. 34.   [2] Rom. iv. 25.
[3] 1 Pet. i. 21 ; cf. iii. 18–22.   [4] Heb. xiii. 20.
[5] Rev. i. 18.

God. *There* was accomplished—at least consummated—the great work of Atonement for human sin ! Christ, as the Epistle to the Hebrews declares, " put away sin by the sacrifice of Himself." [1]

It seems superfluous to quote passages in illustration of a truth of which the Apostolic writings are literally full. Jesus Himself laid stress on His death as a means of salvation to the world,[2] and, theories apart, every principal writer in the New Testament reiterates the idea in every form of expression which the vocabulary of Redemption can yield. But, if this is the true light in which the death of Jesus through and for the sin of man is to be conceived, how does the Resurrection of Jesus stand related to it ? Is it an accident ? Or is there not connexion of the most vital kind ? Manifestly there is, and that in various respects.[3]

(1) The connexion at the outset is an essential one with *Christ's own work* as Redeemer. One need only follow here the familiar lines of Apostolic teaching, in which the Resurrection is represented under such aspects as the following :—

i. As the natural and necessary *completion* of the work of Redemption itself. Accepting the

[1] Heb. ix. 26.
[2] Matt. xx. 28 ; xxvi. 26-28 ; John iii. 14-16, etc.
[3] For an interesting treatment of this whole subject, cf. Milligan, *The Resurrection of Our Lord*, Lects. IV., V. and VI.

above interpretation of Christ's death, it seems evident that, if Christ died for men—in Atonement for their sins—it could not be that He should remain permanently in the state of death. That, had it been possible, would have been the frustration of the very end of His dying, for if He remained Himself a prey to death, how could He redeem others ? Jesus Himself seldom spoke of His death without coupling it with the prediction of His Resurrection.[1] St. Peter in Acts assumes it as self-evident that it was not possible that death should hold Him.[2] St. Paul constantly speaks of the Resurrection as the necessary sequel of the Crucifixion, and directly connects it with justification.[3] The further point —that a complete Redemption of man includes the redemption of the body—is dwelt upon below.

ii. As *the Father's seal* on Christ's completed work, and public declaration of its *acceptance*. Had Christ remained a prey to death, where would have been the knowledge, the certainty, the assurance that full Atonement had indeed been made, that the Father had accepted that holy work on behalf of our sinful race, that the foundation of perfect reconciliation between God and man had indeed been laid ? With the Resurrection a public demonstration was given, not only, as before, of Christ's divine Sonship and Messiahship, but of the

[1] Matt. xvi. 21 ; xvii. 23 ; xx. 19 ; John x. 17, 18, etc.
[2] Acts ii. 24. [3] Rom. iv. 25.

Father's perfect satisfaction with, and full acceptance of the whole work of Christ as man's Saviour,
but peculiarly His work as Atoner for sin, expressed
in such words as " Christ died for the ungodly," [1]
"Who His own self bare our sins in His body upon
the tree." [2] It is this which leads St. Paul to connect the assurance of justification—of forgiveness,
of freedom from all condemnation—with faith in
the Resurrection.[3] The ground of acceptance was
the obedience unto death upon the Cross, but it was
the Resurrection which gave the joyful confidence
that the work had accomplished its result.

iii. As the entrance of Christ on a new life as the
risen and exalted Head of His Church and *universal
Lord.* The Resurrection of Jesus is everywhere
viewed as the commencement of His Exaltation.
Resurrection, Ascension, Exaltation to the throne
of universal dominion go together as parts of the
same transaction.[4] St. Paul, in Acts, connects the
Resurrection with the words of the second Psalm,
" Thou art My Son, this day have I begotten Thee." [5]
But the Resurrection, as the New Testament writers

[1] Rom. v. 6.   [2] 1 Pet. ii. 24.
[3] Rom. iv. 24, 25 ; viii. 35 ; x. 9.
[4] Cf. e.g. Rom. viii. 34 ; Eph. i. 20–22 ; iii. 9, 10 ; Heb.
iv. 14 ; x. 12 ; 1 Pet. iii. 21–2. On this ground Harnack
argues against the separation of the Ascension from the
Resurrection in the Creed (*Das. Apost. Glaubensbekenntniss*
p. 25). But cf. Swete, *The Apostles' Creed,* pp. 64 ff.).
[5] Acts xiii. 33.

likewise testify, was a change of *state*—from the temporal to the eternal, from humiliation to glory, above all, from a condition which had to do with sin, and the taking away of sin, to one which is " apart from sin " ($\chi\omega\rho\grave{\iota}s$ $\dot{\alpha}\mu\alpha\rho\tau\acute{\iota}\alpha s$),[1] and is marked by the plenitude of spiritual power. This is a prevailing view in St. Paul and in the Epistle to the Hebrews. " The death that He died," says the former, " He died unto sin once : but the life that He liveth, He liveth unto God." [2]   " The last Adam became a life-giving Spirit." [3]   " When He had made purification of sins," says the latter, He " sat down on the right hand of the Majesty on high." [4] " Having been made perfect, He became unto all them that obey Him the author of eternal salvation." [5]   " He, when He had offered one sacrifice for sins for ever, sat down on the right hand of God, from henceforth expecting till His enemies be made the footstool of His feet." [6]   A priest " after the power of an endless life." [7]   With His exaltation is connected the gift of the Spirit. " Being therefore," said St. Peter, " by the right hand of God exalted, and having received of the Father the promise of the Holy Ghost, He hath poured forth this, which ye see and hear." [8]

[1] Heb. ix. 28.
[2] Rom. vi. 10.   [3] 1 Cor. xv. 45.   [4] Heb. i. 3.
[5] Heb. v. 9.   [6] Heb. x. 12, 13.   [7] Heb. vii. 16.
[8] Acts ii. 33.   Cf. Christ's own promises, John xiv. 16, 26 ; xv. 26 ; xvi. 7.

On this view of Jesus as having died to sin, and risen
in power to a new life with God, and having become
the principle of spiritual quickening to His people,
is based what is sometimes spoken of as St. Paul's
" mystical " doctrine of the union of believers with
Christ. Through faith, and symbolically in baptism, the Christian dies with Christ to sin—is thence-
forth done with it as something put away and
belonging to the past—and rises with Him in spiritual power to newness of life.[1] Christ lives in him
by His Spirit.[2] He is risen with Christ, and shares
a life the spring of which is hid with Christ in God.[3]
Is it possible to review such testimonies without
realizing how tremendous is the significance attached
in Apostolic Christianity to this fact of the Resurrection ?

(2) A further aspect of the doctrinal significance
of the resurrection is opened when it is observed
that the Resurrection is not simply the completion of Christ's redemptive work, but, in one important particular, itself sheds light on the *nature*
of that redemption. It does so inasmuch as it
gives its due place to the *body* of man in the constitution of his total personality. Man is a com-
pound being. The body as well as the soul enters
into the complete conception of his nature. The
redemption of the whole man, therefore, includes,

[1] Rom. vi. 3–11.
[2] Rom. viii. 9–11 ; Gal. i. 20.   [3] Col. iii. 1–3.

as St. Paul phrases it, " the adoption, to wit, the redemption of the body." [1]   From this point of view it may be said that the Resurrection was essential in that the redemption of man meant the redemption of his whole personality, body and soul together.   A mere *spiritual* survival of Christ— an " immortality of the soul " only—would not have been sufficient.   This is a consideration which has its roots deep in the Scripture doctrine of man, and has important bearings on the subject of resurrection.

It was remarked earlier that the Christian doctrine of immortality is not simply that of a survival of death, and future state of existence of the *soul.* The spiritual part of man is indeed that in which his God-like qualities reveal themselves—in which he bears the stamp of the divine image.   It is the seat of his rational, moral, self-conscious, personal life.   It is that which proves him to be more than a being of nature—a transient bubble on the heaving sea of physical change, and proclaims his affinity with the Eternal.   Idealism emphasizes this side of man's nature, and almost forgets that there is another equally real.   For, if man is a spiritual existence, he appears not less as the crown of nature's development, and as bound by a thousand ties through a finely-adjusted bodily organisation to the physical and animal world from which he has

[1] Rom. viii. 23.

emerged.   Naturalism, in turn, lays stress on the latter side of his being, and is tempted to ignore the former.   It explains man as a product of physical forces, and treats immortality as a chimera. A true view of man's nature will embrace both sides. It will acknowledge the spiritual dignity of man, but will recognize that he is not, and was never intended to be, pure spirit ; that he is likewise a denizen of the natural world endowed with corporeity, residing in, and acting through a body which is as truly a part of *himself* as life or soul itself is. He is, in short, the preordained link between two worlds—the natural and the spiritual; and has relation in his personality to both.   He is not spirit simply, but incorporated spirit.

If this is a true view to take of man's nature—and it is held here to be the Biblical view,[1] it directly affects the ideas to be formed of death and immortality.   Death, in the case of such a being, however it may be with the animal, can never be a merely natural event. Body and soul—integral elements in man's personality—cannot be sundered without mutilation and loss to the spiritual part.   The dream that death is an emancipation of the spiritual essence from a body that imprisons and clogs it, and is in itself the entrance on a freer, larger life, belongs to the schools, not to Christianity. The

[1] The subject is more fully treated by the present writer in his *Christian View of God and the World*, Lect. V., with Appendix, and *God's Image in Man*, Lect. VI.

disembodied state is never presented in Scripture
—Old Testament or New—as other than one of
incomplete being—of enfeebled life, diminished
powers, restricted capacities of action. " Sheol,"
" Hades," is not the abode of true immortality.
It follows that salvation from a state of sin which
has brought man under the law of death must
include deliverance from this incomplete condition. It must include deliverance from Sheol—
" the redemption of the body." The Redeemer
must be One who holds " the keys of death and of
Hades." ¹ It must embrace resurrection.

In a previous chapter it was hinted that this is
probably the proper direction in which to look
for the origin of the Biblical idea of resurrection,
and of the form which the hope of immortality
assumed in the Old Testament. The believing
relation to God is felt to carry in it the pledge of
deliverance even from Sheol, and of a restored and
perfected life in God's presence. It is significant
that Jesus quotes the declaration, " I am the God
of Abraham, and the God of Isaac, and the God
of Jacob " ² in proof, not simply of the continued
subsistence of the patriarchs in some state of being,
but of the resurrection of the dead. The late
Dr. A. B. Davidson unexceptionably states the
point in the following words of his *Commentary on
Job*. " The human spirit," he says, " is conscious

¹ Rev. i. 18. ² Matt. xxii. 23.

of fellowship with God, and this fellowship, from the nature of God, is a thing imperishable, and, in spite of obscurations, it must yet be fully manifested by God. This principle, grasped with convulsive earnestness in the prospect of death, became the Hebrew doctrine of immortality. This doctrine was but the necessary corollary of religion. In this life the true relations of men to God were felt to be realized ; and the Hebrew faith of immortality—never a belief in the mere existence of the soul after death, for the lowest superstition assumed this—was a faith that the dark and mysterious event of death would not interrupt the life of the person with God, enjoyed in this world. . . . The doctrine of immortality in the book [of Job] is 'the same as that of other parts of the Old Testament. Immortality is the corollary of religion. If there be religion—that is, if God be—there is immortality, not of the soul, but of the whole personal being of man (Ps. xvi. 9). This teaching of the whole Old Testament is expressed by our Lord with a surprising incisiveness in two sentences, ' I am the *God* of Abraham, God is not the God of the dead but the God of the *living*.' " [1]

How essential the Resurrection of Jesus is as an integral part of a doctrine of Redemption will appear from such considerations without further comment.

[1] *Com. on Job*, Appendix, pp. 293-5.

(3) A last aspect, intimately connected with the foregoing, in which the doctrinal significance of the Resurrection is perceived, is in its relation to the *believer's own hope* of resurrection. This is the point of view from which the Resurrection is treated in that great pæan of resurrection hope— the fifteenth chapter of 1 Corinthians. Christ's Resurrection is the ground and pledge of the resurrection of believers. If Christ has not risen, neither can they rise. The Christian dead have perished.[1] So completely does St. Paul bind up survival after death with the hope of resurrection that, in the denial of the latter, he apparently feels the ground to be taken from the former as well. Immortality, with him, for the Christian, is " incorruption "[2]— victory over death in body as in soul. In Christ's Resurrection, the assurance of that victory is given. " But now hath Christ been raised, the first fruits of them that are asleep . . . Christ the firstfruits : then they that are Christ's, at His coming."[3] This sheds again a broad, clear light on the nature of the Christian's hope of immortality. It is no mere futurity of existence—no mere ghostly persistence after death. It is an immortality of positive life, of holiness, of blessedness, of glory—of perfected likeness to Christ in body, soul and spirit.[4] It is here that the thought of resurrection

[1] 1 Cor. xv. 18. [2] 1 Cor. xv. 42, 52–4 ; 2 Tim. i. 10.
[3] Cor. xv. 20, 23. [4] Phil. iii. 20–21 ; cf. 1 John iii. 2.

helps, for once more the Redemption of Christ is seen to be a redemption of the whole man—body and soul together.

The difficulties which present themselves on the subject of the resurrection of the body are, of course, manifold, and cannot be ignored. The difficulty is greater even than in the case of Jesus, for there Resurrection took place within three days, in a body which had not seen corruption. But the bodies of the generations of the Christian dead have utterly perished. How is resurrection possible for them? The Apostle does indeed speak of the bodies of those who are alive at the Parousia being "changed."[1] But this obviously leaves untouched the case of the vast majority who have died "in faith" in the interval.

The subject is full of mystery. The error lies in conceiving of the resurrection of the body of the Christian as necessarily the raising again of the very material form that was deposited in the grave. This, though the notion has been defended, loads the doctrine of the resurrection with a needless weight and is not required by anything contained in Scripture. St. Paul, indeed, using the analogy of the seed-corn, says expressly: "Thou sowest not the body that shall be. . . . But God giveth it a body as it pleased Him."[2] There is here iden-

---

[1] 1 Cor. xv. 51-2 ; 1 Thess. iv. 15-18.
[2] 1 Cor. xv. 37-8.

tity between the old self and the new even as regards the body. But it is not identity of the same
material substance. In truth, as has often been
pointed out, the identity of our bodies, even on
earth, does not consist in sameness of material
particles. The matter in our bodies is continually
changing : in the course of a few years has entirely
changed. The bond of identity is in something
deeper, in the abiding organizing principle which
serves as the thread of connexion amidst all changes.
That endures, is not allowed to be destroyed at
death; and stamps its individuality and all it in-
herits from the old body upon the new.

Questions innumerable doubtless may be asked
which it is not possible to answer. How, for example, can a body so transformed as to be called
" spiritual " yet retain the true character of a
" body " ? What place is there for " body " in
a spiritual realm at all ? No place, assuredly, for
the body of " flesh " ($\sigma\acute{a}\rho\xi$) ; but for a body ($\sigma\hat{\omega}\mu a$)
of another kind, there not only may be, but, if Jesus
has passed into the heavens, there *is*, place. " There
are also," the Apostle says, " celestial bodies, and
bodies terrestrial." [1] Such a body, adapted to
celestial conditions, will be the resurrection body of
the believer. Even already a hidden tie connects

[1] I Cor. xv. 40. The remarks on this subject in Stewart
and Tait's book, *The Unseen Universe*, are worth consulting as coming from men of scientific eminence. Cf. pp.
26–7, but specially pp. 157–163.

this future resurrection-body with the Resurrection life of the Redeemer. For the production of this body the possession of the Spirit of the Risen Lord is necessary. On the other hand, where that Spirit is present, the forces for the production of the resurrection-body are at work—conceivably the basis of it is being already laid within the body that now is. Hardly less seems to be the meaning of the Apostle's words : " If Christ be in you, the body is dead because of sin ; but the Spirit is life because of righteousness. But if the Spirit of Him that raised up Jesus from the dead dwell in you, He that raised up Christ Jesus from the dead shall quicken also your mortal bodies through His Spirit that dwelleth in you." [1]

In conclusion, the Resurrection of Jesus stands fast as a fact, unaffected by the boastful waves of scepticism that ceaselessly through the ages beat themselves against it ; retains its significance as a corner-stone in the edifice of human redemption ; and holds within it the vastest hope for time and for eternity that humanity can ever know.

" Blessed be the God and Father of our Lord Jesus Christ, who, according to His great mercy, begat us again unto a living hope, by the Resurrection of Jesus Christ from the dead, unto an inheritance incorruptible, undefiled, and that fadeth not away." [2]

---

[1] Rom. viii. 10, 11.   [2] I Pet. i. 3, 4.

INDEX